Drugs, Labor,
and Colonial Expansion

Drugs, Labor, and Colonial Expansion

edited by William Jankowiak
and Daniel Bradburd

The University of Arizona Press
Tucson

The University of Arizona Press

© 2003 The Arizona Board of Regents

First Printing

All rights reserved

♾ This book is printed on acid-free, archival-quality paper.

Manufactured in the United States of America

08 07 06 05 04 03 6 5 4 3 2 1

Library of Congress Cataloging-in-Publication Data

Drugs, labor, and colonial expansion / edited by William Jankowiak and Daniel Bradburd.

    p. cm.

Includes bibliographical references and index.

    ISBN 0-8165-2351-7 (cloth : alk. paper)

    1. Indigenous peoples--Drug use--History. 2. Drug abuse--Cross-cultural studies. I. Jankowiak, William R. II. Bradburd, Daniel.

HV5824.I48 D78 2003

306.3'6--dc21

                2003005025

British Library Cataloguing-in-Publication Data

A catalogue record for this book is available from the British Library.

Contents

Contents

Preface

This manuscript began as a chance encounter at an intersection in downtown Phoenix at the 1988 American Anthropological Association meeting. At that intersection the question that shaped the entire manuscript was first posed: Do drugs (or chemical stimulants) have specific properties that make them a compelling "tool" with which to extend control over individuals? We did not know the answer but thought it might be worth a look, so we made a tacit agreement to co-research and write a paper on the relationship (assuming there was one). With the help of some students, we conducted a cross-cultural survey that examined the way drugs were used, if at all, within a labor context and/or first contact trade exchanges. A preliminary report of our findings was published in the 1996 issue of *Current Anthropology*. We began testing responses to our ideas as we presented papers at meetings.

Believing our thesis needed a more in-depth ethnographic and historical treatment, we began extending our research.

In 1996 at the Addiction and Culture Conference at the Claremont Graduate Humanities Center we met Chuck Ambler. After fruitful conversations with him, we decided to invite anthropologists and historians to participate in an interdisciplinary book project that explored regional and local responses to the introduction of non-indigenous drug foods. In 1998, in Philadelphia, we brought together a panel of many of the contributors to this volume. We also kept reading, learning more and more about drugs and the history and nature of their use. This volume is thus the result of a long intellectual journey that has taken the two of us far from our original research foci in China and Iran. We have learned a great deal. We hope that the fruitfulness of our ongoing intellectual exchange among ourselves and our contributors has resulted in an informed and readable book.

First authorship of the book was determined by the flip of a coin in a hotel coffee shop, at another American Anthropological Association meeting. Bradburd called heads; it was tails and thus Jankowiak became the first author of the book, with Bradburd becoming the first author of the book's introductory and concluding chapters. In this and in so many other ways, this project has been a truly collaborative partnership where the conceptual framework and analysis have been refined through the years via e-mail messages, phone conversations, and personal meetings.

The following individuals assisted in the collection of the data used in preparing portions of the introduction and conclusion: Laura Boland, Edward Fischer, Jeff Klein, Michele Mendell, Gerald Morris, Joyce Naylon, Micheal Vavrik, Shana Walton, and Peter Woodruff. Portions of the manuscript were written at the National Science Foundation–sponsored 1992 Summer Institute in Comparative Anthropological Research at the University of California, Los Angeles.

We thank Michael Angrosino, Gene Anderson, Victoria Bricker, Jim Bell, Carol Ember, Mel Ember, Richard Fox, Pat Gray, Carol Greenhouse, Ray Hames, Dwight Health, Rena Lederman, Lee Munroe, Wendy Locknear, Thomas Paladino, Robin Room, and several anonymous reviewers for helping us sharpen our understanding of the complexities involved in understanding this issue. We would also like to thank Ivy Taksee for a diligent effort at proofreading each author's references and in-text citations, Yvonne Reineke and Christine Szuter for guiding the manuscript through the review process at the University of Arizona Press, and Mary Hill for superb copyediting.

Finally, we want to especially thank our families who urged us on, while we were all growing old together in anticipation of this project's eventual completion.

Drugs, Labor,
and Colonial Expansion

1

Drugs, Desire, and European Economic Expansion

Daniel Bradburd and William Jankowiak

In grand events like the Opium Wars of the nineteenth century and in small, unrecorded, localized encounters, drugs played a prominent role in Europe's economic expansion. Often, the drugs introduced by Europeans replaced, or significantly transformed, indigenous drugs, whose consumption was tied to the labor process. The essays in this volume explore this nexus of drugs, economic expansion, and labor, attempting to clarify how and why drugs were introduced and used and how prior patterns of their consumption—European and indigenous—shaped postcontact use.

We argue that drugs were a common feature of European expansion because their characteristics made them a particularly effective means of propagating trade or increasing the extent and intensity of labor. We suggest that in the early stages of European expansion drugs were introduced to draw people, quite literally, into relations of dependency with European trade partners; that in later periods of contact, when control over labor power had been consolidated through other means, drugs were used to increase the amount or the intensity of labor drawn from laboring populations; and, finally, that later still the drugs used to intensify the amount and duration of labor shifted from alcohol, opium, and marijuana, which were used to overcome both the drudgery of long, hard, physical labor and the pain and discomfort that come with it, to caffeine-based stimulants, which provided a more sober and alert workforce.

Today people everywhere consume sugar, chocolate, coffee, tea, and other caffeinated beverages; smoke cigarettes; drink "spirits" along with beer and wine; and, to a lesser extent, use drugs derived from opium poppies, coca leaves, and the hemp plant. The near universal availability of these drugs is a recent phenomenon. Before the sixteenth century, tobacco and chocolate were found only in the New World, tea and coffee were restricted largely to their areas of origin in China and the Horn of Africa, respectively, and distilled spirits, while known in antiquity, remained uncommon. Coca use was confined to South America, and opium, known in Asia and Europe primarily as a medicine, was not broadly used.[1]

After the fifteenth century, European economic expansion entailed the movement of vast numbers of plants, animals, and peoples throughout the world, transforming the physical environment, the distribution of species, and the lives of millions of people. This movement and transformation were largely driven by the demand of an ever-expanding "world market system" for finished goods, raw materials, and the labor to collect, grow, and transform those materials into commodities, themselves traded throughout the world. This is not surprising. European geographic expansion was driven by the growth of what became a capitalist economy, with its constant need for increased production, increased consumption, increased intensity and duration of labor, and increased trade. Drugs played a vital role in this process.

This is not a secret history, and the literatures on both drugs and European expansion and colonialism often note the association of drug trade and drug use with work and labor. Beginning with Sidney Mintz's seminal *Sweetness and Power* (1985), a series of works have examined trade in goods that Mintz called "drug foods" (e.g., sugar, tea, coffee, tobacco, alcohol, chocolate) and harder drugs (opium and coca and their derivatives). Many studies provide a broad historical perspective, tracking numerous drugs from their original use in their native regions to their becoming commodities consumed the world over. Some examine a single drug in great detail, often beginning with a discussion of its first "discovery" by the local peoples who became aware of its psychoactive properties, then describing its "traditional" use, its later "discovery" by Europeans, the details of the drug's entry into the European market, and finally its subsequent worldwide diffusion. Other works have still more specific foci, for example, examining the impact of a particular drug on a particular group of native peoples. These studies repeatedly show that drugs are associated with attempts to gain access to goods or labor and that people's use of drugs are deeply intertwined with the circumstances of their working lives. The far larger literature on European economic expansion also frequently notes an association of drug trade and use with access to goods and to labor as well as the use of drugs in work and leisure.[2]

However, discussions of drugs and labor have but a small part in most works, and even those that discuss the relationship through time and over space (e.g., Courtwright's recent work [2001]) rarely make it their central focus. Convinced that there is real merit in exploring the general parameters of the relationship between drug trade and access to or control of labor but conscious of the danger of losing the sharp detail of studying a specific case, we have structured this volume as a compromise. Our introductory chapter provides an overview of the links of drugs with trade and labor, including our model of their role in European economic expansion.[3] Thereafter, individual chapters explore particular instances of this relationship. In combination, this provides a context for considering the specific cases, and a richness of detail reveals how the conjunction of cultural and historical forces shapes local outcomes.

Some Characteristics of Drugs

While many factors shaped the outcome of introducing any drug into a new environment, a powerful common thread runs through all accounts: *drugs are not like other products,* and the historical process of the introduction of drugs into new places is not the same as, for example, the introduction of spinach or potatoes. Drugs are pharmacologically active;[4] they operate by stimulating or interfering with neurotransmitters that control brain functions associated with pleasure or pain, resulting in the formation of specific patterns of reinforcement and learning; they alter human consciousness and, literally, physically transform people's experience of their world and their own condition. Drugs are powerful substances that, whether sought after or proscribed, are quickly seen as special by both those who provide them in trade and those who consume them. Thus, although the patterns of drug use in any society cannot be understood without recognizing that they are culturally constituted and that use is shaped by drugs' symbolic associations, attempts to understand drugs, the drug trade, and the relationship of this trade to labor that do not distinguish drugs from other goods risk ignoring a key point: drugs' pharmacological

5

properties as often addicting stimulants, depressants, and analgesics shape the role they play in *all* human societies and, consequently, the role they played in European expansion. Their pharmacological properties led to widespread drug use prior to European contact and then, after contact and the globalization of trade, to the rapidly spreading demand for them. The drug trade was (as it remains today) largely demand driven.

Alcohol and nicotine are the primary drugs considered in this essay. The latter "can act as both a stimulant and a sedative." Its initial and immediate effect is "stimulation of the adrenal glands…[with] a resulting discharge of epinephrine." This causes "a sudden release of glucose…[and an] increase in blood pressure, respiration and heart rate." Nicotine also "indirectly causes a release of dopamine," causing "a reaction similar to that seen with other drugs of abuse." It appears that nicotine's dopamine-releasing mechanism is responsible both for the sensation of pleasure derived from its use and for its addictive qualities (National Institute on Drug Abuse 1998:2). While the mechanism is incompletely understood, "alcohol consumption also leads to dopamine release" (National Institute on Alcohol Abuse 1998; see National Institute on Alcohol Abuse 1996 for a fuller discussion of dopamine and reinforcement in alcohol addiction). This is probably responsible for the feelings of euphoria and increased self-confidence associated with moderate consumption; it is also the likely mechanism that leads to alcohol addiction. When it is first consumed, alcohol is also a stimulant, and, consumed in greater quantities, it is a central nervous system depressant. These multiple effects seem closely tied to the ways it is used in both pre- and postcontact situations. Caffeine also produces "increased dopaminergic transmission within the brain" (Ferre 1997), which, in turn, "could possibly produce behavioral effects similar to other dopaminergic mediated stimulants" (Garrett and Griffiths 1997).

Historically, stimulants have been used to enhance physical and mental performance by increasing endurance, concentration, and the intensity of physical and mental work. Not surprisingly, the use of stimulants is associated with work, and the use of stimulants to enhance labor is broadly documented. More surprising is the association with work of drugs often thought of as depressants, like alcohol, opium, and marijuana, whose use would seem unlikely to increase either the intensity or the duration of labor. Both the broader literature and the essays included here help explain this unexpected association. First, these drugs are themselves complex and, under some conditions, may act as stimulants of mental, physical, or social activity. Second, the drugs are analgesic, and

the importance of pain relief for enabling workers to sustain labor under difficult physical conditions should not be underestimated. By reducing feelings of
pain, drugs permit people to work when their own physical conditions or the
impact of their environment might otherwise make it impossible. Depressants
also help sick, cold, hungry, and hurting workers sleep, which may also permit
them to labor longer and harder than they otherwise might.

The use of drugs to enhance performance is widespread. Rajputs throughout the nineteenth century took opium prior to battle to "steady their nerves
and to inhibit untimely bowel movements" (Carstairs 1954:297); nineteenth-
century Tibetan state couriers often used opium to overcome fatigue (Washburne 1961). The Barasana, who live near the border of Brazil and Colombia,
said that "coca gives them energy, stamina, and concentration and that it staves
off hunger" (Hugh-Jones 1995:52). Padden claims that whenever the Aztec state
found "itself in the midst of large construction projects, it judiciously used alcoholic beverages to obtain additional efforts from its laborers" (1967). Cassinelli reports that in Yemen *qat* was used "by stonecutters and dock and
construction workers to energize…them for their exhausting tasks" (1986:238).
In Papua New Guinea and Southeast Asia betel nuts were chewed to alleviate
hunger, thirst, and fatigue (Lepowsky 1982; Hirsch 1995). In West Africa "[k]ola
was…distributed during communal work parties (gayya) of young men….
[T]he kola was both a method of compensating the youths and a way of com-
batting fatigue during the hard work" (Lovejoy 1995:115). Writing of Qing
Chinese opium use, Jonathan Spence notes that "in the nineteenth century…
[c]oolie laborers also began to take opium, either by smoking it or by licking
tiny pellets of the drug, to overcome the drudgery and pain of hauling huge
loads day after day." He then adds, "[S]hrewd yet ruthless employers, observ-
ing that the coolies could carry heavier loads if they were under the influence
of opium, even made the drug available to their workers" (Spence 1990:131).

Manipulation of addiction was not unknown. Drug use was a means of
keeping labor captive or rewarding people who worked long and hard. Angrosino (this volume) shows that Caribbean planters who compelled their Indian
indentured workers to consume rum rather than marijuana as their drug of
choice enhanced the economic return on their laborers as well as the intensity
of their labor.

The pain of hard labor is not all physical. Workers separated from their
families, often by force, working long hours under difficult conditions, living in
poverty and squalor, and exposed to death and disease suffered emotionally.

Drugs' consciousness-deadening or consciousness-altering power let people blot out or deflect this pain. Like their analgesic quality, which helped people suppress their physical pain and thus work longer and harder, drugs' consciousness-altering power enabled people to overcome or suppress their emotional pain, allowing them "to tune out the wretchedness of life" (Angrosino, this volume) and continue working in conditions where that might otherwise have been impossible (see also Anderson; Gordon; and Cassman, Cartmell, and Belmonte, this volume).

Drugs, Meaning, and the Organization of Labor

Like other important goods, drugs are embedded in systems of meaning and of power that affect the ways they are distributed and used. Considering their social and symbolic association with work helps clarify the role drugs play in the organization of labor and ways in which drugs become the basis of social rituals that make workers' lives more meaningful and more sustainable.

In this volume, drugs are often set off from other goods. Suggs and Lewis's essay recounts the important social and symbolic role of alcohol in BaTswana society. Hays shows that traditional tobacco use was ritualized in Papua New Guinea. Angrosino notes that marijuana had quasi-religious connotations in India and among Indian laborers in Trinidad. Von Gernet's (1995) discussion of indigenous tobacco use in northeastern North America stresses its use as a means of mediating relations with the spirit world. Coca was not simply used to overcome the physical challenges of working in South American silver and tin mines, it was also used to build and bind social relations among humans and between humans and supernatural forces (Nash 1993; Hugh-Jones 1995; and Cassman, Cartmell, and Belmonte, this volume).

Where drug use is restricted (as was the case among the BaTswana or as it is in Europe and America today) or where those restrictions are imposed on others (e.g., throughout much of southern Africa in the twentieth century), drugs fall into a marked category. They are, to appropriate Appadurai's term, "enclaved" commodities. Writing of these enclaved goods, Appadurai argues, "The reasons for such hedging are quite variable, but...the moral bases of the restriction have clear implications for...political, social, and commercial exchanges of a more mundane sort." He goes on to suggest that "wherever... any other visible act of consumption is subject to external regulation, we can see that demand is subject to social definition and control" (Appadurai 1986:24, 31–32).

There are numerous reasons drugs are enclaved. Perhaps the most obvious is that they are addictive, and their use can generate significant social disloca-tion.[5] The potential for this dislocation becomes apparent when drugs are seen through the lens of Appadurai's general criteria for the exchangeability of com-modities. Appadurai writes of "two kinds of situations...where the standards and criteria that govern exchange are so attenuated as to seem virtually absent[:]...transactions across cultural boundaries...[and] intracultural exchanges where, despite a vast universe of shared understandings, a specific exchange is based on deeply divergent perceptions of the value of the objects being exchanged." The best examples of the latter, he suggests, "are to be found in situations of extreme hardship (such as famine or warfare) when exchanges are made whose logic has little to do with the commensuration of sacrifices." He provides as examples "a Bengali man who abandons his wife to prostitution in exchange for a meal, or a Turkana woman who sells critical pieces of her per-sonal jewelry for a week's food." In these situations, he says, "value and price have become almost completely unyoked" (Appadurai 1986:14).

Appadurai's discussion strikingly corresponds to the conditions of drug trade, which, in contact situations, was often *a deliberate attempt to bring about enormous incommensurabilities of exchange.* In other instances (e.g., trade in heroin or crack cocaine), these incommensurabilities, while not perhaps intend-ed, remain the stereotypical result (Ratner 1993). *Drugs thus are goods that, by their nature, create and maintain exchanges or contexts where "value and price have become...completely unyoked" outside situations of extreme hardship.* Drugs possess characteristics that cause users to behave as they otherwise might only in extraordinary circumstances. Drugs thus are extraordinary goods, and attempts to limit or control drugs, whether in trade or in indigenous use, make considerable sense. In this volume, Hays's discussion of what people would do or what they would give up to obtain tobacco provides a clear case of drugs promoting incommensurable exchange.

Drugs' powers, their attractions, and their ability to disrupt society and ordered economic relations help explain both attempts to limit access to them and the sacralization and ritualization of their use. While their ability to induce states of altered consciousness may be one reason for drugs' association with the supernatural and with ritual, an equally important reason for this association may be the need to make restrictions on their use stand up in the face of their powerful attractions. Ritualized enclaving of drugs embodies the literal mean-ing of making something sacred, declaring or making it a thing "dedicated" or "set apart." Access to the enclaved goods was often limited to those with status, power, and privilege (see Suggs and Lewis; Gordon; Ambler; Brady and Long; and Cassman, Cartmell, and Belmonte, this volume). Restriction by status is, of course, a defining feature of sumptuary laws, but restriction of use also reinforces the aura of power, distinction, and, perhaps, mystery that surrounds drug use. As sacred goods, set aside for ritualized use by prominent members of society, drugs become embedded in multiple matrices of meaning associated with power and control. Misusing them is a violation of the social and the cosmic order. Ritualized enclaving is thus a means of mobilizing social and symbolic power against the powerful attraction of drug use.

Simultaneously, the controls can be manipulated to create incentives for labor. Linking sanctioned access to drugs to labor (e.g., the provision of alcohol at the end of communal labor) can be a powerful incentive to participate in the labor process. It not only gives access to a pharmacologically powerful substance that may make people feel good, it also gives access to a good symbolically freighted in ways that make its consumption, or, more appropriately, the acceptable participation in its consumption, an event that marks and conveys status and gives the consumer an association with that which is powerful and meaningful. Thus, as Appadurai's notion of incommensurable exchange suggests one reason for restricting access to drugs, applying to drugs his notion that restrictions of *any* commodity are generally linked to "facilitating political, social, and commercial exchanges" reminds us that their socially sanctioned access gives them symbolic force that may amplify their already powerful attraction, making control and manipulation of their access a potent means of influencing the organization of labor.

The role of drugs or of their provision in association with labor may be particularly important in societies with what Wolf has called "the kinship mode of production" (1982). In contrast to capitalist or tributary modes of production in which coercion (however symbolically veiled) may underlie the control of labor, in the kinship mode of production, symbolic systems like genealogies and mythic charters play vital roles in allocating access to labor, which is, really, control over people. This control is often tenuous, involving conflicting claims, conflicting interests, and the potential for breakup or fission. The vast anthropological literature on kinship and exchange suggests that a key means of mobilizing labor is the controlled distribution of highly valued goods, of which women, who embody both current and future labor, are perhaps the archetype. Drugs that are also highly valued, set apart, and filled with power, including the ability to make labor more productive and sustainable, are another of the goods whose distribution is associated with access to labor and whose distribution is, therefore, commonly restricted, limited, or controlled, often through a form of symbolic elaboration that makes their possession, consumption, and distribution deeply meaningful.

Recognizing that drugs are agents sufficiently powerful to create incommensurable exchanges also helps clarify why they have such a devastating impact in contact situations. Their antisocial power is hard to control where the social fabric has broken down, so embedding drugs in matrices of meaning and ritualization becomes all the more difficult. Enforcing limits on who will use drugs or how they will be used then becomes more difficult to enact or enforce. It is in contexts such as these that we would expect to see the particularly destructive or at least uncontrolled effects Hays reports. Similarly, in the case of the BaTswana that Suggs and Lewis discuss, chiefs and elders who are upset about untraditional access to untraditional brews are responding to consumption that both challenges the social order and is, through its existence, a manifestation of the breakdown of the older social order that empowered and privileged them.

One additional aspect of drugs' relation to labor is worth stressing. Several drugs promote a sense of euphoria, social ease, and energy that, taken together, provides a strong sense of conviviality.[6] Labor is social, and the allocation and deployment of groups shape society. If some drugs promote sociability, then where groups already exist, ritualized consumption of drugs may enhance this feeling. Where the social order is more fragmented (e.g., in South African mine compounds or on plantations in Trinidad), then ritualized consumption of drugs may ease the formation of groups or help create a sense of group identity. This enhancement of sociability and hence of group feeling seems likely to amplify other elements of the association of drugs with labor. Misery shared with friends may make the drudgery of labor easier to sustain; group solidarity may make the labor process run more smoothly, easing the individual burden as friends take up the slack; the promise of drugs as a reward and the ritualization of their consumption may facilitate calling together groups for collective labor and enhance the organization of labor in the absence of coercive means. At the same time, drugs provide loci for political or emotional resistance to oppression and colonization. Where drugs were used prior to contact (e.g., alcohol in southern Africa or coca in highland South America), their continued use became a means of preserving elements of precontact life, and where drug use was discouraged, their consumption became an act of resistance. Even where it was permitted or encouraged, drug use created spaces of resistance, unoccupied by and out of the reach of an employer's control (see Scully 1992). Whether the social groups formed around drug consumption led to political action remains an open question.

Drugs as Trade Goods

In addition to their pharmacological properties, drugs have certain other characteristics that make them "good to trade" and "good to exchange." Many drugs, for example, can be processed into forms that are relatively easy to transport and that keep well.[7] This was important when traders traveled over long distances or for long periods. While alcohol is more cumbersome to ship than some other drugs, it provides an excellent medium for the storage of surplus grains, sugars, and fruits, which are difficult to store in an unprocessed form. Moreover, at least in North America, trade alcohol was often greatly adulterated and diluted, dramatically increasing the concentration of its purer form. In all cases, drugs' high values meant that they fit into the luxury trade that characterized early European expansion.

Many drugs can be combined in ways that enhance their impact or attractiveness. Sugar combines well with the bitter tropical drugs coffee, tea, and cacao; they become synergistic mixtures, as are alcohol and tobacco.[8] One hallmark of market expansion was the combination of drugs and their recombination as they moved from localized to international trade. Finally, unlike trade goods such as metal or cloth, all drugs share a singular and—from the perspective of the trader—very valuable feature: using them consumes them. To use drugs and still have them, the user must constantly replace his or her supply. Moreover, some drugs create a tolerance in users who then not only need to replace what they have consumed but need to consume more to achieve the same effect. In either case, exchange must be continuous. This was a feature of alcohol and tobacco that was clearly recognized by traders in North America and the Pacific.

Drugs and Trade: A Model and Its Details

The introduction of drugs was a significant and deliberate technique for the capture of labor and commodities in market expansion; they were first a tool of seduction, inducing people to provide goods or labor. When labor could be controlled by other means, drugs became a way of increasing the intensity or duration of labor. This pattern of drug use is associated with the trajectory of European expansion, which saw European presence precede control. Thus the introduction of drugs throughout the world by agents of Western economic expansion provided an effective, efficient, and profitable means of drawing people into the market and creating in them an insatiable demand for its products.[9] The introduction of drugs provided a "euphemization of economic power" that Scott has claimed to be "necessary both where direct physical coercion is not possible and where the pure indirect domination of the capitalist market is not yet sufficient to ensure appropriation by itself" (1985:307). By both increasing demand and capturing labor, drugs were a near ideal medium for promoting European economic expansion. After control was established and more coercive means of gaining access to labor were generally employed, the problem facing colonial and imperial agents was not getting labor but getting the most from it. Drugs worked here too.

In the remainder of this essay we concentrate on describing this pattern and accounting for it. We do so fully aware that this is not the complete story of postcontact drug use. Precontact patterns of drug use helped shape cultural attitudes toward introduced goods. Historical conditions of contact varied greatly, also shaping how introduced drugs were accepted and used. Traders or others did not merely show up with any drug in any context and have their fortune made. The notion strongly articulated by Mintz that "when unfamiliar substances are taken up by new uses, they enter into pre-existing social and psychological contexts and acquire—or are given—contextual meaning by those who use them" (1985:6) is borne out by our research, which shows instance after instance of some goods being accepted while others were rejected for reasons that often remain obscure. Drugs acquired meanings and were incorporated into the symbolic and cultural systems of contacted peoples, and the means and meanings of their use became complex and overdetermined. Still, the broad pattern we have identified is clear enough for us to feel that the recognition, manipulation, and satisfaction of people's desires for drugs played an integral role in European economic expansion and the growth of the world market system and that it ought to be directly explored.

Drugs in Europe

Sahlins has suggested that "the development of Western 'civilization' has depended on an enormous soft drug culture...marked by the daily consumption of such substances as tea, coffee, chocolate, and sugar" (1988:43). This is supported in the history of European and European American drug use, which shows that from the early sixteenth century until the early twentieth century, one drug after another was (ultimately) accepted and often welcomed as the new panacea.[10]

Numerous studies detail drugs' entry into European trade, the ways in which they were described and used, conflicts over their qualities, and the histories of their use.[11] All reveal the diversity of views and purposes of those engaged in trade, even in single locations at particular historic moments, let alone at different times in different locations. In Europe itself the nature, meaning, and appropriate use and distribution of goods like sugar, alcohol, coffee, tea, and tobacco were as vigorously contested as were the goals and appropriate methods of overseas expansion (see, e.g., Goodman 1995; Mintz 1985; Schivelbusch 1992; Smith 1995; Wills 1993).

Still, patterns emerge. Goodman discusses European promotional literature on tea, coffee, chocolate, and tobacco in which they are presented as means of assuaging hunger and thirst. Europeans recognized that the substances "were psychoactive...in their predominantly humoral terms" (Goodman 1995:134, 137). Europeans also seemed aware of the addictive nature of these goods, and "the primary literature [on early European contact with the New World] contains numerous allusions to the tobacco addiction of Europeans who lingered... in the nascent colonies" (von Gernet 1995:77). Early notions of addiction seem common to ours. By the early seventeenth century, people were aware of the hazard of addiction to opium, including the observation that it "being once used, must daily be continued on paine of death" (Purchas, quoted in Booth 1998:30), though through the eighteenth century there seemed to be no moral judgment attached to its use (Booth 1998:33).[12]

Coffeehouses and other similar establishments that rose to prominence in Europe were closely linked to merchants and trade. Smith (1995:154) and Schivelbusch discuss the transformation of Lloyd's Coffee House (established ca. 1687) from a place in which "people in maritime occupations" met to discuss "the latest trade news" (1992:49ff.) into the marine insurance brokerage firm Lloyd's of London. Since "the combination of tobacco plus either tea, coffee or chocolate...with sugar was a critical component of diet and ritual in the eighteenth century" (Goodman 1995:137), and there was early recognition of tobacco's addictive characteristics, it seems likely that those who shipped and traded coffee, tea, and sugar knew their characteristics and how those characteristics could create or sustain trade. If sailors who possessed and consumed drugs on their own understood their properties and their value in establishing informal trade, it is likely that merchants who financed trade and trade companies and who contended over the meanings and uses of drugs were also aware of and appreciated (if that is the correct word) the power of drugs. This knowledge circulated within a culture increasingly attuned to the link between expanded notions of need and economic growth (Burke 1996:85), in part enabling the conscious use of drugs in overseas trade.[13]

Drugs and European Expansion

In the fifteenth and sixteenth centuries, Europeans came into contact with new goods, including drugs such as coffee, tea, tobacco, coca, and chocolate. The expansion of trade also brought Europeans into new or closer contact with numerous peoples. In China, Southwest Asia, and the Indian subcontinent, people lived in polities larger, richer, and more complex than those in Europe. In the Valley of Mexico and Andean South America there were also complex societies and state systems. In much of North America, parts of the Caribbean, lowland South America, Africa, and the insular Pacific, the people encountered were members of less complex societies, including many whose leaders often lacked political power and the ability to coerce and control labor.

Drugs were commonly introduced into trade where combinations of the following factors occurred: the contacted people had an egalitarian political organization with few traditional mechanisms for controlling labor or claiming rights to materials; the contacted people lived in an environment or a fashion that made flight easy and pressure difficult to apply; those creating contact were relatively few in number and had little power relative to the contacted population. Thus drugs were most commonly introduced by isolated traders operating well beyond the frontiers of their own society or when the people contacted were highly mobile (e.g., were foragers or nomadic pastoralists) and were therefore not susceptible to controls introduced by Europeans or indigenous leaders acting as their agents. These conditions most resemble those occurring in what White (1991) calls the "Middle Ground" and that Wolf (1982) associates with the "forward edges of capitalist expansion." These were areas in which Europeans had not established control, in which they were outnumbered (often enormously), and in which European culture was not dominant. Here, where "merchants created commodity frontiers and labor frontiers... exchanging... [goods from the industrial centers] for local products" (Wolf

15

1982:306), the introduction of drugs played a significant role in promoting, establishing, and maintaining exchanges that could not otherwise be easily controlled.[14]

Our data show that the introduction and use of drugs to draw people into exchanges for labor and goods seem strongly associated with the contacted group's level of political organization. Over 86 percent of the small-scale societies in our sample (thirty-seven of forty-three cases) showed evidence of drugs used to gain access to trade or labor, while less than half that rate (five of twelve cases) is reported for complex societies. Conversely, figures for the distribution of drugs used as a means of increasing the duration or intensity of labor virtually reverse this pattern: fewer than 20 percent (four of twenty-three) of foraging and fishing societies, which generally are small and lack elaborate political organization or stratification, show evidence of drug use to increase the intensity or duration of labor, while drugs were used this way in all (thirty-seven of thirty-seven cases) of the more complex and industrial societies in our sample.[15]

Numerous accounts of contact illustrate drugs introduced to gain access to goods or labor. In 1785, Bernardo de Gálvez, the viceroy of New Spain, insisted that the Apaches be given generous amounts of distilled spirits such as brandy or mescal so that "they will acquire a taste for these drinks [to] ... oblige them to recognize their dependence on us" (1951:47). Mining in the west and northwest of the Valley of Mexico was labor intensive, and there was always a shortage of labor (Taylor 1972), so "gifts" of food and, more importantly, alcohol were "given" to workers to recruit and maintain a large labor force. In the end, gifts of alcohol let mining operators accomplish something even the Aztecs were unable to do: transform the Chichimecas (the generic name for northwestern Mexican bands of foragers) into a sedentary population inhabiting the newly constructed mining towns. In 1715 a typical Hudson's Bay Company trading post gave away to native peoples "2,900 lbs. of Brazilian tobacco, 170 lbs. of leaf tobacco, 190 lbs. of rolled tobacco and 950 gals. of brandy.... Liquor was not the only trade commodity that was dispensed extravagantly in an effort to win the loyalty of Indians" (Yerbury 1986:44, 70). Bishop's analysis of the Hudson's Bay Company's fur trading with the Ojibwas shows that between 1780 and 1829 brandy, rum, and wine were the primary media of exchange. Bishop also claims that the Ojibwas learned to bargain for "stronger" rum by playing one trader off against another (1974:15–247).

Peter Mancall notes, "By the eighteenth century, traders in furs and skins... knew that liquor, particularly rum, was an ideal trade good, and they pursued it vigorously" (1995a:43). Russian and Yakut traders took advantage of the Yukagirs by fostering their dependency on trade items that included brandy, tobacco, sugar, and tea (Graburn and Strong 1973:43). Chinese merchant traders also managed to foster dependency relations with border peoples. The Mongols developed such a craving for caffeine taken in the form of bulk tea *(zhan cha)* that, at the turn of the twentieth century, they were trading three sheep for one five-pound slab of the poorest grade of Chinese pressed tea (Jankowiak 1993). A late-eighteenth-century traveler described "Bushmen" as "free from many wants and desires, that torment the rest of mankind" and "detesting all manners of labour yet easily induced into slavery by a little meat and tobacco" (Sparrman 1975, quoted in Pratt 1986:46; see also Gordon 1996). Crais notes that though seventeenth- and eighteenth-century Dutch merchants eschewed trade of alcohol in southern Africa, they did trade tobacco, which Crais calls "a rapidly consumable luxury." He also explicitly comments that "for this reason, [it was] recommended that the Company emphasize it." Crais provides a clear example of drugs creating incommensurable exchange when he quotes a late-seventeenth-century account describing Khoikoi selling cattle for tobacco until they became the impoverished servants of those supplying it (1992:166–67).[16]

A closer examination of the Pacific sandalwood trade and North American fur trade reveals more details of the roles of traders and natives. In the 1840s, as part of a larger triangular trade network that balanced trade of two drug foods, tobacco and tea, on a fulcrum of sandalwood, Australian entrepreneurs began to trade extensively in the islands of Southwest Melanesia. Shineberg (1967) reports that at the outset of the trade, the islands on which the Australians established their trade—New Caledonia, the New Hebrides, and the Loyalty Islands—were both isolated and virtually unknown. Their inhabitants, like other Pacific islanders, lacked iron, which became the primary item of initial trade. Shineberg also notes that European traders who sailed long distances on relatively small boats could not maintain control over the local populations with whom they traded.

Shineberg describes "a discernable trend in Melanesian imports," noting that "the goods required by a community varied...with the length and intensity of its contact." This developmental cycle of trade demands tended to proceed as follows: "1. Hoop or bar iron, metal fish-hooks, beads, cheap iron-mongery...glass bottles and calico. 2. A wider range of metal tools...as well as axes, adzes, cloth and drapery of all sorts. 3. Tobacco and pipes. 4.

Muskets, powder, superior edge tools, *and still more tobacco*" (Shineberg 1967:146, emphasis added).

Local demand and desire played a strong role in shaping trade. Shineberg writes, "The keen competition [between traders] of 1847–9 strengthened the bargaining power of the islanders," and "the tastes of Melanesian buyers were carefully studied to obtain advantage over rivals." Sandalwood traders were forced to keep up with the constant shift in desired goods, increasing not only the difficulty (in 1848 a Captain Towns wrote to his merchant backer that "we have great difficulty in hitting on the Article to suit the fancy of the natives") but the cost of trade. "What was 'good trade' at a certain place and time was a matter of great moment to contending traders: it was therefore a common subject of letters from captains and traders to Sydney" (Shineberg 1967:146, 149), providing further evidence that traders' selection of trade goods was shaped by native desires.

The introduction of tobacco provided relief from the natives' constantly changing tastes and "the problem posed...of hitting upon 'the fancy of the natives.'...[B]y the middle of the [nineteenth] century...[p]ipes and tobacco became indispensable items of trade.... The passion for tobacco suited the trader admirably. It was comparatively cheap trade, it was small and compact to carry, and, above all, it was expendable, creating as much demand as it satisfied." Moreover, while other items went in and out of fashion, tobacco remained a constant, such that "after the end of 1849 there was no export cargo destined for the islands that did not include tobacco" (Shineberg 1967:150, 151).[17]

In North America, alcohol parallels tobacco's role in the sandalwood trade. "The logic of the trade was obvious. The Indians' demand for durable commodities such as guns and blankets declined over time as they acquired as many of them as they could reasonably use. Their demand for alcohol, by contrast, seemed to be constant[,]...and since no alcoholic drink lasted long, Indian drinkers had to return to traders to get more" (Mancall 1995a:43). The striking parallel is not surprising. In North America, as in the South Pacific, isolated traders at great distances from larger European American populations sought goods from the native peoples among whom they traveled.

The diary of Archibald McLeod, a bourgeois of the North West Company who ran a trading post at Fort Alexandria, west of Lake Winnipeg, shows that in North America, as in Melanesia, pressure for the trade of alcohol and tobacco was not all one-sided. Phillips's massive study of the fur trade shows Europeans trading alcohol to attract trade and also natives demanding it. Phillips also documents both native and European resistance to its use in trade (1961: 109, 214, 401, 620–21; see also White 1983; Mancall 1995a). In the 1670s, when the French attempted to outlaw trade in alcohol, Iroquois who were on their way to Montreal with furs to trade "immediately...turned and took their pelts to Albany, where Dutch traders willingly supplied their desires."[18] In fact, "*the Indians demanded these beverages* [wine, spirits, and especially brandy]" such that "the *coureurs de bois* found their largest profits in the sale of brandy to Indians who had collected furs" (Phillips 1961:214, 212–13, emphasis added; see also Phillips 1961:401 for when Quakers tried to end the trading of alcohol in Pennsylvania).[19]

Competition and alternate sources of alcohol played a prominent role in shaping trade. Phillips provides evidence of this competition in Rhode Island and notes that in 1731 two French fur traders in western New York, claiming that stopping the sale of brandy had hurt their trade, stated that they "must allow the Indians some drink or they would take all their furs to the English" (1961:144, 456). While the use of drugs may have begun as a European gambit, native demand powerfully shaped the trade.

McLeod's diary reveals his attempts to use tobacco and alcohol to gain or maintain trade but also shows the impact of native demand. In one entry McLeod records an attempt to use tobacco to induce people to come to his post to trade with him. "Saturday 15th November 1800...Sent La Rose with Roy's step-son to the Thunder's tent, to try to prevail with his wife...to send her fine [?] furs here. I sent 3 feet of Tobacco for an encouragement of them to do so." About one month later, McLeod supplied alcohol in place of tobacco and tried to bring a group rather than an individual in to trade. He also openly notes that he was being played off against a competitor and had to provide the alcohol for free as a means of keeping the trade at his post. Native demand is again reflected in a diary entry telling that locals he wanted to hunt for him were "not at all ashamed to send me word if I do not send them rum they'll not hunt for the Fort" (1965:129, 143, 130).

If McLeod sometimes gave away alcohol or tobacco to induce people to trade with him, in his view it was because people often demanded tobacco and alcohol from him, in effect inducing him to provide them with those goods if he wanted their trade. Once the trade in drug foods was established, it could take on a life of its own.[20]

These accounts of the sandalwood trade and the fur trade reveal some of the pressures and complexities that shaped the role of drugs in early European

19

trade with small-scale societies. Where the European population was small and distant (in both time and space) from larger European populations, Europeans did not control the conditions of trade. Accounts further suggest that even where Europeans were able to create demand through the introduction of drugs and drug foods, they were still unable to completely control that trade. Contacted populations played an active role in shaping trade. They had desires and made demands, and they were willing to insist on the satisfaction of those desires.[21] While Europeans created trade and tried to control it, there is evidence that native preferences, even for certain kinds of alcohol and tobacco, strongly influenced the market basket of goods that Europeans supplied.[22]

Moreover, European competition for access to or control over indigenous resources provided local populations with the ability to seek alternative and, from their perspective, better trade offerings. Competition thus further reduced the control that early European traders had over local populations and the conditions of trade, shifting the balance of power in trade toward the local populations. That under competitive conditions alcohol and tobacco became, and remained, important items of trade suggests both the degree to which trade was driven by local desire for drug foods and that, from a European point of view, these drugs were powerful weapons for inducing trade, the heavy artillery of competition.

In sum, Europeans turned to the drug trade when they lacked the means for controlling with whom and under what circumstances native peoples would trade, so the dominant period for the introduction of drugs, almost by definition, occurred prior to effective establishment of imperial or colonial control over indigenous peoples and their territories. In these circumstances drug foods were used to induce trade, and traders were very conscious of the role these goods could play; they used them and fought to be able to use them.[23] Both this reality and an intimation of what would follow are captured in Caliban's lines from Shakespeare's *The Tempest*:

> *When thou cam'st first,*
> *Thou strok'st me and made much of me, wouldst give me*
> *Water with berries in't, . . .*
> . . . .
> *. . . and then I lov'd thee*
> *And show'd thee all the qualities o' th' isle.*
>
> (I.ii.332–37)

Brady and Long, Hays, Ambler, and Mancall provide accounts of trade in Australia, Melanesia, Africa, and North America, respectively, that clarify the kinds of goods sought in return for drugs, the ways precontact use shaped demand, and the ways in which larger economic imperatives led Europeans to press this trade.

Drugs and the Intensity or Duration of Labor

People have frequently used drugs in their struggle against the drudgery of hard, repetitive, or difficult labor. Labor-enhancing drugs were employed well before the advent of mercantilism or market capitalism and are by no means a European contribution to world culture. After areas were colonized and incorporated into European empires, the goal was not gaining access to labor or goods—that was taken care of by means of slavery, corvée, debt peonage, the *mita,* the *encomienda,* indenture, and other means of forcing indigenous labor to work on colonial projects. Only rarely after these measures were in place and generally in the face of competing demands for labor (as in parts of southern Africa) did the provision of alcohol or tobacco remain a means of acquiring or retaining a labor force.[24] Assuming that the workers were already present and that they could not simply melt away, drug use was promoted or condoned as a cheap means of keeping people working longer and perhaps harder than they otherwise might have. Drugs became a reward to make people more willing to work long hours under difficult conditions; they were used as stimulants or pain relievers to permit people who might have been subject to coercion to work longer and harder than they might otherwise have been able; drugs were also used to create debts or physical addictions that kept laborers bound to the job.[25]

Once European colonies were well established, the relationship of drugs to labor and trade became more complex. Although the parameters of early contact were relatively similar the world over, there was great variation in the nature of the colonial or imperial enterprise, including differences in the kind and degree of control these systems were able to (or wished to) impose and in the nature of the resources and sources of wealth being sought. Differences between particular imperial or colonial systems also evolved over time. Moreover, the European approach to drugs and drug use changed, sometimes driven by new attitudes toward drugs and their use in Europe, sometimes as a result of new circumstances in the colony or the colonial project. Indigenous use patterns also influenced colonial patterns of drug use. Carefully documented cases—like alcohol in southern Africa (see Crush and Ambler 1992; Gordon, this volume) and North America (see Mancall 1995a; Eber 1995)—show that drugs were favored and opposed by many parties for many reasons, precluding any one European conception of appropriate drug use or any single local response. Local preferences and restrictions shaped consumption patterns. However, the inflections arising from local preference do not obscure an important common theme: in an attempt to increase productivity, drugs were regularly supplied as a means of making difficult, dangerous, and unpleasant work physically and emotionally sustainable.

Roughly thirty years after the conquest of the Incas gave the Spaniards control over a highly stratified society with a precontact means of compelling labor, "perhaps 90 percent of the increase in coca leaf production was directed to the newly concentrated population in Potosí," and "neither the use of coca in that way [i.e., in the mines at Potosí] nor the large population was a traditional circumstance or condition" (Murra 1986:51–52). Traditional or not, coca was seen as an important means of labor management. A sixteenth-century mine owner arguing against attempts to ban coca chewing as a "pagan" custom claimed, "If coca were abolished the Indians would not go to Potosí. Neither would they work nor mine" (Gagliano 1963, quoted in Sanabria 1993:40). From this owner's perspective, coca was being used to attract labor, though others have suggested it was needed to help Potosí's workers function under the harsh conditions they endured, and using coca to drawing out more, and more intense, labor is well documented. June Nash's *We Eat the Mines and the Mines Eat Us* shows coca being used by miners and being provided by mine owners as a means of overcoming and perhaps making possible work that takes place in unimaginably difficult conditions. Nash writes at the beginning of a section titled "Coca," "The one solace that workers have on the job is coca...to help them endure physical discomfort, fatigue, and despair." She goes on: "Coca breaks in the morning and afternoon are as established a part of the routine of the mine as the coffee break is of the office." The importance of coca (and alcohol) in making people willing to engage in unpleasant tasks is apparent when, elsewhere in her book, Nash quotes at length a miner discussing his life in the 1920s. Having joined the army to escape poverty, he had been "forced to become a strike breaker." Recounting that experience, the miner says, "The company paid us all. They gave us cigarettes, coca, and alcohol, and when the strike was over, they gave us fifty to one hundred pesos as a tip." Nash concludes her discussion of coca by noting, "Management is well aware of the importance of coca in that it makes the inhuman conditions of the mine tolerable. As a result they keep the pulpería [the company store] well supplied with good coca.... 'If we ran out of coca,' one administrative clerk told me, 'we would really have a revolution on our hands'" (1993:198, 36, 200).

Elsewhere, alcohol was the drug of choice.[26] Arguments were made for providing beer to miners on the South African Rand, like the one claiming that "at Kimberly [the diamond mines,] familiarity with the glass has built moderation in the black man, while it is admitted that better work is got out of him if he sees the prospect of a cheering glass at the end of a day's labor.... On these [Transvaal] fields also...the 'boy' so humored and refreshed [with alcohol] is the better labourer" (van Onselen, 1976:50). Scully (1992) shows how agricultural labor in South Africa was enhanced through the notorious "tot" system, which saw field workers receive cheap wine and liquor as part of their pay. Eber provides similar evidence for alcohol's use in highland Chiapas during the 1930s, citing Ruth Bunzel, who quoted a coffee planter's lament: "[T]ake aguardiente [raw brandy] away from the Indian and what will become of coffee? Coffee plantations run on aguardiente as an automobile runs on gasoline" (1940:363, quoted in Eber 1995:30).

Less potent drugs were also employed to enhance labor. Audrey Richards noted that since the Bemba did not customarily eat a morning meal on awakening, when they began working in copper mines (drawn to them by corvées and the need for cash payment of hut taxes), mine operators thought the Bemba's lack of breakfast slowed their work. Breakfasts of cocoa and white bread then became compulsory for the miners (Richards 1939). Timothy Burke's wonderful study of commodification and consumption in Zimbabwe shows European colonists attempting to increase the demand for tea by marketing it as a labor enhancer:

> [M]arketers actively sought to give public expression to the anxieties and complaints that characterized African daily life in the cities[:]...obtaining work, staying employed, fending off crippling sickness, and achieving upward mobility.... [A]dvertisements also played very strongly, especially in the 1940s and 1950s, to white preconceptions about lazy and indolent African workers.... In one ad, a son tells his father that he is always exhausted and will lose his job soon. His father wisely suggests, "Do as I do my son. Drink a cup of refreshing tea when you feel tired." The son's white employer notes the subsequent improvement and tells him, "I am going to give you a better job." (1996:152–53)[27]

While we cannot always ascertain exactly what drug consumers hoped to gain (relief from physical discomfort, good company, emotional comfort), the consumption of tea or cocoa and perhaps of coca or alcohol as well followed less from a desire to achieve an altered state of consciousness than from the need to overcome the fatigue of daily labor. This seems so even for the initial use of opium among nineteenth-century Chinese coolie laborers and Javanese manual laborers. They received it from their employers, who presumably knew that though "from a clinical point of view morphine does not act as a stimulant in humans, by removing the dull irritation of routine aches and pains, opium would surely induce a feeling of vigor, alertness and energy" (Rush 1990:35) that would help people overcome the pain of hard labor and thus help them work longer and harder than they could have without the drug.

Using drugs to increase the intensity or duration of labor was not an outcome of European expansion. Prior to contact, non-European populations had appreciated drugs' energizing effects, which had been provided by those organizing labor and sought out by laborers themselves.[28] European expansion did create a massive number of people who needed to be spurred on to produce under constraints of time and cost. This and the replacement of traditional with new and often much more powerful drugs—most prominently, distilled liquors but also coca(ine) and opium—as well as softer drugs like caffeine and nicotine greatly intensified the relationship of drugs to labor. Details of how this process of intensification played out in particular cases, the rich complexity of the outcomes, and the motivations of both workers and their employers are revealed in the essays by Angrosino, Suggs and Lewis, Gordon, and Cassman, Cartmell, and Belmonte.

Coffee and Tea and a New Role for Alcohol

During the nineteenth and twentieth centuries a modern, industrialized chemical industry emerged with the ability to isolate, mass produce, and deliver (both globally and, through the development of hypodermic syringes and wooden matches, individually) large quantities of drugs far more potent than their preindustrial predecessors. Industrialized drug production occurred even though many drugs, including alcohol, were increasingly stigmatized, while caffeine and nicotine became the preferred, socially accepted choices.

From their introduction in Europe, coffee and tea stood in contrast to alcohol. If alcohol caused inebriation, coffee and tea sobered (Burnett 1999;

Schivelbusch 1992). If alcohol was associated with vice, coffee and tea were associated with virtue.[29] Unlike taverns, coffeehouses were places where sober men gathered as equals to intelligently consider their affairs and the affairs of the day. In the eighteenth century coffeehouses replaced taverns as sites at which businessmen gathered, and coffee conveyed not only the image of "sobriety" but also of "honesty, reliability and moderation" (Smith 1995:154ff.). While not all coffeehouses evolved into Lloyd's of London, they were associated with business, and a man who wished to make his way in business was far better seen in a coffeehouse than a tavern (Schivelbusch 1992; Smith 1995; Courtwright 2001; Burnett 1999; Pendergrast 1999; Weinberg and Bealer 2001).

Coffee's association with sobriety was partly a continuation of its roles in Ethiopia, Yemen, and then the Muslim Middle East, whence it came to Europe. While coffee's increased popularity in Europe is often linked to the rise of capitalism (it was perceived as the ideal beverage for sober, ascetic businessmen rationally calculating their costs), in the Middle East coffee was first considered an aid to concentration, valued in Sufism and study (Weinberg and Bealer 2001). People in the Middle East and later in Europe shared the perception that coffee consumption drew together gatherings of men who engaged in lively but sober discourse; this led to attempts by rulers to restrict its consumption on the grounds that it promoted sedition (Mathee 1995; Anderson, this volume; Weinberg and Bealer 2001; Schivelbusch 1992). As with many drugs, prohibition failed, and, at least in Europe, coffee and tea became the accepted beverages of the rising, sober middle class. Drinking coffee or tea came to be considered not only an aid to work but also a means of marking oneself as a sober, respectable member of society; their consumption increased.

Later, the consumption of caffeinated beverages no longer demonstrated bourgeois respectability, but their association with energy, with mental acuity, and, particularly, with sobriety remained. As legal and social pressures restricted the consumption of alcohol and hard drugs, the drinking of coffee, tea, and cacao, often consumed with sugar, either directly or in sweets, cakes, and candy, increased. The active agents in these drugs are the methylxanthines discussed by Anderson. Stimulants and hunger suppressants, they are felt to promote clear thinking and provide energy, and they have few deleterious side effects.[30]

The change of preference occurred in everyday life and within institutional structures. As European and American military technology and battle strategy changed from tasks that relied on brute force to tasks that required more sustained and focused attention (i.e., flying an airplane and operating computer-controlled artillery), the preferred drug foods for enhancing job performance changed from alcohol, often used prior to World War II as a stimulant, however momentary, to overcome physical fatigue and thus sustain the work effort, to other drugs, including synthetic manufactured drugs, that enhance a person's ability to concentrate. Pilots in both the Vietnam War and the Persian Gulf War used caffeine pills, ritalin, methadone, methamphetamine, and dextrose tablets as temporary means to enhance concentration and thus performance.

From the mid-nineteenth century onward, the consumption of coffee, tea, and then caffeinated cola beverages increased (see Pendergrast 1993, 1999; Burnett 1999; Anderson, this volume) as these beverages became part of daily life at home and at work, and the promotion of stimulants continues to be significant in our own day. A recent *New York Times* article, for example, reported that some companies such as Snapple, Celestial Seasonings, Coca-Cola, and Procter & Gamble are expanding their beverage labels to include herbal drinks that, much like the early-twentieth-century Coca-Cola ads, claim to enhance a person's alertness, concentration, and memory retention (Barnes and Winter 2001:A1). That these products emerged first in a less commercialized "health food" market suggests that the demand for them is driven by twenty-first-century clerical and professional workers self-medicating to enhance their productivity.[31]

Conversely, the increased antagonism toward alcohol (and later to opiate and coca derivatives and marijuana) seems linked to the rise of capitalism, the incorporation of large-scale, expensive machinery into production, and the concomitant rise in and need for work discipline. E. P. Thompson's classic "Time, Work Discipline, and Industrial Capitalism" stresses that undisciplined alcohol use and an artisan's control over his labor time were part of preindustrial work patterns. The famous "Saint Monday" that workers celebrated in Great Britain was not simply a day off but a day for continuing heavy drinking, and attempts to control the consumption of alcohol were part of an overall attempt to discipline labor and rationalize the production process (Thompson 1967; Gutman 1977 describes similar holidays in U.S. labor history).

Though prior to industrialization plantation workers, miners, sailors, and others doing hard physical labor were often given alcohol as a portion of their wages, throughout the nineteenth century alcohol lost favor with employers, and they often attempted to limit or prohibit its consumption. As Courtwright pithily notes, "As the social environment changed, becoming more rationalized, bureaucratic, and mechanized, the distribution of cheap intoxicants became more troublesome and divisive. *A drunken field hand was one thing, a drunken railroad brakeman quite another*" (2001:178, emphasis added).[32] Worries about the effect of drug use on control over labor, coupled with xenophobic concerns about Asian immigrants, racist attitudes toward African Americans, worries about crime, evidence of an increased use of purer and more powerful products such as morphine and then heroin, and social reforms, including the professionalization of medicine and increased government regulation, led to similar pressures for restrictions on the use of opiates, cocaine, and marijuana (Courtwright 2001; Pendergrast 1993).[33]

If manufacturers sought a sober workforce, some labor leaders did too, arguing that alcohol, not religion, was the opiate of the masses and that sober workers would be more capable of promoting their class interests. Others in the labor movement claimed that taverns were the workers' political clubs and that attempts at prohibition were in fact attacks on the institutions in which worker solidarity was constructed and maintained both by fostering conviviality and camaraderie and by providing a venue for political discussion and organization. Drink was thus seen as both the friend and foe of the working man.

These oppositions barely scratch the surface of the complexities of drug consumption.[34] *Rivethead,* Ben Hamper's autobiographical account of life on the General Motors assembly line, describes workers drinking and using drugs on the job with attitudes that clearly make consumption acts of quiet resistance. But drinking to blot out the mind-numbing repetitiveness of life on the assembly line is also what permitted Hamper to work day in and day out. Drinking may thus have paradoxically kept an experienced worker on the job. Indeed, on-the-job drinking may simultaneously be an act of shared resistance that makes the work experience more meaningful and more sustainable even as it embodies opposition. To close the circle, Hamper's graphic description of the physical and emotional toll of his drinking highlights the cost of using alcohol and drugs as an anodyne. In Hamper's account, drinking created worker solidarity and was an act of resistance, an anodyne to drudgery, and a labor enhancer. It played a role in the social reproduction of the working class and wreaked havoc with his family life, first as the child of a drinking father and in his own adult life, and with his health.

From at least the eighteenth century on, these contradictions and complexities abound wherever one looks at conjunctions of drink and labor within the metropolitan arenas of European American culture.[35] Still, the broad trend was for the restriction of alcohol consumption or opiates and the acceptance of stimulating bitter beverages like coffee and tea.

The increased consumption of bitter brews was not solely driven by the attempts of employers and reformers to sober up their workers. Mintz (1985) has pointed out that the British urban laboring class's switch to sweetened tea was part of a complex shift in labor patterns, gender roles, and diet that saw it occupy several new niches in new workers' lives. Those who consumed tea or coffee and sugar were not simply the passive victims of soft drug lords who pushed these goods, they demanded them just as the natives of the New World and the South Pacific demanded alcohol and tobacco. Consumers wanted hot, bitter beverages because they fit in with their new lives, making possible, for example, quick and cheap warm meals. Stimulants, coupled with large doses of sucrose, also gave cold, hungry, poor workers a noticeable kick of energy. It is an irony worth noting that when members of the new European and American ruling class promoted their workers' consumption of bitter beverages they were promoting drugs once prohibited because of their "revolutionary" potential, revealing again how much the perceptions of drugs' qualities and hence the conditions of their "proper" use are socially constructed.

Not surprisingly, ferment over drug use in Europe and among "white" Americans affected the attitude toward the use of "hard" drugs and alcohol in the colonies, and the ambiguities, contradictions, and disputes surrounding metropolitan consumption are also manifest in colonial drug use. Van Onselen (1976) shows that as mining operations on the Transvaal shifted from relatively simple surface mining to deep pit mines requiring elaborate technology, great capital investment, and steady labor, the mine owners tried to restrict miners' access to liquor. Essays in Crush and Ambler (1992) detail the complexity of this process. They—and van Onselen—describe the conflicts among Europeans who were, sometimes simultaneously, trying to restrict (see, e.g., Courtwright 2001:175), control, and profit from native liquor consumption in southern Africa.

The combination of gender roles, indigenous attitudes toward drink and work, residential and organizational patterns associated with an industrialized labor process, and the ways in which state pressure for temperance were imposed made some drinking behavior simultaneously an act of resistance, an attempt to overcome the drudgery of labor, and an effort to enact continuities of local custom. Thus if the big picture of drug use following industrialization reveals a general pattern of pressure to restrict alcohol and hard drugs and to replace them with the stimulants found in bitter beverages, a closer look reveals a broad stream composed of numerous eddies and whirls. In the end, drug use in colonial circumstances takes on all the complexities of drug use in metropolitan areas with the added complexities of precontact patterns of use and multiple loci of power and interest.

Still, through all the complexities of considering different stages of contact or relations of production, an underlying pattern remains: humans find drugs attractive; they are powerful agents for gaining access to labor power, for gaining some control over it, and for increasing people's ability or willingness to work long and hard under difficult conditions. The chapters that follow detail variations on these themes.

2

Mutual Exploitation?

Aboriginal Australian Encounters with Europeans, Southeast Asians, and Tobacco

Maggie Brady and Jeremy Long

Eighteen years after Capt. James Cook claimed the eastern coast of Australia, "New Holland," for Britain in 1770, a new settlement at Port Jackson (now Sydney) was established as a penal colony. The intention was that the prisoners transported from England would undertake the hard labor of clearing land and planting crops that would make the settlement self-sufficient. The eleven ships of the First Fleet that arrived in January 1788 carried some fifteen hundred Britons, more than half of whom were convicts, to a country whose people, flora, fauna, and geography were almost entirely unknown (Tench 1996). They found a population of indigenous people—hunters, gatherers, and fishers—who neither tilled the soil nor altered or "improved" the landscape in the way it was thought by Europeans that landowners should.[1] The indigenous people were considered by the Europeans not to have advanced far enough beyond the "state of nature" to be recognized as having "sovereignty," so the land was regarded as *terra nullius,* having no recognizable owners and therefore as unencumbered, free for the taking. The motivation for the colonization of Australia was primarily economic: taking, controlling, and using the land were central to the purpose of the British invasion (Atkinson and Aveling 1987:205).

The steadily increasing number of convicts provided free or cheap labor for

31

military and civil officials and other free (and freed) settlers who were soon on the lookout for exploitable natural resources. Sheep were found to flourish and increase, and within thirty years stock owners' flocks had spread over the inland plains. In the 1830s men made fortunes sending wool to the mills of Britain, and "squatters" took up land under license beyond the official limits of settlement, to the south, west, and north of the original settlement, in Tasmania (then Van Diemen's Land), and later in South Australia and Western Australia, where more colonies were established.[2] The convict shepherds employed by stock owners, many of whom were absentees living far away in the towns, sometimes came into violent conflict with the Aboriginal inhabitants whose land was being taken over. The military was at times called in to quell the resistance on the frontiers of settlement. The Aborigines showed little interest in manual work, and for the first fifty years convict labor was abundant enough to meet the demand. But in the 1840s, as transportation ceased and the gold rushes of the 1850s created acute labor shortages, the squatters argued unsuccessfully for the importation of "coolie labor" from India. In the settled areas introduced diseases and intermittent guerrilla warfare on the advancing pastoral frontiers drastically reduced the Aboriginal population. Surviving groups tended to gather at townships and at those sheep stations where they were offered food and clothing and work as shepherds and domestic servants. In the tropical north, where cattle proved to do better than sheep, Aboriginal people became an increasingly important, even vital, source of labor for the industry. Not all the country was suitable for pastoral development, and in the large areas of desert in the center and some of the rugged and remote coastal areas in the far north the Aboriginal inhabitants remained relatively untouched; colonial endeavors there were mediated by missionaries. As Peterson (1998) points out, land, labor, and resources were not systematically appropriated until after World War II.

Most of the convicts, marines, and soldiers were heavy users of alcohol. They came from an England where drunkenness was rife and where only a few years before Australia was settled six million people managed to consume eleven million gallons of gin. Most cargoes landed in Sydney included rum, and all inhabitants soon gained access to spirits, despite official attempts to restrict supply to both convicts and settlers. A chronic shortage of coins and the desirability of alcohol meant that rum became an item of barter, indeed, a currency within the colony (Dingle 1980; Langton 1993). Convicts, laborers, officers, and even the builders of the first church in 1793 were paid in liquor. Illicit stills were common, and attempts were made to establish local wine and hop industries, initially with mixed success. With the spread of settlement the tyranny of distance came to influence European consumption styles, and the great distances separating workplace and pub produced a "work and bust" pattern in which workers from the bush "knocked down" their paychecks in spells of binge drinking. The new settlers were also heavy users of tobacco. In 1819 it was reported that every second adult British male was addicted to tobacco. As white settlement took hold of the continent both alcohol and opium had their uses, but tobacco had a particularly powerful influence by mediating a wide range of interchanges between whites and indigenes and as an inducement to labor. In this process the indigenous people were often active and engaged participants, seeking out the sources of desired substances as they had done prior to the invasion. The indigenous populations already made use of naturally occurring and regionally specific drug substances, including both alcohol and tobaccos, but they were unprepared for the powerful attraction that introduced alcohol, commercially produced tobacco, and opium would hold and the impact on their world that the desire for these substances would produce. Marcia Langton (1993) has suggested that alcohol was used as a device for seducing Aboriginal people to engage economically, politically, and socially with the colony. Tobacco may have been even more addictive, more seductive, and more persuasive than alcohol in this process.

Indigenous Use of Tobaccos

The indigenous peoples of Australia have generally been thought to have had no knowledge of alcohol and only limited knowledge of other mood-altering substances prior to the arrival of the British in 1788. In fact, the indigenous peoples of the continent and its islands had a thorough understanding of the uses of psychoactive plant substances and exploited them with considerable skill. Apart from using what was already on the continent, some groups assiduously incorporated new drug substances that were introduced by visitors long before the British arrived.

Of preexisting uses of alcohol we know a little from some early commentators. According to the Tasmanian journals (1829–34) of G. A. Robinson, mildly intoxicating drinks were made from the sap of the "mellifluous" cider gum, *Eucalyptus gunnii*. The trees were tapped to release the sap, and Robinson was told that this juice frequently made the Aborigines drunk (Plomley 1966:534;

Low 1990). In 1904 Roth documented the use in Western Australia of man-gaitch, a fermented liquor made from the soaked cones and flowers of a banksia, the consumption of which was said to produce "excessive volubility." There are also reports of the consumption of fermented beverages made from the honey of soaked blossoms and from other plants in the Northern Territory that caused "indubitable merriment" (Basedow 1929:154) and on the Diamantina River in southwestern Queensland (Duncan-Kemp 1933). It was reported that the Aborigines of Lake Boga, Victoria, made a stupefying drink from the root and bark of the ming, *Santalum murrayanum (T. L. Mitchell)* (Stone 1911), and another such drink was derived from the corkwood tree, *Duboisia myoporoides,* by Aborigines in the Shoalhaven/Illawarra districts of New South Wales (Johnston and Cleland 1933–34; MacPherson 1921). These are scattered vignettes, and there are few eyewitness accounts. We know nothing about the social circumstances under which these drinks might have been consumed or whether their use was rule governed.

Much more widespread and far better documented was the use of a variety of indigenous nicotine-bearing plants, which were used not just as stimulants but sometimes as a means to alter consciousness. Before the arrival of outsiders, Aboriginal people did not smoke any form of tobacco but instead chewed the leaves of several plants, some of which were nicotine containing.[3] Linguist and Pallotine father A. R. Peile (1997) lists nine different plants used by just one language group, the Kukatja of Western Australia. The nicotine-bearing plants include *Nicotiana excelsior, N. suaveolens, N. ingulba,* and *N. gossei.* The leaves are dried in the sun and rolled into balls or lumps, which are wetted with saliva before use and dipped in and mixed with ash from the bark, leaf, or twigs of particular trees. This alkaline ash is added in order to give more tang or bite to the quid; it also speeds the absorption of the nicotine (Watson 1983; Goddard and Kalotas 1995). People say that the ash makes the quid juicy and yellow "like a custard." Wads of mixed ash and tobacco are stored behind the ear, where they not only deliver a mild dose of nicotine (Watson 1983) but also are believed by some groups to have the power to improve a person's hearing (Peile 1997). Bush tobacco such as this was and still is used as a stimulant and a depressant. When chewed, it has a narcotic effect and is used as a medicament to alleviate physical stress, mental weariness, pain, headache, and dryness of mouth and to still hunger pangs.[4]

The leaves of the most highly favored tobacco bush found in central Australia, *N. gossei,* contain 1.1 percent nicotine (Carr and Carr 1981; Jessop 1985).

Women from this region have stated that bush tobacco is so strong that it makes people sick until they become used to it (Brady, personal communication). Some species are said to be "hot" and "biting," with the ability to blister the mouth. Bush tobacco is so desired that people refer to themselves as "starving" for it (Peterson 1997:179). It is highly sought after, prized, and chewed with enthusiasm by young and old. A photograph from the Kimberley region of Western Australia, for example, depicts a Worora boy of about twelve years of age being bitten on the chin "as part of the admission-rite to tobacco chewing" (McCarthy 1957:138).[5] A Yankunytjatjara man from central Australia describes the joys of mingkulpa (bush tobacco) in this translated account: "Then his eyes'd lift up, from chewing that tobacco. 'oh yes! I'm chewing tobacco at last! I've been without it for ages! Oh quick, and I can sleep with it in my mouth!' They would talk about sleeping with it in the mouth. 'Oh, to sleep with the stuff!' As it gets dark, they'd be saying, 'Oh! I'm going to sleep with it!'...[a]nd would travel around contented, with it held in the mouth. They'd feel satisfied. They put some in the mouth and travel around, looking out for game" (Goddard and Kalotas 1995:98).

Aborigines did not cultivate tobacco, although according to eyewitness accounts, Torres Strait Islanders grew tobacco of unknown species.[6] Native tobacco was traded over long distances and still is today. There are accounts dating from the 1940s of it being traded from the "stone" country in northern South Australia to the edge of the Nullarbor Plain hundreds of miles south; fifty years later, one of us (Brady) saw a woman from this area with a tin of mingkulpa that she had obtained in trade from the same stony country to the north.

A Psychoactive Drug

As well as these indigenous tobaccos, an even more powerful nicotine-containing drug, known as pituri, was used that was made from the cured leaves of the shrub *Duboisia hopwoodii* of the Solanaceae family (Peterson 1979). Like native tobaccos, the leaves were dried, mixed with ash, and chewed.[7] Prepared and chewed quids were stuck behind the ear.[8] In the prime growing areas, pituri plants appear to have contained up to 8 percent nicotine (commercial cigarettes contain about 2 percent). There are numerous descriptions of its opium-like effects. It was a powerful stimulant and an addictive anesthetic, and it was widely traded; distant groups sent message sticks requesting supplies (Carr and Carr 1981; Roth 1904; Watson 1983). Apart from its use as a stimulant,

the drug was used in southwestern Queensland as an offering to a mythologi-
cal being associated with the rain ceremony (Duncan-Kemp 1964). It is likely
that users were addicted rather than merely habituated to the drug. For all these
reasons, pituri has been described as the "gold standard" for exchange and
barter.

Duncan-Kemp, an acute local observer from the Channel Country of southwestern Queensland, where the most potent pituri grows, declared that a sev-
enty-pound bag of undried pituri leaf represented untold wealth.[9] She observed
that it was the highest currency possible and was only used among tribes whose
country did not grow the priceless product. Rolled into tight balls or pellets
and wrapped in bark or plant fibers, it kept its narcotic properties for months
(Duncan-Kemp 1933:221; Roth 1984; Horne and Aiston 1924). The country was
(and still is, in some regions) crisscrossed by trade routes or "roads" along which
a complex series of economic exchanges took place; religious cults were also
transmitted and exchanged along these routes (Akerman 1980). Pituri passed
along particular trade routes in association with numerous other articles such as
pearl shell, eagle-hawk feathers, stone tools, ocher, boomerangs, human-hair
belts, blankets, and red cloth (Roth 1984). In contrast to these expected means
of exchange, there is an unusual account of large-scale open-market trading for
pituri taking place in the early twentieth century at some rural settlements
such as Goyder's Lagoon and Birdsville (Watson 1983, citing Aiston 1937).
The market involved large numbers of Aborigines (up to five hundred), much
haggling over the barter price, and professional Aboriginal traders.

An unusual feature of *Duboisia hopwoodii* is that although it was so highly valued and traded across a particular region of the country, it was not used
as a mood-altering drug by Aborigines everywhere. In fact, in central Australia it was placed in waterholes in order to stun game, as its leaves contain
alkaloids that are poisonous to animals (Cleland and Johnston 1937–38; Jessop 1985; Duncan-Kemp 1964:72; Spencer and Gillen 1904:20). Unfortunately, both historical and contemporary accounts of its use become confused,
because, as with the term *kangaroo,* the term *pituri,* rapidly assimilated into
English and Aboriginal English, was applied to all indigenous chewing tobacco,
not just the product made from *Duboisia*.[10] "Pituri" has even been used to
describe cigarettes: "We are all eating that *pitcheri* [*sic*] which is from the
white man, cigarettes and tobacco, it is very good *pitcheri*" (Peterson 1979:179).
Johnston and Cleland noted in 1933–34 that Cooper's Creek Aborigines referred
to tobacco as "white fellow *pitchiri* [*sic*]."

True pituri undoubtedly had several social and physiological functions, and its use was almost certainly restricted to older men.[11] Watson (1983) cites a number of sources indicating that it was used to promote sociality, with the quid being passed from person to person to chew, each person deriving an additional stimulus from its psychoactive qualities. The ethnography reveals that, traditionally, communities exerted a number of social control mechanisms over nicotine-containing plants. There were restraints on production, distribution, and consumption that are particularly apparent in the case of pituri. Mature men were the retainers of restricted knowledge of the processing of pituri, particularly, the artificial drying techniques used to enhance its psychoactive properties. Watson believes that the rapid decimation of Aborigines brought about by disease and massacre meant that the pituri clans became extinct, and with them was lost the religious and economic knowledge associated with it. As a result, its use declined at a time when tobacco, alcohol, and opium were becoming available and taking its place (Watson 1983; Evans, Saunders, and Cronin 1975).

The entrenched use of native tobacco and pituri by Aboriginal people in many areas meant that a habituated clientele had been created for the commercially produced tobacco brought in by Europeans and other visitors.[12] Aborigines went to considerable lengths to obtain this tobacco and quickly became addicted to it. The manner in which pituri and tobacco had been traded and the fact that a wide variety of goods were obtained in exchange for these drugs provided the sociocultural basis for the way in which imported tobacco was obtained, exchanged, and traded with Europeans. In a sense, people simply transferred their gathering behavior into gathering from Europeans. It is not clear, though, whether Aborigines used native tobaccos in every part of the continent. This is particularly difficult to ascertain for northern coastal regions, where the record is confounded by the fact that Aborigines had smoked introduced tobacco for at least a century before Europeans settled there, and for regions in the southeast first settled by the British. There is also the question of the rapidity with which groups that used no native tobacco became addicted to introduced tobacco. Lumholtz, for example, noted in 1889 that the Aborigines of the Herbert River (Queensland) had no stimulants. He proposed that "this is the secret of the influence of tobacco, which they value so highly that they sometimes wrap a small piece of about three to four inches long in grass, in order to enjoy it later with allied tribes with whom they are on a friendly footing, or they may send it in exchange for other advantages to another tribe

37

...The tobacco is not chewed, but only smoked, and they believe that it is good for everybody" (1980:115).

Another suggestion made by Lumholtz was that smoking tobacco, like wearing "the garments and ornaments of white people," was a marker of "civilization" among Aborigines and a means of distinguishing themselves from their myall, or "wild," contemporaries. If Aborigines did have access to strong native tobaccos, why were they so desirous of introduced tobacco? One answer to this may be that as with introduced staple foods such as flour and sugar (which quickly replaced their traditional counterparts), tobacco was rapidly adopted because it was available in volume and represented a great saving in labor (Baker 1999:128).

The Incorporation of Novel Substances

Macassan seafarers were the first major distributors of imported tobacco to Aboriginal Australians. They visited northern Australia from around 1700 until the early twentieth century to fish for trepang, and they used tobacco to facilitate good relations with the Aboriginal owners of the land. Described by early European observers as "Malays," these traders were in fact Macassarese, a distinct linguistic group from the southwest of the island of Sulawesi in present-day Indonesia. Trepang, or bêche-de-mer, is a marine invertebrate found on shallow seabeds. It was a major item of commerce throughout the great archipelago to the north of Australia and a vital ingredient in the commercial relationship between China and the seaport city of Macassar (Macknight 1976:14).

The Macassarese had no use for trepang themselves, and the product fished from Australian waters was exported to an international market. The trepang trade became increasingly important once the Dutch destroyed the role of Macassar in the spice trade in the seventeenth century (Macknight 1976:11), but because of its location at the intersection of numerous trade routes in the archipelago, the city formed a natural center for trade in maritime products and continued to flourish. The trepang fishing trade was a highly enterprising exercise: at least a thousand men made the voyage to Australia each year in large seaworthy praus, sailing from Macassar on the northwest monsoon and back again several months later when the winds changed to the southeast. This went on for most of the nineteenth century, bringing hundreds of Bugis and Macassarese seamen into regular and extended contact with coastal Aboriginal residents over an area from the Kimberley region in the west to the Gulf of Carpenteria in the east.[13]

The Macassans introduced numerous items, including language terms (such as *balanda,* derived from "Hollander," now used for all white people), dugout canoes, detachable harpoon heads, and shovel-nosed spears. They brought liquor, particularly arrack (probably derived from palms) and brandy, and left behind bottles that once contained Dutch gin. The term remembered by Aborigines and still used in the region to refer to alcohol is *anitja,* derived from the Macassan *anisi,* meaning anisette (Macknight 1976:30–31). Imported drug substances included betel nuts, tobacco, and smoking pipes (Love 1915; Macknight 1976; Spencer and Gillen 1904). Of these, tobacco and tobacco pipes have had the most enduring influence, and the long Macassan pipe became incorporated into Aboriginal social and ceremonial life. In the 1950s ethnographic photographer Axel Poignant observed two ceremonial leaders in Arnhem Land sharing such a pipe after a cleansing ceremony and noted its use when men were sitting around yarning (Poignant 1996:64; Thomson 1939). Tobacco received in association with particular ceremonies was declared taboo to all but the fully initiated members of the totemic group (Thomson 1939:76). The prestigious nature of Macassar-style pipes is indicated in this region by the fact that special pipes were incised and dedicated by their owners, thus restricting their use. This was interpreted by the ethnographer Donald Thomson as a ruse enabling the "hoarding or conserving [of] tobacco without giving the legitimate ground for ill-feeling, or the risk of openly incurring a charge of meanness that must otherwise result" (1939:76). Since demands for tobacco were common, this strategy was highly effective (Peterson 1993).

The Macassan voyagers recognized Aboriginal ownership of the land and paid tribute (or at least kept the peace) each season with the owners of the territories for the right to fish for trepang and pearls. Thomson's informants told him that Aborigines did not actually work for the trepangers, but occasionally, when men were short, they helped to make up the crews of canoes that operated as tenders from the praus in diving for trepang (1949:51–52).[14] The items with which the Macassans "paid" for the right to use Aboriginal marine resources (and to utilize coastal camping places where they boiled and smoked the trepang) became highly valued trade goods known as *gerri* (goods, possessions). Axes, iron, wire, calico, tobacco, and pipes acquired in this way passed far inland to people who had never met the Macassans, long before any British settlement in the Northern Territory. Tobacco was said to be one of the most popular items obtained from the Macassans.[15] Searcy noted, "The niggers [*sic*] were either assisting the Malays, or lolling about smoking cigarettes made of

Malay tobacco, rolled up in pandanus palm-leaf" (1909:27).

Tobacco was also introduced into Cape York, the northernmost tip of Australia near the border with Papua New Guinea and the Torres Strait Islands, although it is not clear by whom (Creed 1878:267). An eyewitness account from a shipwrecked white woman named Barbara Thompson who was stranded on an island in the Torres Strait for four or five years (1844–49) described the islanders smoking tobacco that they had obtained from mainland blacks (i.e., Cape York Aborigines). It "had come from the ship [i.e., a visiting European ship,] some of the men fainting away, and some getting quite sick" (Moore 1979:190). The islanders used smoking pipes of bamboo, traded from other islands, and perfected a method of inhaling deep into the lungs: "The effect of this kind of smoking appears to be very severe. The men always seem quite dazed for a second or two, or even longer, and their eyes water; but they enjoy it greatly, and value tobacco highly, they will usually sell almost anything they possess for some. I have seen an old man reel and stagger from the effects of one pull at a bamboo pipe, and I have heard of a man even dropping down on the ground from its effects" (Haddon 1901:75–76).

The crews and passengers of the first British ships to make landfall in South Australia were also users of tobacco. It seems likely that the officers and members of the upper social echelons took snuff and later smoked cigars, while the seamen and the convicts they transported smoked tobacco in pipes. Not surprisingly, the habit most widely introduced to Aboriginal people in the first sixty to seventy years of contact was that of pipe smoking. Early reports and illustrations from the 1820s show that Aboriginal men and women quickly took to smoking tobacco from the ubiquitous clay pipe of the day—the pipe of the manual workers (Walker 1980; Wilson and Kelly 1987; Backhouse 1843).[16] The clay pipe was fragile, cheap, and disposable, and pipes were manufactured in the colony as early as 1804. A million pipes were imported into New South Wales in 1836.[17] British servants, ticket-of-leave men, and convicts alike were issued with tobacco as an incentive for good behavior and in order to induce them to work. One report from 1828 declared that the convicts in the interior "cannot or will not work without it" (Walker 1984:12–13). It was not long before the same technique was brought to bear on attempts at Aboriginal labor. The squatters who enticed Aborigines to work for them created a form of bondage by addiction to a product grown by black slaves on the other side of the world. A popular tobacco in the colonies was a Virginia leaf called "Negrohead" (Atkinson and Aveling 1987:171).

In the early days of settlement, tobacco supplies were scarce enough for everyone to discourage indiscriminate distribution; there was argument and theft on both sides, with the ill feeling exacerbated by the tit-for-tat killings of soldiers and natives as Aboriginal land was taken over.[18] The missionary and linguist Reverend L. Threlkeld, for example, in 1825 tells of a "croppy" (a prisoner or convict) snatching away an Aborigine's tobacco and keeping it for himself (Gunson 1974:44). In 1837 parties of men overlanding with sheep and cattle to Port Phillip and Adelaide annoyed local Aborigines by not sharing their supplies of food and tobacco. Strife over Aboriginal women occurred when whites refused to supply their relatives with food, tobacco, and clothing on request (Reece 1974:53–54). Aborigines raided European farms, flocks, and outposts and conducted systematic attacks on individual properties; they often stole tobacco supplies along with food and other goods (Reynolds 1981; Plomley 1966). As with the Macassan trade items in the north, material objects and food emanating from the British in the south found their way to the "other" side of the frontier to be used by Aboriginal people who had not yet encountered the invaders. Objects included teapots, wheat, flour, horseshoe nails, bottle glass, belt buckles, and tobacco. In Queensland in 1889 it was reported that Aborigines bartered for tobacco and wrapped it up in leaves for transportation and trade (Reynolds 1981:43). In this way it reached people well beyond direct contact with whites.

Tobacco as a Means of Conciliation

Despite the shortages, early gifts of tobacco were made in order to exact good relations with the natives, to conciliate them, and in some instances a sense of reciprocity is apparent. The diary of Governor Lachlan Macquarie in 1821, thirty-three years after the establishment of the colony, described an excursion by boat near Port Stephens and contains one of the earliest accounts of the giving of tobacco: "A single native came running after us, holding up a fish in his hand, which he seemed disposed to give us. We put back to the shore to speak to him; he approached towards the boat with great caution and apparently under fear of being molested. He however ventured near enough to the boat to hand his fish to Mrs M. who gave him a piece of tobacco in return, with which he seemed much pleased" (1821:8).

Early commissioners of crown lands and later the police gave food and tobacco in order to parley with Aborigines or in payment of services by them

(Walker 1980:268), but diarists and letter writers seem to have been too focused on drunkenness among the natives to make much mention of smoking (see Tench 1996; Backhouse 1843). Tobacco was frequently used in the first encounter between white men and the indigenous people they met. Searcy observed that he "always carried tobacco to assist in establishing friendly relations with the blacks" (1909:49).

Imported tobacco rapidly became a highly desired commodity, and there are numerous accounts—mostly lamenting in tone—of importunate Aborigines, declaring that their "only desires" were for spirits and tobacco (Gunson 1974:347). These accounts depict Aborigines as being demeaned and degraded as a result, although whether this was a reaction to the so-called begging in which they engaged or whether it was thought smoking or drinking in itself was degrading to the otherwise "noble savages" is not clear. Certainly, there are accounts of children being allowed to smoke that seem alarming today. For example, in his journal of 3 June 1825, Threlkeld observed a child crying during a funeral: "[T]o my surprise it was an infant at the breast screaming for a pipe of tobacco which its mother was smoking. It obtained the pipe but owing to its infancy was not able to convey it to its mouth. The mother aided it and the little infant actually whiffed it, the smoke coming out of its mouth and then as though exhausted by the effects of the tobacco fell back on the breast and washed it down with its mother's milk" (Gunson 1974:89). A railway employee stationed on the edge of the Great Victoria Desert in South Australia in the 1920s also observed a child sucking on an adult's pipe (Bolam 1978); and Garry (1930), who kept a diary in a buffalo camp in the Northern Territory Kakadu region, noted a child as young as six smoking a pipe (cf. Lumholtz 1980:115). Among the many artifacts he collected in northern Australia, Thomson obtained miniature smoking pipes that were used as toys by children (1939; Haagen 1994).

Aboriginal demands were interpreted by most whites as being unwarranted and were invariably described as "begging," despite the obvious fact that their land was being taken over without treaty or payment by the unwelcome visitors. Curr describes a hostile incident in 1841 in which two naked Aborigines, after having attempted an attack, begged hard for tobacco and food (1883:57). From the Aboriginal point of view, it is clear that they were expecting European men living on and using their land and waters to behave henceforth as classificatory brothers, sons, and nephews and to provide for their "relatives" without question (Reynolds 1981). Despite already having given up at least some of the land, many people continued to offer gifts to Europeans (as with the gift of fish to Mrs. Macquarie) in anticipation of an exchange; but reciprocity quickly became skewed and remained so. A patrol officer wrote of contact with Aboriginal people (which occurred a century later in some parts of central Australia): "When contacts are first made the aborigine likes to give presents in appreciation of gifts he may receive. It is perhaps natural that the white refuses the gift of some half cooked kangaroo or mangey looking rabbit (even though he is not obliged to eat it) but the result is that very quickly the aborigine believes that the white will provide free and continuing food from his inexhaustible supply for nothing in return—the genesis of a life of parasitic and demoralising beggary by the aborigine" (MacDougall 1956).

In the early twentieth century a chief protector of Aborigines, W. G. Stretton, implied that reciprocity was important and argued that tobacco could be used as a civilizing influence: "There can be no better civilising influence than that of continually moving about among the various tribes, each time taking a little tobacco or coloured cloth. How often has the weary traveller had to trust to the natives for a drink of water!" (cited in Rowse 1998:29).

The Power of Tobacco

"Under the 'drive' for tobacco," wrote Thomson, "the natives will undertake long journeys and endure unbelievable hardships, to obtain a few ounces of trade tobacco" (1939:83). Tobacco and other desired goods were commodities that, intentionally or unintentionally, caused hundreds of Aboriginal people to leave their traditional homelands and that brought them into contact with white settlements. Langton (1993) writes of this process as "taming" Aborigines by drawing them into ration depots and towns. Movement of this sort was not usually a one-time affair but a more gradual, subtle detachment of people from their homelands and a reattachment to a new milieu. Desert people, for example, describe how, as more and more of their relatives moved into missions or settlements, those remaining became increasingly anxious about their ability to care for the land and its sacred places. Survival became more difficult as the populations dwindled and water sources were untended (Brady 1987). In many areas small groups of people continued to move in and back out over many years, with the momentum gradually decreasing so that the periods of settlement in proximity to whites grew longer. Stanner wrote despairingly of this trend in the Daly River region of the Northern Territory: "Each enterprise after

43

the 1870s had drawn more Aborigines towards the river and had made them more familiar with Europeans and more dependent on their goods.... In places where no European had ever set foot, or was to do so for many years, a demand had grown up for iron goods, tobacco, tea, sugar and clothes" (1979:81).

One of the most remarkable accounts of premeditated movement—and unpremeditated eventual relocation—by Aborigines in order to obtain supplies of tobacco was given to Peter Read by a Warlmala man, Engineer Jack Japaljarri (Read and Japaljarri 1978). Engineer Jack told how in 1926 his group encountered several wandering European bushmen with whom they established economic relations, including the receipt of tobacco. In return for flour and tobacco they showed one man, a Mr. Hamilton, routes through the desert; they camped and hunted wild camels with him. When these supplies ran out, it was decided the group should visit Wave Hill cattle station for more. In order to do this, they had to traverse country belonging to another group, the Kurintji, with whom they used to "make a war." The necessity now was to get friendly in order "to gettem longa tobacco, go longa tobacco, get it tobacco." Two formal "peace" ceremonies were negotiated with the Kurintji in order to allow safe passage, and the group of fifty Warlmala finally arrived at the station. Once there they were given tobacco, and they camped some miles away. They desired more and approached the station, where the manager demanded work in return for rations. "Whatever their intentions [i.e., to return to the desert] two months after leaving the desert, many of the Warlmala were enduring conditions in a road gang little short of slavery" (Read and Japaljarri 1978:146; Read and Read 1991:87–90). In this and many other cases, the European cattle station managers were ready and waiting to exploit the supply of cheap labor that had been created by a desire for tobacco.

Appropriating Intellectual and Cultural Property

The realization of the power of tobacco provided those Europeans who wanted something from Aborigines—whether their intellectual, cultural, or physical property or their labor—with a persuasive weapon. Christian missions of various denominations used tobacco and other items in order to procure converts and congregations, although some denominations, such as German missionaries at Moreton Bay in Queensland, were at a disadvantage as they were nonsmokers and would not give away tobacco (Walker 1980:269). Missions also used gifts of tobacco to placate men whose arranged marriages they had intercepted (Berndt and Berndt 1951–52). Aboriginal labor was essential for the cost-effectiveness of missions. Work itself was a key element in the Christian ideology of the time, which associated constancy, self-determination, and social responsibility with work. In addition, industriousness was believed to have a remedial effect on the pauperized classes and the uncivilized (Kidd 1997:23). Many missions had small-scale farming and other projects, vegetable gardens, and herds of goats for which Aborigines provided labor. At a mission near Lake Macquarie, for example, natives were employed to clear land at the settlement for the planting of corn and wheat. The mission supplied them "for their labor with food and slops, tobacco and fishhooks. They worked well while under the direction of a free man and his two sons" (Woolmington 1973:88).

In 1948 an argument erupted over tobacco distribution in the establishments of the Church Missionary Society in northern Australia. One missionary at Oenpelli lobbied against and ultimately succeeded in halting the distribution of tobacco rations, undertaken on behalf of the government, on the grounds that it was an addictive substance and detrimental to the Christian principle of healthy living.[19] Two prominent Australian anthropologists, Ronald and Catherine Berndt, working at Oenpelli complained that the ban was causing quarrels and fights among the people. Eventually the Northern Territory administration instructed the mission to resume distribution at the risk of forfeiting its license to conduct missions. In the end the matter was resolved when the mission agreed to make tobacco available for sale at the mission store on condition it was not to be available to children (Cole 1980; Berndt and Berndt 1951–52; Long 1992).[20]

Apart from those who attempted to appropriate the souls of the indigenes, the colonial enterprise brought with it an interest in the acquisition of their culture. Both anthropologists and less scrupulous collectors sought out items of material culture and intellectual knowledge in exchange for items valued by Aborigines. Languages too could be transmitted using tobacco as a facilitator. Threlkeld, appointed to work at the Lake Macquarie, New South Wales, mission in 1825, devoted a good deal of time to learning the local language, compiling a dictionary, and translating the Bible in order to civilize and instruct the Aborigines. He enticed them to his tent by gifts of tobacco, and as he noted in his 1825 reminiscences, "[T]he tent drew many who s[a]t smoking their pipes around a charcoal fire answering such questions as I proposed, until the fumes of the fire, the everlasting stench of Tobacco, and the disagreeable smell of their own persons would compel me frequently to take refuge in the open air.... [B]y supplying the Blacks with fish-hooks, tobacco and other little articles I could secure a party at any time when the weather was favourable" (Gunson 1974:46).

There is no doubt that Aborigines parted with sacred and other objects in return for valued goods. Charles Chewings noted in 1936: "The native has arrived at the stage when he willingly parts with his most sacred *tjuringa* [secret or sacred ceremonial boards] and other ceremonial objects to the whites for a little tea or sugar, flour or clothing.... If you desire some article they possess and value you can offer nothing more tempting than tobacco in exchange for it. More *tjuringa*, pointing bones and weapons have been purchased from them by tobacco than anything else" (cited in Anderson 1995:102).

In many instances, however, the anthropologists were giving away a commodity that was highly valued for things of much less value from the Aboriginal point of view such as samples of flora and fauna, ritual that was being performed anyway, items of material culture that could be readily replaced, and information that was not lost by being shared. There are many recorded instances of these exchanges. One example is that of W. Baldwin Spencer, a biologist who advised the federal government on Aboriginal policy and who was collecting animal specimens as part of his research at Charlotte Waters in the Northern Territory. He noted in his diary for April 1901: "I have started the *lubras* [slang for Aboriginal women] out hunting for beasts, with the provision of flour and baccy if they get any. The highest price is two sticks of tobacco for one special kind of 'rat' but I'm afraid they won't get it" (1901:127).[21] On their 1901–2 expedition, Spencer and his companion, F. W. Gillen, carried provisions "enough to allow of trade with the natives," including forty bags of flour (each weighing two hundred pounds), seven hundred pounds of sugar, and four hundred pounds of tobacco as well as "innumerable" pipes (Spencer and Gillen 1912:230). He describes a welcoming deputation of Arunta (central Australia) men:

> They were naturally much interested in our stores and quite ready to share in them at once. Of course we gave them some flour, tea, pipes and tobacco in return for their courteous welcome, but not too much, indicating that further supplies would be available in payment for work done in the way of collecting, or for things that we wanted, such as boomerangs, spears, shields and spear-throwers. They went back to their camps with the news of our ideas on the subject of disposing of our supplies of food and other things they desired, in return for what we

wanted. The result was that we soon had all manner of things brought, from a common beetle or butterfly, hopelessly squashed in the tight grasp of a picaninny's little fist, to a big fighting boomerang four or five feet long.... Prices were not excessive and everything was paid for in "trade," the bush natives having then fortunately no use for money. A stick of black-twist tobacco, value about a penny-halfpenny, would easily buy a boomerang; the owner of a good shield readily parted with it for a pipe that cost sixpence. (Spencer 1928:370–71)

Lumholtz in Queensland also describes using tobacco as money, which he paid out together with pipes in small quantities so as to maintain its value, procuring (as just one example) a beautiful headband: "I offered him a stick of tobacco, and he immediately untied it and gave it to me.... I saw two others who sold me their brow-bands for tobacco" (1980:132). The multidisciplinary Cambridge expedition to the Torres Strait Islands in 1898 offered cigars to the islanders that "they were polite enough to pretend to relish" (Haddon 1901:75). The Berndts paid their informants in tobacco both at Ooldea in South Australia in the 1940s and Oenpelli in northern Australia in the 1950s. When the Church Missionary Society ban on tobacco rations came into force at Oenpelli, they continued to pay their informants in tobacco.[22] They noted with apparent irritation that the Aborigines with whom they worked at Ooldea had come to expect presents and contributions of various kinds and could not understand that some "service—eg. a period of talk and stories, was necessary before such could be obtained from us" (Berndt and Berndt 1942:312).

Poignant, working at Nagalarramba in Arnhem Land in 1952, bartered with and paid people in tobacco for items of material culture, for giving him permission to take their photographs, and for allowing him to witness ceremonies: "There was much in the way of barter: introduced food for fresh food; tobacco for food and services; tobacco, trade goods and food for assisting with photographs, and for being photographed; transfers of goods as tokens of esteem or regret, as a social lubricant, or as a gift. Every transaction seems to have been on an ad hoc basis; no notion of equivalence is discernible, until one begins to take into account the social invisibles" (1996:64).[23]

Tobacco and Labor

From the first days of settlement, Europeans had unambiguous plans for the wild blacks who came in from the bush: it was argued that they could be induced to give up their wild and unsettled habits and become progressively useful to the colony (Reynolds 1981). Industrial colonialism recognized the economic value of both the land and the native (Rowley 1978:91). As Reynolds points out, the move from bush to white society was more than spatial, it was a transfer from one economic system to another: from the domestic mode of production to the burgeoning capitalist economy of colonial Australia. Work as the Europeans knew it meant submitting to regular habits, learning the rules of subordination of servant to master, and understanding the values associated with economic incentives and with accumulation. None of these were part of the social world of Aboriginal people, and there was increasing frustration at the inability of the whites to excite the natives' interest in work. In the early 1800s officials reported that Aborigines were "more ready to work for Blankets and Tobacco than any other kind of payment" on the Lachlan River (HRA 1925, 25:562); a Mr. Bligh on the Gwydir River in 1847 refers to "the food and tobacco which form the common remuneration of their labours," and in Wellington, New South Wales, workers were "rewarded" with food and tobacco, said to be "their prime luxury" (HRA 1925, 26:396, 399).

The account of an isolated European adventurer in far northern Queensland highlights the clash between the dissonant worldviews on work. Jack McLaren was born in 1884, ran away to sea, and after some ten years "in various romantic occupations in tropical places" ceased wandering to try to start a coconut plantation on an isolated beach near Cape York. Quite alone, he had to rely on "patience and diplomacy" in his efforts to persuade the local inhabitants not only to accept his presence but also to work for him. Tobacco was the key to success. His first encounter was with a man, "tall and muscular, smoky black of skin and entirely naked," who had silently approached, "dragging between his toes," McLaren observed after a short and silent confrontation, "a spear which, by a quick raising of his foot, he could place in his hand."

> I produced a piece of "trade" tobacco, and at the same time got my rifle. He took the tobacco, smelt it, broke it in two pieces and placed one behind each ear. Then he made an almost imperceptible sign, and another native, nude and smoky black as the first, stepped out from the jungle so silently that there was not even the crackling of leaves beneath his feet. I gave him a piece of tobacco also, and he returned to the jungle and a moment later reappeared with a number of spears and throwing-clubs, which he laid in a heap on the ground before me; whereupon the first man came right up to me and held out his hand in

48

the European manner of greeting, save only that it was the left hand instead of the right, and in an English the most mutilated and full of antiphrasis I have ever heard said that he was my friend and that his companion was my friend, and then with engaging frankness asked if I had any more tobacco.

When I told them that I had, they produced some tree-bark thin as paper and made cigarettes and lit them with a coal from my cooking-fire and squatting on their haunches smoked them.

Then they asked the reason of my building a house there, and whether it was to be a trepang-station or a place wherein to store pearl-shell, but asking it as though they were only slightly curious about these things, but were more interested in the fact that I possessed a considerable quantity of tobacco. (1973:29–30)

McLaren explained his purpose and that he "needed labourers for the work and was depending on the natives to supply that need": "They shook their heads; they were hunters they said in effect, not workers—a statement that caused me to deliver a homily on the advantages of working, and having a regular supply of food, over the uncertainties of the chase, and which they considered to the extent of agreeing with me and declaring that while they themselves were disinclined for work, no doubt there were some in the tribe who would like it. Meanwhile, they would like some more tobacco" (1973:30).

Later that day, the rest of the tribe came to camp on the beach, and next day McLaren expected to be busy hiring laborers and setting them to work. No one rose until midmorning, when he visited the camp and explained his needs to a man who looked like "a chief or leader of some kind." No answer. "But the interview turned out quite satisfactorily, for presently, when I had given him a piece of tobacco—which in the most casual fashion he placed behind his ear— my listener gave me to understand that the thing did not rest with him, but with the individual members of the tribe: that they could please themselves in the matter; whereupon the others . . . informed me that they would be willing to accept the things I spoke of in return for a little work" (McLaren 1973:32). These Cape York people could see no advantage in agriculture and no need for it, and McLaren found that unless he supervised them at all times, they would sit down, smoke, or go to sleep. More than anything else, his account provides us with an understanding of why it was that the habit of labor had to be induced.

Tobacco was commonly part of the "payment" of stockmen together with food and a regular issue of clothing: "No, no money that time, we bin work early days. Just for bread and beef and clothes. Shirt and trousers, boot, hat, black tobacco, that's all. No money, that's all" (Kaiser Bill Jaluba in Read and Read 1991:185). To some extent, the feeding of relatives, the aged, and the infirm was the trade-off for the nonpayment of cash wages (Love 1915; Berndt and Berndt 1987; Lyon and Parsons 1989). In the Northern Territory, it was not until 1947 that cash payments were made to Aboriginal pastoral workers, and the figures included the value of keep and tobacco supplied by the employers.[24] Many employers had no intention of paying in cash until they were absolutely forced to do so (Lyon and Parsons 1989:22). Angelo observed that in the Kimberley region in the 1940s, "[i]f it were not for the lure of tobacco they would not go through the long, hard mustering seasons as there is plenty of native food available in the Kimberleys.... Tobacco, however, holds their allegiance.... [T]hey return starving, not for food, but for tobacco" (1948:44).

Farther south, white squatters frequently complained that Aborigines were unwilling to work or, if they did, that they were erratic and unreliable. However, work with sheep and, in particular, cattle in the north and south allowed people to maintain contact with their land, enabled them to travel through it, and made it possible to continue with ceremonial life (Goodall 1996; Baker 1999). Workers were recruited from the groups resident on the land, and, unlike the transient white workers, they offered white pastoralists continuity of labor. Aborigines became skilled horsemen and -women (the enhanced mobility must have seemed revolutionary to them); they knew the country intimately, its sources of water and good feed for animals, and they also came to realize that the white pastoralists recognized their value. This, together with pride in their skills at horse breaking and mustering, contributed to a sense of self-esteem and confidence in those associated with the cattle industry that has persisted to the present day (McGrath 1987; Brady 1992; Goodall 1996). All this is not to suggest that Aboriginal laborers and stockmen were treated humanely. The unwillingness to submit to regular work was overcome to some extent by coercion (Lyon and Parsons 1989). In Queensland the Aboriginal settlement fulfilled the role of colonized village, where the family was maintained by the government and the men worked on contract at the stations (Rowley 1978:93). Conditions and attitudes varied widely across the country but were everywhere demanding, and people were poorly rewarded (Love 1915; Stevens 1974; Lyon and Parsons 1989; Read and Read 1991).[25] Stanner said that all the white men on the Northern Territory Daly River farms in the 1930s were hard on their natives. They and the Aborigines were mutually dependent, and no love was lost on either side. He described it as a "barbarous frontier—more, a rotted frontier, with a smell of old failure, vice, and decadence" (Stanner 1979:80). The sexual services of Aboriginal women were exchanged for tobacco, sugar, and tea, and the workers were paid "nothing but were given a meagre daily ration of the foods which the farmers themselves ate, together with a small allowance of tobacco.... Pitiably small as this real income was, it attracted far more natives than could be employed. Each one at work had others battening on him as adhesively as he on his employer" (Stanner 1979:78).

Although many pastoralists used the Aboriginal labor already resident on their land, some station owners also took Aborigines from their own territories to work on properties, persuading them by a variety of means: "When once the station owner secures the native, who has a love for his own country, and who does not care to remain in one place too long, he practically makes a slave of him, because the black cannot get away.... It often happens that the lubra [Aboriginal woman] is taken away from the blackfellow, who is promised a bag of flour, or something of that sort, or some promise is made to him to leave his own country for another place in the shape of 'plenty tucker [food]; plenty 'baccy'" (Select Committee of the Legislative Council 1899:item 13). During World War II, when some areas were under military control, Aborigines in parts of the Northern Territory lived in army settlements at which a number worked, full time, for wages. For many this was the first time they had received regular cash wages, and they contrasted this state of affairs with their previous experience at the stations (Berndt and Berndt 1987:165). In addition, the army supplied food, and there was a fortnightly distribution of tobacco.

Other industries used indigenous labor and paid in tobacco. A. C. Haddon, leader of the Cambridge expedition to the Torres Strait Islands in 1898, noted that Murray Islanders hired to obtain black-lip shell were paid in wages of calico and tobacco (1901: 20). He observed that continuous labor was irksome to them. Aborigines also worked as divers in the pearling industry in Western Australia. Whereas once they had to be captured for this work by white men known as "blackbirders," when they became accustomed to the food and tobacco they volunteered their services (Angelo 1948:43). Queensland in the nineteenth century was particularly notorious for its trade in human laborers for its sugarcane plantations and the pearl shell and trepang trades. It is estimated that up to one thousand indigenous divers worked every year on the pearling luggers (Kidd 1997:33). Men working on the boats could buy tobacco on credit, booking it up under what was called the "slop chest" system; they said a smoke before going into the water warmed them up (Jeremy Beckett, personal communication, 21 September 1997). Some reportedly bartered their women for flour and tobacco (Kidd 1997:33). Narcotic dependency was a cheap means of keeping a regular Aboriginal workforce, and employers commonly enticed men and women with bribes of tobacco, adulterated liquor, and the dregs of opium. These workers included Pacific Islanders, who were employed on sheep stations and in tropical agriculture in Queensland. Thousands of Melanesians, known as Kanakas, were indentured to these operations in the 1880s, where overwork, poor feeding, bad water, and lack of medical care wreaked huge loss of life, and the atmosphere was not unlike the Deep South of the United States, with segregation an accepted practice (Corris 1970).[26] Tobacco was used as an inducement to work, and its withdrawal was a form of punishment for fighting, which was common among Chinese, Japanese, Melanesian, and Pacific Island gamblers, drinkers, and opium addicts (Corris 1970:56). Labor recruiters from Queensland also sought workers from islands in the Louisiade Archipelago, Papua New Guinea, in the 1880s, and many were forcibly abducted or tricked into sailing with the Europeans with promises of guns, iron axes, and tobacco.[27] These recruiters created a desire for tobacco that ensured the local inhabitants would be eager to barter with them whenever they appeared (Lepowsky 1982:327).

Alcohol and opium were also used as wages for Aborigines in the nineteenth century.[28] Nevertheless, in New South Wales in the 1860s it was the pastoralists who lobbied the government to regulate the supply of alcohol to Aboriginal people in order to protect their workforce from its ravages. This ostensibly altruistic gesture, Goodall notes, was "motivated less by a concern for Aboriginal health than by the fear expressed by a member of Parliament for the Lower Darling in 1868 that alcohol would make 'previously valuable' Aboriginal workers 'useless in pastoral and grazing occupations'" (1996:64). In Queensland and the Northern Territory opium was obtained freely from the Chinese, who came to work in the goldfields and in the tin mines, and whites. It was distributed as rations, like tobacco, to Chinese laborers (Rolls 1993). White scalpers paid their Aboriginal hunters with opium.

While agents of the government expressed horror at the ravages of opium, they were not averse to manipulating addiction per se. A Queensland police commissioner, for example, suggested that confidence in the police could be bought through the introduction of tobacco. It was so addictive that "even the wildest, when once they have smoked, try and become friends with and hang around the haunts of whites." Such addicts, he reasoned, could prove very handy as police informers (Kidd 1997:45).

The Question of Aboriginal Agency

We have described the high value invested in tobacco and pituri by indigenous peoples before the widespread introduction of commercial tobacco and the extreme lengths to which they went in order to obtain both kinds of tobacco. We have also illustrated the extent to which this intensity was made use of by outsiders, first the Macassans and later the Europeans, in order to procure Aboriginal compliance with the desires of these outsiders. Many of the historical descriptions we have cited are couched in a discourse that deprives Aboriginal people of agency in the relationship between the object of desire and the means of obtaining it. Stanner, for example, writes of people "tending to drift away from their traditional tribal lands to live near white settlements where they can secure more readily the tobacco, tea, sugar, new foods, clothing...they have learned to value and to crave" (1979:12). They were described as engaging in "intelligent parasitism" with Europeans (Elkin 1951; cf. Stanner 1979:12). In a detailed study of the role of rations in the lives of Aboriginal people, Rowse analyzes this discourse in which people are described as being transformed by a European material culture that was seen to render them passive and dependent, devious and scheming ("a colonialism of goods and desires"). He observes that these are "images of loss and inversion, a process of cultural decay as sudden and obvious as the donning of trousers—these descriptions demonstrate the ideological potency of pity" (Rowse 1998:32–33). Other commentators have since implied that the exploitation was mutual between colonists and colonized. Historian Mervyn Hartwig, for example, presented indigenous people as adventurous and enterprising in their quest for food, clothes, and tobacco (Rowse 1998:42).

There is certainly strong evidence that the exploitation was mutual rather than being entirely one-sided. Europeans were used in numerous ways for Aboriginal ends, and it only takes a slight shift of perspective to understand Aboriginal "begging" and "demanding" in a different light. Anthropological studies of giving and sharing among foraging societies suggest that a more apposite description of what takes place could be termed "demand sharing" or even mutual taking (Peterson 1993:871). While this is true of many foods and other resources, tobacco, both indigenous and introduced, was especially valued by

Aboriginal people to the extent that it was jealously hoarded.[29] This apparently selfish behavior is associated with the deeply embedded and intense social
pressure on Aboriginal people to share resources; as Peterson observes, coun-
terstrategies had (and still have) to be adopted in order to prevent exploitation
by the lazy or manipulative among the group. It is deemed socially unacceptable simply to deny someone a request for an item when it is clear that supplies exist. A Pintupi man spoke of hiding wild tobacco, saying, "After
preparing it let us hide it in the shelter, so the women won't grab it from us.
Let us carry it in our pockets. If you keep it where people can see it, they ask
you for it, finish it all up. Not only *pitcheri* [*sic*] but tin of tobacco and cigarettes as well" (Peterson 1993:864, citing Hansen).

The idiom of sharing among Aboriginal people is, Peterson says, embedded within an idiom of demands and claims that carries multiple meanings.
These include testing the state of a relationship, demonstrating assertiveness,
coercing someone into a response as a means of substantiating the rights of
the demander, and making a gift in order to create status asymmetry (Peterson
1993:870–71). All these meanings can be transposed to dealings with Europeans—and any other outsiders—over tobacco. As mentioned earlier, Aboriginal people in the first years of the colony expected there to be symbolic
payment for living on and using the land, and Europeans, after all, offered food
and other items to the indigenous people (albeit for the Europeans' own ends),
which led them to expect acquiescence in their requests. Indeed, Aborigines
accepted the annual issue of blankets in the early days of settlement as a form
of tribute or compensation for the land that had been taken from them (Reece
1974; Miller 1985). From their point of view they had a right to receive goods,
and refusal by whites to engage in proper reciprocal relationships could affront
Aboriginal moral codes (Hamilton 1972). In addition, while the etiquette of
request meant that Aboriginal people would not ask distant kin for tobacco or
food, this shyness did not (and still does not) apply to making requests of Europeans (Peile 1997:123).[30] At the time of colonial expansion and pastoral settlement, Aboriginal people were presented with a fully articulated social and
economic system that was mediated entirely through the personal contacts they
had with particular Europeans. Hamilton (1972) proposed that their ongoing
responses to and expectations of Europeans, indeed, their understandings of
what white society was all about, were based on these early interchanges.

As well as resituating Aboriginal "begging" as a purposive activity embedded in a sociohistorical context, we can relocate Aboriginal movements and

migrations for introduced tobacco as examples of a transformed existing economic process. Aborigines actively sought out tobacco supplies from Europeans as they had actively "hunted" for native tobaccos and pituri. There were occasions when Aborigines welcomed missionaries so that they could have easier access to tobacco. Nevertheless, the degree of agency and intentionality involved in Aboriginal movement into European settlement is complex. Their movement into white settlements, primarily with the intention of utilizing what was seen as an abundance of food, was undertaken largely free of coercion (Hamilton 1972; Brady 1987; Baker 1999) and in some cases specifically targeted tobacco (Read and Japaljarri 1978). Overall, it seems valid to describe this as a form of *accidental migration,* in which the initial movement was deliberate and designed in order to obtain tobacco. Once there, it seems that in many cases no decision was made to remain, but remain people did.[31] The longer they stayed, the more impractical would be a return as people lost knowledge of their country. Read analyzes this thoughtfully, writing: "It may be that the young men had no conscious intention of attaching themselves, still less submitting, to the squatters. But life was lived from day to day: novelty bred a habit, and habit bred a dependence into which the next generation, which knew no other relationship, was born" (Read and Japaljarri 1978:147).

An Aboriginal version of this interpretation was collected in 1990 from a Daly River man, reminiscing not about why people left their country but about why they stayed in a new one: "Them oldfellas got too hungry. They bin sit down now, think la tilip [tea leaves] 'n smoke, tilip 'n smoke. Must be that mob bin forget now, forget him own country. They bin worry for that country alright...but tilip, smoke 'n sugar [were] too strong" (Duelke 1998:186). Baker isolated several reasons for coming in among the Yanyuwa, including the longing for stimulants, the desire for staple foods, economic necessity as a result of environmental damage, curiosity, the fact that others had moved in, disease, and protection from both Europeans and other Aboriginal people (1999:128–29). Even though the movement may in many cases have been "voluntary," once within reach Aborigines became captive to the rations and the work practices or Christian worship demanded for their distribution.

Apart from the oral histories, which emphasize Aboriginal agency in the search for tobacco, Aboriginal people were enterprising and creative in their engagement with the substance. They were inventive, rapidly incorporated the introduced pipe (Macassan or clay), and ingeniously created new smoking implements from crab claw, shell, bone, wood, and drift bamboo. Arnhem Land people now still make bowls for their long Macassan pipes out of spent .303 cartridges and soda siphon sparklet bulbs (Drysdale 1974). Those who chew augment the flavor of introduced tobacco by adding ash to it as they had done with chewed indigenous tobacco and pituri.[32]

Another indication of Aboriginal agency is evident in accounts of Aborigines actively playing off different groups of Europeans against each other, showing that they had an acute comprehension of the politics of interpersonal behavior and an awareness of the potential to exploit competing agendas among whites (Reynolds 1981:156). This was manifest in many dealings with missionaries, during which Aborigines realized their power: they provided the souls upon which the raison d'être of the missionaries was based. At Beagle Bay in Western Australia, Aborigines bargained for more generous supplies of tobacco, with one man arguing that it was a case of "no more tobacco, no more h'allelulia" (Reynolds 1981:156). In another instance, a Church Missionary Society worker in 1834 noted in his journal that Aborigines who had asked for tobacco were directed to ask at the Wellington mission. "Oh no," they replied, "that fellow always *pyhalla* [a vulgar word meaning "to speak"]. We don't want *pyhalla*: we want tobacco, pipes, bread" (Woolmington 1973:71). Similarly, when their labor and expertise were desperately needed by labor recruiters, Aborigines and islanders demanded bonuses of tobacco and flour in advance of their work on coastal luggers (Reynolds 1981:148). Indigenous peoples were indeed active in procuring their supplies of tobacco, demanding it and other desired goods with aplomb. These items were viewed initially as a rightful exchange for the losses of land and resources that had been incurred at the hands of outsiders and later as a commodity more valuable than cash in exchange for labor.

Tobacco: A Multipurpose Substance

As we have illustrated in this discussion, tobacco had numerous uses and purposes for the colonizers of Australia. Its first use by the British and the Macassans was as a means of conciliation and appeasement that also bore rudimentary notions of reciprocity and exchange. Both these foreign nations used tobacco to ease their passage into Aboriginal lands and seas and the resources contained in each. As an inducement to labor, tobacco had a big advantage over both alcohol and opium, as it was a drug that did not interfere with people's ability to work. On the contrary, it not only served as a potent inducement to engage with outsiders (not all of whom were British colonizers), it tied Aboriginal people into a complex of relationships with those who wanted something from them. It was ideal as a currency with which to pay Aborigines for their services, being more valuable than cash prior to their full engagement with the cash economy. The physical labor of indigenous workers was bought in whole or in part with tobacco: shepherds and stockmen, divers for pearls and shellfish, laborers on plantations and peanut farms. The products of Aboriginal intellectual and cultural labor were also bought with tobacco, as missionaries, linguists, anthropologists, and collectors realized tobacco's power to persuade the indigenes to part with items of material culture, to divulge their intellectual property, and to share their languages.

The power of introduced tobacco lay in the fact that it slotted into preexisting Aboriginal drug use: it fulfilled many of the same purposes as the native tobaccos and the psychoactive drug pituri. For these substances social control mechanisms had been developed, with sources of the drug plants being closely guarded and the distribution of supplies well established. Indigenous Australians constituted an already habituated clientele experienced with chewing tobaccos, a clientele open to the use of newly introduced substances. Not only did they actively seek out supplies, people quickly adapted to new methods of ingestion by adopting smoking pipes derived from Macassans and Papuans in the north and from the British in the south. Using these new methods, indigenous people in some regions actively sought to enhance the effects of tobacco by perfecting deep-inhaling techniques. For whatever reason—ease of access, quantity, taste, choice, status, curiosity, or addiction—tobacco became a highly desirable substance, notwithstanding the existence of strong and satisfying indigenous nicotines. Tobacco was treated as traditional drugs were treated in that it was sought over vast distances, exchanged with other items, and bartered with existing as well as new trading partners. Groups who had no apparent prior use of stimulants also rapidly took it up. In most if not all of these ways, Aboriginal people followed the same path that Europeans, Asians, and other peoples had in their responses to a new drug substance or a new version of an old one.

Tobacco's powerful attraction was one of the most important elements in enticing hundreds of these hunting and foraging people out of their homelands and into centers of European activity in a process we have described as a form of unintentional, or accidental, migration. In view of the entrapment that followed, it is ironic that numerous Aboriginal groups actively sought this engagement with Europeans. Once the Aborigines were drawn in, Europeans managing cattle and sheep runs, pearling luggers, plantations, and missions found that the provision or deprivation of tobacco was a potent technique for maintaining control over them.

Acknowledgments

Thanks to George Boeck for research assistance; Barry Cundy of the Australian Institute of Aboriginal and Torres Strait Islander Studies Library; the Pictorial Archive of the National Library of Australia; and Kim Akerman, Nicolas Peterson, and Alan Thorne for their ideas, assistance, and comments on earlier drafts of this essay.

3

"They Are Beginning to Learn the Use of Tobacco"

Cultural Context and the Creation of a Passion in Colonial Papua New Guinea

Terence E. Hays

During the period of European colonization of the non-Western world, the attraction of laborers and the enhancement of their performance were both desired and necessary on the part of employers, whether they were businessmen, government agents, or missionaries. The value of tobacco in this regard is well recorded (Jankowiak and Bradburd 1996), and colonial Papua New Guinea provides another example. The introduction of European manufactured goods disrupted many established New Guinea communities' trading networks (see, e.g., Hughes 1978); more important, the deliberate introduction of "twist" or "trade" tobacco also provided the Europeans with a means by which to manipulate indigenous populations to engage in new work activities.

In this essay I argue that Europeans' success in controlling native labor was largely the result of their control over an addictive American commercial product consisting of cured tobacco twisted into "sticks" and often soaked in molasses. This product, which was followed later by commercial pipe tobacco in some areas and cigarettes almost everywhere else, constituted an important form of payment for native labor and goods, and for Europeans it served as a primary means by which to restructure local populations' economic transactions.

While myths about the origin of tobacco have been recorded for a number of societies in Papua New Guinea, virtually all modern scholars agree that tobacco in New Guinea is the American species, *Nicotiana tabacum,* and that its initial entry was almost certainly in northwestern Irian Jaya not long after the Dutch introduced the plant to Java in 1601 and Ternate in 1605 (Haddon 1946; Riesenfeld 1951; Marshall 1981). Over the next three centuries there probably were additional introductions by so-called Malay traders and hunters of bird of paradise plumes for the European and American fashion markets along the northern coastline, but the geographical distribution of the cultivation and smoking of tobacco in New Guinea when the significant presence of Europeans began in the nineteenth century is largely the result of a long process of gradual south- and southeastward diffusion, a process that was nearly complete when Europeans arrived with their twist tobacco—an alternative to the locally grown varieties or, in many areas, an entirely new drug.

European Interests in the Spread of Smoking

The colonial literature of New Guinea is replete with comments by administrators, explorers, missionaries, and traders on the degree to which twist tobacco quickly became a kind of currency, almost universally convertible along the coasts into copra, food, labor, land—whatever one wanted. Representative of this view is the report of Theodore Bevan, an early explorer on the south coast of British New Guinea: "[I]n the autumn of 1884 I made up my mind to visit New Guinea. It was described as a land of gold, yet where a fig of tobacco would buy more than a nugget of the precious metal had power to purchase" (1890:3). Indeed, one could buy a lot—even gold—with little investment, as a few examples will illustrate.

For a stick of tobacco, a local trader at Wanigela could "buy ten or twelve pounds of native sago, or thirty pounds of taro or bananas or yams. As much tobacco as would fill a clay pipe will purchase several crabs, or as many prawns as even Peter would care to eat at a single sitting" (Chignell 1915:60). The local missionaries there also benefited from the exchange rates in the early period: "The current price of everything...is exactly what we like to give.... Roughly, we give a stick of tobacco, which costs about a penny halfpenny, for twenty-five to thirty pounds of taro or yams, and the same for fifteen coconuts, or for eight or ten pounds of sago.... A turtle is worth four or five sticks" (Chignell 1915:133).

In the early colonial period, an economic mainstay for many Europeans was the processing of copra (dried coconut "meat," which was used in making cooking oils, among many other products). Copra was readily supplied by local people, but the price they received for it was, in the view of the administrator, Sir William MacGregor, "far from encouraging; they get two-fifths of a pound of trade tobacco for a full sack of copra. If they sell the coconuts, they get for twenty-eight coconuts the twenty-fifth part of a pound of tobacco. It is wonderful that they care to take so much trouble for such poor returns" (1892:32).

In addition to raw materials for commerce, Europeans also needed food, and fortunately for them (since they were generally disinclined to cultivate their own) it was cheap virtually everywhere. For example, at a German trading company outstation on the northwest coast of New Ireland in 1897 "ten pineapples were obtainable for one stick of tobacco valued at a halfpenny" (Webster 1898:282). Both vegetables and meat were readily available, as in the Duke of York Islands in 1872, where "fowls and pigs are very numerous and cheap: three small plugs of tobacco for a pig of 30 lbs. weight" (Redlich 1874:32).

In addition to food, all European colonials, as keen on other forms of work as they were on gardening, required labor, and this too was available in return for tobacco. On Goodenough Island "two sticks of tobacco [at most, a few cents] a day is considered high wages, and a man will often work for only one" (Jenness and Ballantyne 1920:164). And at another mission being established at Wedau in 1891, missionary Albert Maclaren wrote, "Some of the posts for the mission house are twelve feet long and very heavy, and it is with difficulty that we are getting them taken up the hill. I gave five sticks of tobacco for every post taken to the top, and we have twenty up already, but it is slow work" (Synge 1908:140).

Still another example of tobacco's use as a labor incentive is recorded by A. E. Pratt, who in 1902 wrote that when local men were hired to erect mission buildings in Dinawa they required "occasional supplies of tobacco as a gratuity." He elaborated that "[t]he average wage per day was three sticks of tobacco, or one rami, which would mean about 1¼ yards of scarlet calico. At the end of the time each man was to receive a large 18-inch knife, or an axe, and a certain number of sticks of tobacco" (Pratt 1906:111). Not only buildings were erected with the inducement of tobacco, but land clearing and drainage ditch construction also depended on this form of payment, as at Dogura, where in 1891 Maclaren wrote, "It took twenty men five days to accomplish it, but it has been well done. We paid them in tobacco and matches, thirty-five pounds of tobacco and 350 boxes of matches" (Synge 1908:151–52).

In addition to labor itself, enhanced performance was also an explicit desideratum on the part of European employers. On Goodenough Island the missionary A. Ballantyne commented:

> [A] stick of tobacco would hardly be used up under a week. During hard toil, such as constant paddling or rowing, the native naturally requires more, for betel and tobacco are the only stimulants he knows. Tobacco does really appear to stimulate him, much more than it does us. Every now and then a native will pause in his task to inhale a whiff or two from his cigarette or a mouthful of smoke from his pipe. A whale-boat crew with a stick of tobacco will row twice as far in the same time as a crew with none. The tobacco appears to renew their strength, while the betel-nut takes away hunger and thirst. (Jenness and Ballantyne 1920:163)

Gold prospectors and miners as well as missionaries typically paid their laborers with stick tobacco and sometimes even traded tobacco for the precious metal itself: on Sudest Island in the late 1880s, "in one case a native had sold some 4 ounces of gold, value about £15, to a miner for two sticks of tobacco, worth about a halfpenny" (Thomson 1889:514).

A final example pertains to the most priceless commodity of all, at least for missionaries—people's souls. Not all missions engaged in the practice of trading tobacco for attendance at worship services, but at least some did (see Hays 1991 for a late-nineteenth-century controversy about the use of tobacco in the London Missionary Society). At Maiva on the south coast in 1897 Thompson reported: "The teachers naively submitted to us the question of the expediency of following something like the plan which they said was adopted by the Roman Catholic priests." According to their description, it was the practice of the priest to go through the village on "Sunday morning with a basket containing a supply of tobacco. He promised a piece of tobacco to every man who attended service, and, in consequence, his ministrations were greatly esteemed by a considerable number of the heathen" (Thompson 1900:76).

These examples illustrate the powerful economic motivation for Europeans to take an active role in the spread of tobacco smoking. "The passion for tobacco suited the trader admirably," as Shineberg (1967:151) notes, but only if the Europeans were in control of its supply. The prevailing view is well expressed by Sir William MacGregor, speaking of the Rossel Islanders in 1892: "They have taken kindly to tobacco, and will consequently be willing to trade. Tobacco is not grown on the island" (1894:7). This last point was important, for it clearly was not in the colonists' interests for the local people to cultivate the plant.

Stimulating Trade: Stick Tobacco

While conversion rates varied regionally and over time, Europeans in the period from the 1870s to the 1930s typically paid about a penny or less for a stick of tobacco, which, as seen in the examples above, yielded coconuts for the burgeoning copra trade, food, labor, gold, and converts (or at least church attenders) for the missions. But in addition to being cheap, twist tobacco had many advantages over other European goods. Throughout the Pacific, according to Shineberg, "It was comparatively cheap trade, it was small and compact to carry and, above all, it was expendable, creating as much demand as it satisfied. After the end of 1849 there was no export cargo destined for the islands that did not include tobacco and many traders did not even bother to take anything else, while others took little besides" (1967:151). In Papua New Guinea, European involvement began somewhat later, but the same considerations applied. Stick tobacco was more portable and weighed much less than hoop iron or bolts of cloth, it was easily divided into thin slices, and—perhaps most important—it was consumable. Once a demand could be established, given the addictive nature of nicotine, it was constant and ever-increasing.

In some places, establishing a demand was not easy, such as on Goodenough Island, where, among the "inverted ethnic jokes which they tell against themselves...there is the one about the first men to be offered black twist tobacco by exploring Europeans: thinking it to be pigshit the bewildered recipients threw it away" (Young 1977:76). Thus the appearance of stick tobacco as well as the sight of smoke pouring out of white mouths and noses in some cases stimulated little initial interest in sharing such pleasures. Instead, sometimes such a sight evoked fear, as when the first London Missionary Society representatives arrived at Divinai on the East Cape in 1877: "The clothing on the visitors was a very striking feature to the natives. Also the fact that some of the party smoked increased the memetua [something supernatural] impression, as smoking was unknown" (Wetherell 1998:112).

63

One solution to the "problem" (as far as Europeans were concerned) was, as on New Ireland, to set up "schools for smoking...with traders as instructors, in which the new pastime was propagated, so that in a few years time tobacco was the most coveted and indispensable commodity among the natives" (Hernsheim 1983:60, quoted in Rubel and Rosman 1991:341). Similarly, in the Trobriand Islands, "when Whitten and Oscar Solberg had a trading station on the north-west end of Kiriwina, they could not get the natives to smoke, until one day Whitten persuaded one of the Toliwaga chiefs to have a draw from his cigarette. After that, smoking spread all over the island, and today [i.e., the 1940s] the Trobriander is the most inveterate smoker throughout Papua" (Austen 1945:24).

Local Responses to European Tobacco

In some places, trade tobacco initially was rejected out of preference for home-grown varieties, but in others the new twist rapidly supplanted native tobacco. In still others, smoking became what can only be called a passion.

On Goodenough Island, where tobacco was unknown in 1891, the long-resident missionary Ballantyne reported in 1912:

> Two things appear to the native almost as necessary as his food—betel-nut and tobacco. Abundance of both makes life rosy, their absence robs it of all pleasure. Sometimes the natives assert that they could not live if they were deprived of tobacco. A man would often come to us and say, "My tobacco was all used up, so I stayed at home in my hamlet. My strength all left me; I existed, and that was all. At last I thought to myself, 'I will go to my father [i.e., the missionary] and he will give me some tobacco.'" (Jenness and Ballantyne 1920:163)

On Kiriwina, less than a decade after the introduction of tobacco, Sir William MacGregor cautioned that renewed tribal fighting would result in withdrawing European tobacco, which people had become accustomed to. He urged the local big men that "peace must now prevail, and that they must at once recognise the superior authority of the Government. One of them promptly replied that it was true that I saw a great many men with spears, but they had brought them not to fight, but for barter; and if I liked I could purchase all that was there. And he added, 'If I were to fight, where should I get my tobacco from?'" (MacGregor 1893:4).

As a final example, in the Motu-speaking Port Moresby area, virtually all early European visitors remarked on Kuku, the "God of the Motuites," as stick tobacco was called by the adventurer Octavius Stone: "[T]he first words I heard in landing were *kuku, kuku iasi*, repeated several times in an interrogatory voice.... [S]ince then, those words rang constantly in my ears.... Even little babies learn to utter the word *kuku* before *tinana*, 'mother.' I never knew a people so fearfully fond of this weed. *Kuku* is their god, whom alone they worship and adore. The word *kuku* escapes their lips more than any other in the course of the day, and is ever in their thoughts" (1880:39, 89).

Visiting missionary William Turner summed up the European perception of native populations' nicotine addiction: "There is one foreign habit which the Motu have adopted: this is the use, with them also the abuse, of tobacco. The weed is largely used by men, women, and children; mothers give it to their infants to make them sleep while they are away at their plantations.... The natives have become slaves to the weed, and will rather want anything than their smoke, in fact, when food is scarce, they almost live upon tobacco" (1878:494).

A Question of Taste?

These reports, which I located in the course of nearly two decades tracing the spread of tobacco cultivation and use throughout New Guinea, have struck me as perhaps the most intriguing of all. It is difficult even for long-time Western smokers, fully appreciating the power of a "nicotine fit," to identify with the man met by Italian explorer-naturalist Luigi Maria d'Albertis on the south coast in 1876: "To-day an old man came from Matzingare and, having nothing else to offer me for the tobacco he wanted, he brought me a wig, roughly made, and ornamented in front with seeds.... I believe that to get tobacco this old man would sell, if not his wife, at least his soul" (1881:203–4).

If we are dealing here simply with addiction, then the striking range of variation in response to twist tobacco needs to be explained. As mentioned earlier, in some areas trade tobacco was rejected out of preference for the locally grown native variety, and in others there was interest but reportedly not to any extraordinary degree. It is possible that quality was a major consideration. Unfortunately, it is not possible from existing records to compare in a systematic way the qualities of locally grown tobaccos with receptivity to trade varieties, but reports that do exist are suggestive of a possible relationship.

Certainly, in some locations tobacco cultivators went to great lengths to grow and cure fine tobaccos, as with the Sipisipoia Gogodala, who, according to A. P. Lyons, "manure the ground in the beds in which they plant tobacco. To do this, they undertake the laborious task of collecting the dung of wallabies, and wild pigs, and carrying it to the gardens. When an old genama [communal longhouse] is abandoned for a new one erected on another site, it is left standing until just before the commencement of the wet season, when it is burnt. The ashes are mixed with the earth, which is dug up at the site of the old village, and then formed into raised beds in which tobacco seed is planted" (1916:7).

Extensive efforts were also made in some areas to cure locally grown tobacco, as reported by Roy Wagner for the Daribi people of the southern highlands: "I should [say] that Daribi tobacco is the richest, sweetest, and smoothest tobacco I have ever smoked.... [This is probably because] Daribi take a great deal of trouble to cure their tobacco, which, when harvested, is draped over poles and hung at various places beneath the roof of the longhouse. It then cures slowly in the woodsmoke of the cooking fires" (personal communication). On the other hand, on the northeast coast the lack of curing was a notable feature of local tobacco production, as reported by Otto Finsch: "The leaf is not fermented but usually picked green, dried over the fire, and then smoked.... [T]he natives smoke plump cigarettes wrapped in tree leaves, which understandably burn very poorly. There and everywhere our cigars—even the smallest stubs—were the choicest of objects, a position occupied otherwise by trade tobacco in stick form, which also was found" (1887:549–50, my translation).

There is little doubt that native tobacco varied widely in quality, at least according to European tastes. But it should not be supposed that the quality of twist tobacco was high (not surprising, given the economic incentive behind its production and export). Peter Ryan describes Australian soldiers during the Second World War in the Markham Valley as smoking "the trade twist that was issued to the natives—foul black stuff made, I should say, from the sweepings from cigar factories and bound together with molasses in plaited sticks" (1959:12). The early missionary André Dupeyrat describes the twist tobacco he commonly distributed to would-be converts as follows: "These plugs were made from poor quality leaves, which were first soaked in a mixture consisting mainly of treacle, and then compressed into small sticks, as hard as iron and black as ebony. They were acrid to the palate, and strong enough to choke a bullock, but the natives much preferred them to their own tobacco" (1955:117). Dupeyrat's remarks concerning the strength of twist tobacco may help explain its appeal, at least in most cases. The molasses or treacle in which it was typically soaked gave trade tobacco a sweetness that was appealing to some, for example, the Gebusi, for whom "trade tobacco came to have a special value among...men, and was desired as being particularly sweet, *despite the fact that it was also regarded as less potent*" (Knauft 1987:96–97, emphasis added). More common was the view attributed to the people of the Kokoda region, where tobacco "is grown in gardens in the mountains, but the leaves do not furnish as strong a tobacco, and are looked on as a poor substitute for those who are badly off" (Cheesman 1935:45–46). In general, the potency of tobacco (like that of alcohol in West Africa; see Ambler, this volume) was the major consideration among smokers and was a well-attested feature of native tobacco where it was grown. This potency was drawn upon in many areas for the induction of trances by spirit mediums and shamanistic healers, as among the Daribi, whose ethnographer, Roy Wagner, reported: "If anybody has any doubts that Daribi tobacco can bring on a trance, I would urge them to try the stuff" (personal communication).

Indeed, I will argue elsewhere that it was precisely the trance-inducing (i.e., psychoactive) properties of tobacco that best explain its rapid precolonial diffusion not only throughout most of New Guinea but throughout the world in general. For now, however, I suggest only that for people who already were smokers, trade tobacco that was perceived as being stronger than local varieties more likely was preferred to and eventually displaced the home-grown product (as also happened in parts of Aboriginal Australia; see Brady and Long, this volume). Yet we are still left with the phenomenon referred to earlier, namely, that in many places in Papua New Guinea trade tobacco was not only appealing but compelling—a powerful lure for which men (mainly) would "give their souls." In this regard, revisiting the precolonial distribution of tobacco cultivation and use may be helpful.

Filling a Pipe and a Void

At first contact, peoples in virtually all parts of Irian Jaya (with the possible exception of the extreme south coast) and most of Papua New Guinea (excluding the northeast and southeast coasts and adjacent island groups) were reported to engage in smoking and cultivation of the tobacco plant, with the exception of a few groups who acquired tobacco in trade with neighboring groups. There can be little doubt that tobacco seeds and knowledge regarding their propagation and subsequent use (sometimes as medicine as well as for smoking) had diffused to and nearly throughout New Guinea in post-Columbian times as they had (though perhaps not as rapidly) everywhere else in the world (Goodman 1993).

One of the most important points to be derived from early accounts by Europeans is that where tobacco was grown and/or used prior to direct Western influence, its use was in most cases surrounded with rules. In a few areas, most notably, in northern Irian Jaya and on the north coast of Papua New Guinea, regions where tobacco cultivation and smoking probably were established earliest, recreational smoking existed in the sense that men, women, and children smoked casually as an everyday practice. More commonly, however, primarily because of its purported potency as a psychoactive agent, tobacco smoking was restricted in terms of both eligible parties and contexts: the former were nearly always adult males, and the latter included ritual or symbolic contexts. It is striking that in almost none of these cases were "tobacco fiends" reported upon the introduction of the European product. Rather, the craving for trade tobacco was limited almost entirely to areas where it was new or had been only recently acquired. While the practical advantages of such items as steel tools and matches seem to have been appreciated nearly everywhere in colonial Papua New Guinea, the terms "craving" and "addiction" are not found in association with these introductions. But tobacco was a different matter.

In this regard, it may be instructive to examine a few cases from the Central Highlands, where tobacco was only beginning to diffuse along traditional trade routes when Europeans first arrived in the 1930s. For example, one of the first European missionaries in the Benabena area around Goroka in the Eastern Highlands, Theo Baas, reported that in the early 1930s smoking was "seldom done by the men and not at all by the women" (quoted in Roux 1948:259, my translation). A survey undertaken in 1981 in the Goroka area found that 77 percent of the men and 80 percent of the women were smokers (Marshall 1991:1332). In the Lufa area, southeast of Goroka, when gold prospector Michael Leahy entered the area in 1930, "smoking and betel-nut chewing [appeared] to be unknown" (1936:232); in 1970 60 percent of the men and 51 percent of the women were smokers (Marshall 1991:1332). Similarly, in the Mount Hagen area to the west of Goroka, the first European administrative patrol officer to visit said that "smoking is not indulged in" (Taylor 1933:61);

in 1968, 74.5 percent of the men and 78.3 percent of the women were smokers (Marshall 1991:1332). Such enormous increases in rates of smoking arguably are a product of the European introduction of trade tobacco and, later, factory-made cigarettes. Moreover, they suggest, for these inland regions where tobacco was only beginning to diffuse when Europeans arrived in the 1930s, a similar phenomenon to that in the coastal regions discussed above—if not craving, then at least an explosion in use and popularity.

In all of this, Papua New Guinea may only be a specific instance of a worldwide pattern. Sidney Mintz has proposed in a broader context that

> highly desirable substances appear to function differently in areas where they are old (and perhaps less pure) from the way they function in areas where they are newer (and perhaps purer). The sacred tobacco of the Plains Indians did not evoke the use-patterns that have come to typify it in the Western world; whiskey has serious consequences for Europeans, but it wreaked even greater havoc upon American Indians; coca leaves do not do in the Andes what cocaine has done in New York City. Is it possible that substances, even harmful substances, do relatively less harm when the social contexts for their ingestion have had a very long time to take shape? (1987:194–95)

While information regarding precolonial rates of smoking-related diseases and other harm attributable to tobacco is not available, the current situation in Papua New Guinea is reasonably clear (Marshall 1991). What is also clear is that postcolonial tobacco use patterns contrast markedly with traditional ones: increased and less restricted use among peoples who probably had not possessed the drug for very long and widespread addiction where it was brand new.

We cannot know, of course, whether tobacco smoking would eventually have become recreational throughout Papua New Guinea—as it is today—without the assistance of Europeans, although patterns in parts of Irian Jaya and north coast Papua New Guinea where tobacco probably has been present for centuries suggest that this might have happened with time, as it apparently did among Native Americans, who first domesticated the plant (von Gernet 1995). Indeed, I would hypothesize that, for New Guinea as a whole, tobacco smoking (and probably its cultivation) diffused in precolonial times primarily as a perceived psychoactive agent (as it had done earlier in Europe; see Goodman 1995), hence its incorporation into ceremonies and rituals and restrictions upon its use to specific sex and age categories, restrictions observable in many interior societies where tobacco smoking was a fairly recent phenomenon. But the very properties of nicotine that allow it to alter states of consciousness are those that make it addictive with increased use. What appears to have happened in the case of European twist tobacco is that for those who were unfamiliar with the product and hence had no models or rules for its use, the chemical properties of nicotine introduced into such a void provided an opportunity to Westerners for the acceleration of both processes: diffusion and recreational consumption.

It is important to recognize a contrast in the contexts in which tobacco was introduced in precolonial versus colonial times. In the natural course of events, the plant or at least the custom of smoking it would have been subject to whatever authority structures existed in a given community. If males, say, or senior males controlled most ritual and ceremonial life as well as the trade routes along which the diffusion doubtless occurred (which was the case virtually throughout New Guinea), they were in a position to impose any restrictions they wished and were likely to do so with a psychoactive agent. However, as these authority structures began to crumble in the face of colonial administrations and missions, such restrictions may not have been possible or at least as easy to impose as in the past. For example, on Kiriwina in the Trobriand Islands, where chiefs and village headmen had a monopoly on the ownership of betel nuts (another, though less potent, psychoactive substance), Leo Austen tells us: "Commoners had just as great a craving for the narcotic [i.e., tobacco] as men of rank. They were not prepared to see this become a monopoly; and it never did." Instead, "smoking spread all over the island, and to-day the Trobriander is the most inveterate smoker throughout Papua" (Austen 1945:21, 24).

In the context of European colonization, then, tobacco was introduced either into a void of models and rules for its use or into communities whose usual agents of establishing such rules were rapidly losing their power to do so. Tobacco, a drug whose appeal was hardly limited to New Guineans but instead was a worldwide phenomenon (Goodman 1993), was suddenly available in seemingly limitless quantities and was easily obtainable by all, from food vendors to those willing to put in a few hours of labor to the small children diving into the sea after bits of tobacco tossed from the "Tobacco Ship," as the London Missionary Society vessel was called in its early days at Port Moresby (Turner 1878:494). The stage was set and immediately occupied by those for whom New Guinea would be "a land of gold, yet where a fig of tobacco would buy more than a nugget of the precious metal had power to purchase" (Bevan 1890:3).

Acknowledgments

Since 1983 I have been engaged in a comprehensive study marshaling the botanical, ethnographic, historical, and linguistic evidence to reconstruct the introduction and diffusion of tobacco and smoking in New Guinea. This project has benefited most directly from grants awarded by the Rhode Island College Faculty Research Committee. I am grateful to them and to the many others who have contributed to this work.

4

Alcohol and the Slave Trade in West Africa, 1400–1850

Charles Ambler

Beginning in the early 1400s, European trading ships gradually advanced southward along the west coast of Africa. Within a century, commercial links had been established between various European ports and African coastal communities (Blake 1977). Initially, it was the lure of gold that drew the ships south, but during the seventeenth century the development of the transatlantic slave trade put the new West African coastal trading entrepôts at the center of a far-flung Atlantic commercial system (Curtin 1990). Alcohol was implicated in this commerce from its very foundation, and as the global demand for sugar fueled the expansion of the slave trade, one leg of the infamous if illusory triangle trade came to be associated with that seductive sugar product: rum. By the late eighteenth century, when the Atlantic slave trade reached its violent peak and its impact had cut a destructive swath across vast areas of West Africa, a complex commercial system had emerged that propelled slaves to the coastal trading centers and then into the slave ships. Historical study of this system has focused on the means and impact of enslavement, and scholars have concentrated relatively little attention on the importation of products into Africa (but see Metcalf 1987). Yet slave traders and their merchant allies in the ports along the West African coast were not only the agents in a brutal commerce in human beings but critical functionaries in a complex process in which imported goods flowed into extensive commercial distribution networks, in effect purchasing slaves. Thus, the history of the slave trade in Africa is also the history of the development of demand for imported products and the complicated and highly differentiated evolution of this demand over time and space.

This essay explores the role of rum and other alcoholic beverages in the development and expansion of the slave trade in West Africa and in the transition to "legitimate" commerce in the aftermath of abolition. It is tempting to ascribe an instrumental role to this potent and potentially addictive substance in the process through which merchants captured and sustained the trade in slaves. Yet across the entire history of the slave trade, alcoholic drinks (and another drug food, tobacco) represented a relatively small if significant proportion of imported goods (Eltis 1991:97–119). Moreover, the trade in alcohol emerged and prospered at a time when the parties to the trade, both European and African, constructed the concept of the substance in ways quite different from our present understanding. Still, it is plain that alcoholic beverages represented more than simply another commodity. And if European merchants and their fellow traders based on the West African coast did not conceive of these drinks as addictive stimulants that could be utilized to capture and control a huge slave workforce, they certainly did utilize liquor as a crucial tool in defining and maintaining a set of commercial relationships that ensured the availability of slaves for sale to traders on the coast.

Alcohol and the Slave Trade

From the fragmentary records of the early period of the West African slave trade it appears that from the very beginning of the commerce most ships carried various types of beers and wines both as supplies and as goods for trade. Distilled drinks in the form of brandy and rum had begun to appear in ship inventories by at least the late seventeenth century. European slave traders apparently regarded these kinds of alcoholic drinks as an essential, if relatively minor, trade commodity—hardly surprising, given the ubiquity of alcohol in European and Mediterranean trade at the time (Donnan 1930:179–82; Rodney 1970:179). Among goods imported into West Africa during the seventeenth and eighteenth centuries, both textiles and firearms were substantially more important than alcohol (Hopkins 1973:110–12; Eltis 1991:97–119). It has been estimated, from the analysis of ship cargoes, that liquor ultimately purchased some 5 percent of all the slaves obtained in the West African region (Postma 1990:104). By the late 1770s, the peak of slave trade activity, this proportion may have risen to as high as 10 percent, which represented a substantial expansion in volume (Postma 1990:104; Metcalf 1987:380, 394). In addition, some of the alcohol carried in the holds of these ships was not destined for trade but was provisions for the ship's crew and for the slaves imprisoned on board in an era in which alcohol was often considered a staple food and essential to good health, especially in tropical climates (Postma 1990:234). In fact, alcohol undoubtedly also facilitated trade by providing an illusory prophylactic authority for Europeans visiting or living in dangerously unhealthy West African ports and perhaps too some kind of respite from the fear associated with the deadly realities of the infamous "white man's grave."

The slave traders who frequented the west coast of Africa encountered societies in which alcohol consumption was well established. In the coastal belt, palm wine was a staple, while beers produced from various grains predominated outside areas where palms thrived. These drinks were produced through various fermentation processes that resulted in relatively low levels of alcohol content, usually substantially less than 10 percent. As Joseph Miller has noted in his study of the slave trade to the south in Angola, "[B]eyond the local mood-altering weed, *hamba* or *dihamba,* wealthy lords in the wetter regions maintained groves of palms from which they drew sap that fermented rapidly into wine. Residents of the wooded uplands prepared mead from the honey they collected from the hives of wild bees and farmers in the drier zones brewed millet beers" (1988:83). Distillation was unknown in Africa at that time, and, as a result, there was no long-distance trade in alcohol. Fermented drinks like palm wine were subject to rapid spoilage and thus could only be sold locally and had to be consumed quickly. In contrast, imported spirits could be transported over very long distances and in many cases had virtually unlimited shelf life as well as far higher alcoholic content. Other locally produced stimulants included tobacco, which was grown in many areas of West Africa, and especially kola nuts. Kola was widely used in social and ritual contexts; it was in particular demand in the Muslim areas of West Africa, where alcohol consumption was discouraged or forbidden. From the late eighteenth century, when a series of Muslim revitalization movements, or jihads, swept the interior of West Africa and a more observant Islam took root, the demand for kola increased rapidly (Austin 1995:96).

Local consumers in West Africa would therefore have found quite recognizable the wines and beers carried by the earliest Portuguese and English traders. These drinks may have differed substantially in taste and packaging from West African products, but the fundamental character and alcoholic content did not differ greatly from customary drinks (Rodney 1970:178). The French brandy, rum, and other spirits carried by the merchants who succeeded them in seaborne commerce between Europe and West Africa, however, represented a product that was familiar in terms of its psychoactive properties yet distinctive in taste and strength. Such liquors were sometimes distributed in bottles with a characteristic shape and labeling, and of course these beverages had substantially higher alcohol content than local drinks. Spirits were, however, often shipped in casks and apparently were often sold and distributed in an adulterated form. It is difficult to know whether African consumers initially saw these new distilled drinks as simply a stronger form of a familiar substance or as something plainly quite different. Emmanuel Akyeampong has argued in his recent study of alcohol use in Ghana that imported spirits fit within defined local conceptions of fluids and were essentially integrated into well-established social and ritual systems (1996:6–12). Similarly, in a pioneering article Raymond Dumett (1974) demonstrated that residents of the coastal region of present-day Ghana rapidly drew imported distilled drinks into customary consumption patterns and that no significant problems with alcohol abuse resulted from the growth in this trade. Certainly, there is no evidence that local traders or consumers, all of whom were familiar with indigenous forms of alcoholic drinks, developed any addictive cravings for imported spirits.

The various kinds of imported alcoholic drinks nevertheless represented a very seductive commodity in the development of trade and in sustaining commercial relations. According to records of fifteenth-century Portuguese traders, "gifts of trinkets and the sale of spirits were used to pacify the warlike tribes," indicating that alcohol was recognized in effect as a weapon in the traders' tactical arsenal (Blake 1977:100). This view was reiterated three hundred years later by a British official who noted that "no arguments are so powerful with the natives as a plentiful supply of rum, of which he has not been sparing" (Brooks 1970:19). Such goods, in other words, made it possible for a small group of European and Afro-European traders to secure positions in trade and to maintain their often tenuous standing in relationship to local African leaders. African customers certainly developed highly articulated tastes and were by no means willing to accept every commodity, whether alcohol or not, that traders proffered (Metcalf 1987:379). In his description of his early-eighteenth-century travels along the West African coast, John Atkins, a Royal Navy surgeon, wrote that "the success of a voyage depends [on among other things]... in drumming well with English spirits, and conforming to the Humours of the Negroes.... To give dispatch, cajole the trades with Dashes of Brandy.... If you look strange and are niggardly of your drams, you frighten him.... [H]e never cares to treat with dry lips, and as the expense in English spirits of two Shillings a gallon brought partly for that purpose; the good Humour it brings them into is found discounted in the sale of goods" (Donnan 1930:264–83). Likewise, a description of the port of Loango from half a century later notes that "in the kingdoms where [traders] buy goods it is customary to give for each slave what is called 'the over and above,' which commonly consists of three or four guns and as many swords; fifteen pots of brandy, fifteen pounds of gunpowder, and some dozens of knives" (Donnan 1930:550). Plainly, the ability and willingness of ship captains to respond to this wide range of demands and in particular to provide varieties of stimulants, such as different alcoholic drinks and tobacco, was a crucial factor in building commercial bridgeheads in West Africa, where alien merchants and the enclaves they established were continually vulnerable to the military and political power of indigenous rulers.

The expansion of commerce along the West African coast gradually resulted in the emergence of a series of trading centers or forts through which most exchange was conducted. Some of these centers were the province of local African or Afro-European "comprador" merchants, while others, notably, the forts along the Gold Coast, were controlled by various European interests—French, English, Dutch, Danish, and German (Hair and Law 1998:241–63). During the peak era of the slave trade, ship captains sometimes engaged in "coasting"—the practice of attempting to trade directly with communities along the coast; but most trade was confined to the established centers. These forts survived for the most part on the sufferance of the leaders of local states, numbers of which expanded in size and power as a consequence of their involvement in overseas commerce.

When slave ships sold off their cargoes, they did so to other traders, men who would resell the various goods involved, including alcohol (Hopkins 1973:110–12). This trade rapidly developed into a very complex enterprise. By the late seventeenth century, one merchant captain emphasized that a ship had to carry 150 separate kinds of goods to trade successfully on the Gold Coast. Ships in the trade thus had to resemble floating superstores, prepared to meet varying local inventory needs (Hopkins 1973:112). Even so, captains often did not carry all of the goods that some slave sellers demanded; these would have to be acquired along the coast. On the Gold Coast, for example, commodities, including alcohol, were frequently traded first for gold, which was then exchanged for slaves, generally in combination with other goods. As late as the 1730s a French ship trading in West Africa was attempting to use brandy to purchase gold (Harms 2002:233). As Joseph Miller has pointed out in his study of the Angolan trade, depending on the particular port, slave sellers developed well-articulated demands for specific mixes and proportions of certain commodities, sometimes from particular sources. Thus, some merchants in Loango demanded not only British muskets and French brandies but Portuguese gunpowder and Brazilian rum that American and European ships would have had to obtain in Luanda or Benguela in Angola (Miller 1988:78).

From fragmentary evidence, it is clear that alcohol served various uses in trade as both a commodity and a currency. Ship captains certainly made direct payments in alcohol for some services, for example, to the Kru canoe men who assisted in loading and unloading ships. In 1731, when the French ship *Diligent* anchored along the coast of the Kingdom of Dahomey (present-day Benin), the captain offered local men who provided barrels of fresh water a bonus bottle of brandy every Sunday, and he promised the local canoe men who moved goods and slaves between the ship and the shore a bottle of brandy every day, whether they worked or not, simply to guarantee their services (Harms 2002:232). Some of the liquor was consumed in the forts and trading establishments that catered to the slave traders, and the managers of these enterprises also used the liquor they had purchased to pay their own employees and reward their retinues (Kea 1995:123). An additional portion was sold for local consumption in the communities that had sprung up along the coast, and finally, some of the liquor was transported inland. Even with the introduction of spirits into the trade, however, trade into the interior remained relatively minor. Although the specter of a river of cheap booze flooding the West African interior would become a stock image of the temperance campaigns of the late nineteenth century, there is little evidence that much of the liquor sold on the West African coast before that time ever got very far beyond the coast.

Transport in West Africa was simply too expensive because of its dependence on human porterage (Austin 1995:98). As late as the 1870s, when the Sierra Leonean Reverend James Johnson made a tour of the hinterland of Lagos colony in present-day southwestern Nigeria, he found little evidence of the use of imported liquor in most communities. Even in Abeokuta, with its long-established and close ties to the nearby port of Lagos, Johnson regarded increased drinking as alarming precisely because imported spirits had been relatively rare until recently (1878:543; Latham 1973:74–75). Similarly, early-nineteenth-century observers who noted some excessive drinking in coastal port towns found little evidence of imported liquor or alcohol abuse in the interior (Hallet 1965).

Spirits also found widespread use as a currency, a means of accumulation, and perhaps an opportunity for conspicuous consumption. Robert Harms's account of the voyage of the *Diligent* suggests that the cost of slaves in the territories of the Bight of Benin were often calculated in terms of kegs of brandy, which in turn had widely understood conversion rates in relation to the value of textiles. Competition among trading ships, however, sometimes had the effect of driving down the value of the brandy in terms of the numbers of slaves that could be obtained (Harms 2002:233–34). Alcohol probably played its most important role as a symbolic and literal lubricant in the performance of exchange, serving as what was often referred to as a "dash," a kind of offering that demonstrated good faith in trade (Latham 1973:74–75; Donnan 1930: 273–79, 550). In 1767 one ship captain drew up a list of "customs imposed at Whydah" that stipulated necessary gifts of brandy for agents such as a conductor, brokers, canoe men, the king's messenger, the captain of the waterside, the "gong gong beater," and others (Donnan 1930:531–32). This ritual, a requirement of trade, revealed the degree to which this imported commodity had developed a "traditional" character but also the relative balance of power between European slave traders and local merchants.

Since the 1970s many studies of the history of West Africa's involvement in international trade in West Africa have drawn attention to the complex relationship between international exchange and underdevelopment. Over time, West African societies exported critical human resources as well as other valuable commodities like gold and in return imported what were essentially disposable consumer items. If such commodities gave substantial pleasure, prestige, or power to those who obtained them, they certainly did little to generate wealth. Some, like guns and perhaps liquor, had some decidedly negative effects (Rodney 1970). Over time, this relationship of exchange drew West Africa into a distinctly disadvantageous position in international commerce. Yet it would be a crass simplification to suggest that African consumers were somehow hoodwinked into purchasing worthless consumer items and destructive and possibly dangerous luxury products like rum and tobacco (Metcalf 1987:

393–94). During the period of the slave trade, this imbalance in trade had not yet translated into extensive direct European power in West or Central Africa or even into controlling positions for European trading interests (Hopkins 1973). Through most of the nineteenth century, indigenous leaders and states continued to dominate the region, and most European settlements and enterprises survived only because of their economic importance—as a source of the commodities, including liquor, imported into West Africa from Europe and North America (Miller 1988:687). Local traders and rulers were most definitely in a position to play merchants off one against the other. As early as 1698 one West African ruler wrote to the king of Portugal that "your Majesty should know that...my country requires foreign goods, such as iron, alcohol, and swords. Your Majesty's Company which is here does not sell me alcohol or iron, nor does it have sufficient goods for my country...nor are the goods of the same quality as those brought by foreigners. Your Majesty should be well aware that the price paid by foreigners for my slaves suits me better than that of the Company" (Rodney 1970:148).

The Rise of the Rum Trade

Although spirits, and especially French brandy, had been a standard trade item from the earliest period of the West African slave trade, alcohol emerged as a really prominent commodity in the commerce in the second half of the seventeenth century. At that point, independent English merchants, attempting to circumvent the chartered company monopolies on the trade, began to export rum directly from the West Indies to West Africa. Ships leaving England obviously targeted for the slave trade were sometimes searched and their cargoes seized in English ports; the direct trade from the Caribbean avoided this scrutiny (Coughtry 1981:107). Because it was clandestine, the trade is not well documented; but the Royal African Company certainly regarded the West Indian traders as serious competition, and by the late 1600s the company had itself become directly involved in the export of rum from the islands. By 1700 rum had replaced brandy as the favored liquor import on the West African coast, and during the first decade of the eighteenth century the Royal African Company sent more than five ships a year loaded with rum from Barbados and other islands to Cape Coast Castle on the Gold Coast of West Africa (Rodney 1970:179; Coughtry 1981:108).

By the early decades of the eighteenth century West Coast agents of the

Royal African Company and other companies acknowledged that rum had become an essential element of local trade. In 1721 it was described as the "chief barter" for Gold Coast gold and was used alone and with other goods to purchase slaves (Coughtry 1981:108). European, Euro-African, and African employees of trading stations along the coast had begun to demand that their salaries be paid at least in part in rum. Residents of the coastal towns had apparently come to regard access to rum as essential in these communities, but their demands for rum wages probably had less to do with unslakable thirst than with a desire for profit. Most employees also acted as local independent traders, and rum was becoming a critical commodity in local commerce (Coughtry 1981:108). Rum had also joined gold as an important currency in the conduct of trade, with the prices of slaves commonly quoted in gallons of rum (Coughtry 1981:108, 111; Metcalf 1987).

From 1689, when the Royal African Company lost its legal monopoly in the English slave trade in West Africa, the company faced growing competition from independent traders and especially from the West Indian merchants active in the rum trade. As demand for rum increased in West Africa, the company felt correspondingly threatened by West Indian competitors (Eltis 2000:127–28). In 1718 the company devised a plan to sweep away competition in the slave trade by manufacturing rum in West Africa itself and in the process driving the West Indians out of the market (Coughtry 1981:109). The plan failed because the company was too weak and poorly financed to carry it off, but its design reveals the important role that rum had come to play in the trade—a role that would expand significantly in subsequent decades. Beginning in the 1720s, merchants and distillers based in the New England colony of Rhode Island saw the potential market on the Gold Coast for Rhode Island rum. Within a decade the New Englanders had pushed the West Indians from the trade and established their product as the liquor of choice in the West African market. In the 1730s Rhode Island was exporting 100,000 gallons of rum to West Africa; by the 1760s the volume had risen to 275,000 gallons; and the trade reached its peak just before the abolition of the slave trade in 1808, when more than 800,000 gallons were exported annually (Coughtry 1981:111).

Rhode Island rum was king among West African consumers. The growing popularity of this particular liquor translated into substantial increases in the trade from New England and was demonstrated in the tenacious loyalty of African traders to this product. (However, when the American Revolution effectively cut off supplies, traders shifted to the Caribbean variety.) On a number of occasions, for example, the commanders of trading forts attempted to replace rum with brandy, which was available at substantially cheaper prices. The governor of Cape Coast Castle noted in the 1750s that it was "madness" to pay nine shillings for a gallon of rum when brandy was available for five shillings and bought up stocks of brandy for sale. Madness it might have been, but employees continually petitioned for a return to rum. They claimed that brandy made them ill and that it had little value as a trade good. The governor finally relented, citing the unhealthful combination of brandy and climate. It is much more likely that the governor simply had to give in to the reality that rum had become entrenched in local trade and popular taste. Traders preferred rum, and if they could not get it from English traders they would turn to competitors such as the nearby Dutch fort or American ships trading along the coast (Coughtry 1981:112). In fact, Gold Coast consumers remained extremely loyal to rum, retaining their preference for it well into the twentieth century, even after neighboring areas of West Africa had succumbed to the cheap gin that flooded the region after 1880.

This demand for rum deserves further scrutiny. It reveals certainly that African traders, and presumably their customers, were by and large not willing to accept any alcohol offered to them by the major commercial houses, even if the price was competitive. George Metcalf's study of goods used to purchase slaves along the coast of present-day Ghana during the 1770s provides very detailed and concrete evidence that the Akan people of this region were sophisticated consumers with well-articulated and discriminating tastes (1987:379). Good quality consumer goods, including textiles, dominated the trade at this time; luxury goods were essentially confined to tobacco and especially rum. Certainly, among detailed lists of trade goods there is no evidence of cheap beads or other gewgaws (Metcalf 1987:382). After well over a century of trade in spirits, African traders and consumers retained substantial economic as well as political independence, and the major commercial interests lacked the power to shift tastes. Yet alcohol was critical to trade, a circumstance that plainly made some European traders uneasy. According to the detailed records of one British trader along the Gold Coast in the 1770s, rum figured in 70 percent of all transactions and accounted for 9 percent of total trade. With imports rising, rum became a commonplace drink in the coastal port towns and surrounding communities (Metcalf 1987:382, 389). The British governor of Cape Coast Castle noted in the mid–eighteenth century that an African trading fort "may be as well without guns as without rum or brandy" (Coughtry 1981:112). This comment was an ironic reminder that these small outposts of European trade scattered along the West African coast thrived and even survived at the pleasure of neighboring African states. If local commercial representatives wanted a certain kind of rum, then it had to be provided.

These circumstances expose not only the relative weakness of the European trading interests on the coast but also the entrenched position of spirits in the slave trade. In the 1760s one observer noted that rum dominated the trade because it is "ten percent stronger than corn spirits, and of consequence of more value to the natives" (Coughtry 1981:113). When brandy and later rum were introduced in the trade, the strength, distinctive tastes, and decorative bottles also proved appealing. The rapid growth of the rum trade during the eighteenth century made alcohol a critical factor in the slave trade but at the same time integrated rum into the social and ritual lives of communities. The conduct of trade negotiations was punctuated by "dashes"—offerings of drinks and presents of bottles of liquor that not only prolonged such discussions but made them more difficult (Brooks 1970:229). William Bosman's description of trade negotiations around 1700 emphasizes the role that alcohol played:

> Excessive Brandy-Drinking seems the innate Vice of all *Negroes,* but these [along the coast of present-day Nigeria]…really herein exceed all others that I have ever Conversed with. They consume in this all they can come at…. If one chance to get but a Mouthful more than another, and they are half Drunk, they immediately fall on Fighting, without any respect to the King, Prince or Priest…. As great Lovers of Brandy as they are, they will not yet, when they first come on Board and are ask'd to Drink, touch a Drop before they have received a Present. And if we should happen to stay too long before we give them any thing, they will boldly ask us if we imagine that they will Drink for nothing; It not being sufficient to content this wretched Crew that they Drink up our Liquor for nothing, but they must besides be hired to it…and he that intends to Trade here, must humour them herein, or he shall not get one Tooth on Board. (1967:403–4)

The Kru canoe men who dominated cargo handling along much of the West African coast had perhaps once been recruited with "gifts" of liquor but by the 1700s routinely demanded such wages as a matter of course (Brooks 1970:235; Donnan 1930:531–32).

As offerings and consumption of imported liquor became commonplace elements in the rituals and exercise of political and economic power, leaders often found themselves dependent on access to liquor to maintain their positions and their lifestyles. A seventeenth-century account of a Senegambian Mandinka ruler noted: "Kings and all will drinke, untill they be starke drunke and fall fast asleepe, so that to describe the life of the Kings truly, is, that they doe eate, drinke and sleep, and keepe company with their women, and in this manner consume their time, untill Time consumes them" (Brooks 1993:249). From this account and the comments by Bosman and others already cited, it is clear that many European traders were convinced that Africans had a particular susceptibility to drink. In his study of Senegambia before 1700 George Brooks asserts that "craving for imported spirits impelled leaders to attack and capture people of neighboring societies and, for the most addicted and debauched, to pillage and enslave their own subjects. Indeed unpredictable behavior induced by alcoholism was part of the fearful aura of rulers and warriors" (1993:249). But such bold claims must be viewed with skepticism. There is in fact no compelling evidence to link the increasing prevalence of imported spirits in trade to excessive alcohol abuse or drunkenness, let alone addiction. In fact, in the coastal region of the Gold Coast, where the alcohol trade was especially extensive, there is little evidence of widespread abuse of alcohol or even excessive drinking (Metcalf 1987:389; Dumett 1974). As William Taylor has pointed out in his perceptive study of drinking in colonial Mexico, there was a tendency for European travelers and observers (or, for that matter, more recent historians) to interpret occasions of African drunkenness through the lens of accepted European drinking practices. Whereas Europeans tended to value the ability to hold one's liquor, it was often perfectly accepted in African societies, as in Mexico, for drinkers to behave raucously, even if they had not consumed large amounts of alcohol (Taylor 1979; see also Ambler and Crush 1992:5–6).

Yet even if imported liquor came in many cases to be an essential element in the demonstration of social status and political power and even if local merchants and rulers routinely demanded spirits as rents or as trade fees as well as goods in trade, these circumstances did not apparently translate into dependency: there was simply too much competition among European traders for access to slaves (Miller 1988:84; Harms 2002:233–34). A mid-eighteenth-century treaty between Portuguese officials and such a leader in what is today Sierra Leone obligated the Portuguese to provide a bottle of rum for each returned escaped slave and to make regular "gifts" of liquor (Rodney 1970:179–80). Alcohol's place in the trappings of power certainly began at the top. In 1679 a

European trader on the Gold Coast described an elaborate dinner at the residence of the Danish governor: "[A]fterwards the general's concubines arrived... all dressed in the finest attire.... They arranged themselves around us and were served sweet oranges, French wine, Palm wine, mum [beer], and brandy" (Akyeampong 1996:xix). In 1817 Thomas Bowdich described the *odwira*, or harvest festival, presided over by the Asantehene, the head of the Asante state, in his capital, Kumase (in present-day Ghana):

> The... King ordered a large quantity of rum to be poured into brass pans, in various parts of the town; the crowd pressing around, and drinking like hogs; freemen and slaves, women and children, striking, kicking, and trampling each other underfoot, pushed head foremost into the pans, and spilling more than they drank. In less than an hour excepting the principal men, not a sober person was to be seen.... All wore their handsomest cloths, which they trailed after them in a length, in a drunken emulation of extravagance and dirtiness. Towards the evening the populace grew sober again.... [T]he kings and the dignitaries were carried in their hammocks. (Akyeampong 1996:6)

Vast supplies of spirits were required to manage such acts of largesse and the more regular gestures of generosity that were the marks of stature and the concrete acts of cementing relations of power and subservience. These kinds of relationships were reproduced continually across Asante society and in many other areas of West Africa as local rulers and "big men" asserted their power and the importance of their offices at political functions and especially at events such as funerals (Akyeampong 1996:39; Dumett 1974:81–82). Thus, for the most part, the consumption of spirits took place in ceremonial confines, which explains the relative absence of public consumption of spirits and drunkenness in West African towns (Dumett 1974:84; Law 1990).

Alcohol, Abolition, and "Legitimate" Commerce

The 1808 abolition of the slave trade by Britain and the United States (followed by other European powers) transformed West African trade. As the efforts of the British especially to ban slaving intensified, the focus of slave commerce shifted south, especially to Angola, although illegal exportation of slaves from Nigeria and other areas of West Africa certainly persisted. Notwithstanding the activities of illicit slavers, abolition had a substantial impact on West

African economies and political systems (Curto 1989; Miller 1988). The transatlantic slave trade had generated a far-flung commercial network, stretching inland from West African ports, organized around the production and transport of slaves. Political structures had emerged rooted in the slave trade economy, and abolition did not eliminate this system, which now increasingly produced slaves for transport and sale within West Africa. This shift was accompanied by a parallel emergence of alternative "legitimate" products for export, chiefly, palm products (Hopkins 1973). The development of these exports was driven, of course, by the need of coast merchants and political leaders to find new sources for the imported goods that they had come to regard as essentials, notably, alcohol. For example, reports of the British Consulate in Bahia show that the cargoes of Brazilian, Portuguese, French, Spanish, British, and American ships bound for Africa in 1831 and 1832 consisted mostly of spirits: wine, rum, and gin as well as tobacco (British Parliamentary Papers 1968, 13:37–38, 43, 105–06). What proportion of these products went to buy slaves is not clear, but official British correspondence describing interdictions of slave ships suggests that almost every ship involved in the illicit South Atlantic slave trade carried as part of its eastbound cargo substantial quantities of tobacco and especially the inexpensive Brazilian rum known as *aguardente* (British Parliamentary Papers 1968, 9). By the second half of the nineteenth century, spirits was one of four items (the others being textiles, salt, and iron) that accounted for more than 75 percent of all West African imports (Hopkins 1973:130). The volume of alcohol imports certainly expanded. According to one estimate, 750,000 gallons of alcohol were imported in the 1780s, 1 million gallons by the 1820s, and more than 6 million gallons by the 1860s. During the same period per capita consumption would have risen from about .03 gallon to .30 gallon (Eltis 1991:109). Per capita statistics, however, don't reveal much about actual consumption, which continued to be centered in coastal towns and dominated by men of substance.

Surveying the nature of interaction between Europeans and West Africans around 1812, a European observer noted that "the natives of this Coast have had intercourse with Europeans about three hundred years, and…have adopted none of their customs but smoking and drinking" (Brooks 1970:10). Certainly, rum's central role in trade remained relatively constant. In a meeting with the Gold Coast governor in 1822 thirteen resident European traders emphasized that "rum is indispensable here" (Brooks 1970:246). Rum continued to figure largely in the rituals of trade (Brooks 1970:225, 228; British Parliamentary Papers 1968, 10:53–54). Moreover, European officials recognized the revenue potential of such an entrenched commodity. As the British, in particular, gradually established enclave colonies in Sierra Leone, on the Gold Coast, and at Lagos, they turned to alcohol as well as to imported tobacco to finance their administration (Brooks 1970:242). During the course of the nineteenth century duties on these imports increased, despite commercial resistance, until more than half the cost to importers was taxation. Notwithstanding the taxation-driven rise in price, demand continued to expand, and by the late second half of the nineteenth century more than half of colonial revenues was derived from these sources. After 1850 cheap German and Dutch mass-produced gin began to enter the market in substantial quantities that increased rapidly with the establishment of direct steamship routes between West Africa and Hamburg (Martin 1997:69; Latham 1973:74–75; Hopkins 1973:129). In a few decades gin had pushed rum out of Nigeria, but rum remained firmly in command in the Gold Coast, which had long been the focus of the American trade.

This dramatic expansion of what came to known as the "liquor traffic" and the growing dependency of colonial treasuries on revenues drawn from this traffic did not escape the attention of the emerging temperance movement. In the 1880s increasingly vocal and strident opponents of the alcohol trade described a bleak future for West African populations addicted to drink and denounced the conspiracy of colonial and economic interests to perpetuate the trade. Such sweeping and unsubstantiated assertions, inscribed with race assumptions, made the alcohol question in West Africa briefly an international moral cause célèbre. Unfortunately, the heated debates that ensued over the following three decades tended to obscure rather than illuminate the complex engagement of alcohol and other drug foods in the incorporation of West African societies in international markets.

Acknowledgments

I wish to express my thanks to Jeff Lucas for assistance in locating references.

5

Alcohol and the Fur Trade in New France and English America, 1600–1800

Peter C. Mancall

Before the arrival of Europeans on their shores, the Native peoples of eastern North America possessed no alcoholic beverages. Over the course of the seventeenth and eighteenth centuries, that situation changed in large part because Europeans were eager for furs, brought by Natives in exchange for liquor, to ship across the Atlantic Ocean. The economic advantages of this commerce to Europeans were many, though some colonizers recognized that alcohol could have dangerous effects, since Native American Indians often behaved violently after drinking. Still, Europeans who stood to gain the most from the trade tended to ignore warnings and restrictions. To them, alcohol had become an ideal commodity. Many American Indians, especially young men in the eastern woodlands, demonstrated their views with their actions: despite the protests of community leaders, they sold their furs to anyone who provided alcohol.

In this situation, was alcohol a "drug food" in the ways that anthropologists have described this phenomenon? (See Jankowiak and Bradburd 1996:717–20.) Was its use intended to persuade indigenes to perform labor for Europeans, or was it instead just one of many products that colonists traded with Indians in a developing interracial economy? The answers to those questions depend to a large extent on the particular circumstances of the transaction.

To assess the situation in its historic complexity, it is necessary to set a few issues aside. First, no known biological or genetic trigger for alcohol abuse has been identified for Native Americans in the eastern woodlands or elsewhere (Goldman et al. 1993:199–204; Bennion and Li 1976:9–13; Segal and Duffy 1992:213–17; Chan 1986: 93–104; Dyck 1993:116–20; Chen et al. 1992: 351–52). Instead, the most current medical information holds that Native American Indians have no physiological deficiency that would make them metabolize alcohol at a rate different from non–Native Americans (Gill et al. 1999:149–58), and there is no genetic evidence suggesting that the desire for alcohol is more pronounced among Indians than non-Indians. If some Native Americans possess a genetic predisposition to abusive drinking, there is no evidence in the clinical literature to suggest that this physiological trait occurs with greater frequency among American Indians than non–American Indians.[1]

Second, there was no concerted plan on the part of colonial officials in England or France (or Spain or Portugal, for that matter) to use alcohol to make Native laborers dependent on Europeans. While colonial traders no doubt used alcohol as a lure, liquor never became part of any preconceived plot on the part of seventeenth- or eighteenth-century Europeans eager to enslave or otherwise compel Native laborers to work; in both New France and English America, as opposed to territory the Spanish claimed, there was little effort on the part of colonizers to use Native labor to develop the newcomers' communities. Thus relations between the indigenous peoples of eastern North America and newcomers from Europe departed from the labor plans that Europeans put into place for transported African slaves, whom the English and French worked, often to death, in their island colonies, and the English continued to do so in the mainland colonies from Maryland and Virginia into Georgia.

Third, surviving documents reveal that English and French colonial officials claimed they wanted to inhibit, not encourage, the liquor trade. In English America, virtually every official proclamation on the subject of providing alcohol to Indians was intended to halt what was perceived as a noxious commerce, an "abominable filthynes," in the memorable words of the Rhode Island legislature in 1673 (Mancall 1995a:103–10). Further, the continuance of the alcohol trade in English America despite its apparent social costs for Native Americans was not another example of what has been termed "salutary neglect": the belief on the part of English men and women on both sides of the Atlantic Ocean that colonists should be allowed to develop their own societies without active intervention from England. English traders did have enormous latitude in their negotiations with Indians; the existing commercial regulations such as the Navigation Act of 1660 and other measures that followed did not place any real restrictions on the ways that British traders in the Western Hemisphere were supposed to deal with Native Americans (Jensen 1955:esp. 354–64). But the fact that traders had liberty to engage in commerce did not mean that they had license from the crown to do whatever they wanted. Imperial bureaucrats weighed in on the alcohol trade precisely because they feared it would endanger peaceful relations between Natives and newcomers; they also feared the possibility of losing Native allies to the French. If anything, there was a British imperial interest in preventing the alcohol trade from becoming threatening. The French, by contrast, had a more complicated imperial posture. The government allowed the trade to continue, but, according to a royal proclamation of 1679, the commerce was to be banned in Native communities (Mancall 1995a). Further, French clerical condemnation of the brandy trade led to the passage of a *cas réservé,* which dictated that only the pope or a bishop could provide absolution for the mortal sin of selling brandy to Native Americans; this spiritual injunction meant that brandy traders in Canada could not be absolved of their sin by a local priest ("Délibération sur le cas réservé du commerce de l'eau-de-vie avec les sauvages" [1678], in Margry 1876–86, 1:407–19).

But despite efforts to limit the commerce, the fact that the alcohol trade flourished in eastern North America suggests that liquor was nonetheless used for profit by colonists engaged in the commerce in furs and deerskins. As such, alcohol was a drug food, according to the definition of Jankowiak and Bradburd, since it was used to "encourage and compel members of the contacted culture to provide the trader or merchant with either goods or labor" (1996:718). Yet intent on the part of alcohol venders needs to be set into the specific cultural and economic context of the early modern fur trade. The most obvious point is worth stressing: alcohol worked as a drug food because of the continued demand for it among at least some American Indians. Traders used alcohol as a lure, to be sure, but the network through which alcohol reached Native communities suggests an ongoing demand for it once it had been introduced. To understand why the trade continued, it is necessary to understand this consumer demand for the substance, a demand that increased when certain Indian groups developed a range of culturally acceptable ways to consume alcohol.

The argument, then, is straightforward. In much of eastern North America, especially in the broad interior region that stretched from Hudson Bay to the Carolina piedmont, European traders tried to organize Native hunters to bring them furs (or, in the South, deerskins). To succeed, they had to convince hunters to alter traditional beliefs that had prevented hunters from killing more animals than a community needed at that time. This change in the relationship between hunters and the hunted presumably led to a deep soul-searching evaluation about some of the fundamental issues of daily life, including its spiritual dimension (Martin 1978; Krech 1981). Whatever motivated Native hunters to bring furs to trade, by the mid- to late seventeenth century one product those hunters received for their furs was alcohol, one of the few trade goods (along with powder and shot) for which there existed potentially infinite demand.

Conquest and Commerce

The alcohol trade began in North America in the mid–seventeenth century. Before then, Europeans did on occasion provide alcohol, probably in the form of wine or beer, to Native Americans, but there was no measurable commerce in any alcoholic beverage. Instead, the initial proffering of alcohol to Indians took place sporadically and probably in most cases as part of a treaty session or in the rituals that took place when Natives met newcomers. Across eastern North America, Europeans quickly learned Natives' trading protocols and soon recognized that the giving of gifts to hosts had to precede any real commercial dealing (Axtell 1988:154–60). The offering of a toast would have made sense to Europeans in these settings, especially given the age-old custom in their home cultures relating to the communal function of drinking.

Yet if there was no alcohol trade per se during the formative decades of colonization, Europeans were nonetheless already altering Native communities. The arrival of Europeans meant the spread of epidemic diseases, most notably smallpox but a range of other potentially lethal microbes as well. Natives and newcomers alike believed that the epidemics had spiritual causes, but the assignment of causality to otherworldly forces had little known effect on mitigating the lethal scourges. As a result, widespread death had a direct impact on relations between Europeans and Native Americans at their formative stage, and the repeated visitations by death-dealing epidemics meant that everything about race relations in eastern North America was invariably set against this gruesome background (see McNeill 1976:176–207; Crosby

1986:195–216; Thornton 1987:42–90; Verano and Ubelaker 1992).

The arrival in the Western Hemisphere of European missionaries hoping to convert Indians to Christianity—Catholicism in territory claimed by France, Protestantism in what would become English America—had another direct impact even in the presettlement period. From the start, Native Americans were aware that their uninvited visitors believed that their traditional beliefs were somehow inadequate. For the visitors, Native Americans' belief systems were often much worse: Indians, to French and English missionaries, dwelled in ignorance and had to be saved from the demonic forces that lurked in the American landscape.[2]

The first colonizers in New France and English America were of course aware that their arrival had altered Native communities, but they had little time to sit back and see what would happen. Instead, many of those involved in the earliest exploratory and settlement ventures realized that they needed to find American goods to ship to Europe to finance their voyages. In both English America and New France, many who traveled across the Atlantic believed that the Western Hemisphere contained untold riches. The Spanish had by that time been extracting gold and silver for decades, a feature of Iberian expansion that had elicited much anxiety among other western Europeans who wanted to enrich own their nations; this national jealousy derived much of its urgency, at least for the English, from the different religious traditions that divided Europe after the Reformation. By the late sixteenth century, the publication of travel accounts and promotional materials across the Continent had given an unmistakable impression: America had a variety of ample natural resources that could be harvested by Europeans (see, for example, Mancall 1995b; Wright 1966).

In New France and English America, the early seventeenth century proved a time of experimentation. In New France, colonial officials tried to determine how to create a viable colony during an age when few French men and women were willing to cross the Atlantic. As a result of limited migration, Catholic missionaries played an enormous role in the formation of colonial settlements and in the early negotiations with Native Americans (Choquette 1991; Moogk 1994). More important for the French, perhaps, was their need to establish trade relations with the Algonquian and Iroquoian peoples who inhabited the territory surrounding the waterway the French called the St. Lawrence River. By the early seventeenth century, French traders had come to the realization that the fur trade would become the most important part of the colonial economy.

But the French who arrived in North America had little experience in this business, and their numbers were small enough that they quickly realized it would be better to enlist Indian hunters in the business to make it succeed.

But in English America the economic circumstances were different. Despite the failure of the first English colonizing ventures, notably at Roanoke in the mid-1580s, the early-seventeenth-century plans for North America included the transplantation of English men and women and the creation of new colonies. For those colonies to survive, the migrants had to be able to send American goods to Europe. Though the English had of course hoped to find gold and silver, they settled on seemingly more mundane products. Beginning in the mid-1610s, colonists in Virginia had discovered the profitability of tobacco, and they proceeded to make the production of that miraculous crop the basis of their economy, a decision that eventually fueled the creation of slavery along the shores of Chesapeake Bay (Morgan 1975; Berlin 1998:109–41).

Although the tobacco economy of the Chesapeake became vital to English America during the seventeenth century, its labor needs had little impact on relations between Native Americans and colonists. By contrast, in New England the first cash crop of any real worth was peltry. Thus, though New England's material contribution to overseas trade paled in significance to the production of tobacco in the Chesapeake Bay region, from the start its economy depended on establishing relations with Native Americans (Salisbury 1982; Cronon 1983). As the governor of Plymouth, William Bradford, and other Puritan leaders recognized, the newcomers needed to encourage local Indians to participate in the fur trade if they were to obtain goods valued in Europe.[3] In this sense, their timing could not have been better; the waning of the Russian fur trade by the end of the sixteenth century had meant continued demand in Europe for a good that seemed in ready supply in the Western Hemisphere (Wolf 1982). The logic that drove the creation of the fur trade in New England remained intact for the remainder of the colonial period. The founding of three colonies after the Restoration—Pennsylvania, New York, and Carolina—all depended at least to some degree on establishing relations with local Indians and encouraging them to hunt animals valued for their fur (in the middle colonies and New England) or their skins (in Carolina, where white-tailed deer were abundant and populations of furbearers were small) (Hatley 1993:32–51; Merrell 1989:49–91; Silver 1990; Richter 1992; Mancall 1991:47–70).

Thus, by the late seventeenth century English and French colonists all had incentive to trade with the Algonquian- or Iroquoian-speaking peoples who remained in eastern North America, but they had additional incentive to do so after the discovery in 1650 of the profitability of distilling liquor from West Indian sugar. It would be a mistake to downplay the significance of the plantation colonies to either the English or the French. Since early in the seventeenth century Europeans had reshaped the islands to make them better fit for sugar production; they had also imported tens of thousands of African slaves to work the lands in the tropics (Dunn 1972; Mintz 1985). For this investment to pay off, plantation owners needed to find markets for sugar and its by-products. For the French, the brandy trade promised great profit; for the English, rum seemed the most profitable product. As a result, by midcentury the planters and their agents in Europe and in the Western Hemisphere had organized the production of liquor from the great volume of sugar being produced in the islands.

By 1650, then, the alcohol trade was ready to go. On the one hand, English and French colonists in North America were seeking ways to continue trade with Native Americans; on the other hand, each of these would-be colonial powers was producing alcohol. If colonists in the Western Hemisphere could convince Native American hunters to demand alcohol, this would be more than a marriage of convenience for the Europeans. Supplying Indians with alcohol and receiving furs or deerskins in exchange would benefit planters in the islands and imperial bureaucrats in London and Paris. What greater incentive could there be to try to get Natives somehow addicted to this product of empire? Although no conspiracy created the trade, a compelling economic logic certainly facilitated it.

The Alcohol Trade

From 1650 through the end of the eighteenth century (and beyond), alcohol became a primary good used in the fur trade in English America and New France. Traders chose to use alcohol because the demand for it was apparently constant, because the profits on it could be substantial (estimated at approximately 400 percent on the sale of watered-down spirits alone; see Norton 1974:69, 113), and because young Native hunters seemingly always proved willing to trade skins or furs for liquor.

The anecdotal evidence for alcohol use in the fur trade is abundant. Colonial travelers frequently took notice of the commerce. So too did imperial officials and missionaries, each of whom believed that the trade posed a substantial threat to their American operations. Native American headmen made complaint after complaint about the trade, noting that the commerce impoverished Native families, eroded the fabric of social relations in countless communities, and threatened nascent religious revivalist movements. Although it is impossible to quantify these observations, there is no doubt that alcohol was, as Neolin, the Delaware Prophet, termed it in the mid-1760s, a "deadly medicine" that was destroying Indian communities. In Neolin's opinion, the trade in liquor did not simply emerge; it was part of a larger plan devised by conquering Europeans. With that idea in mind, he told his followers that they needed to change their ways. "You are to make sacrifices," he told them, urging them "to put off entirely from yourselves the customs which you have adopted since the white people came among us; you are to return to that former happy state, in which we lived in peace and plenty, before these strangers came to disturb us, and above all you must abstain from drinking their deadly *beson* [medicine], which they have forced upon us, for the sake of increasing their gains and diminishing our numbers." (Neolin's speech was recorded by the colonial negotiator Conrad Weiser; see Weiser 1737.) But despite Neolin's claims, the existence of the trade and the fact that it thrived do not necessarily mean that all colonists supported it or that all Native hunters wanted alcohol. In 1678 a group of leading French officials and merchants met in Quebec to discuss the brandy trade. At the meeting, now referred to as the Brandy Parliament, some in attendance recognized the dangers that the commerce posed to Native Americans and to race relations in the struggling colony; one even opposed the trade on the grounds that halting the brandy trade would reduce the fur trade and thus force colonists to turn their energies to the creation of an agricultural economy. But the prevailing sentiment of the meeting was expressed by Robert Cavelier, sieur de La Salle, who noted that the French were trading brandy to perhaps twenty thousand Natives each year and receiving in the fur trade approximately sixty to eighty thousand beaver skins; to reduce the brandy trade would be to cut off at least part of the most lucrative commerce in Canada. Besides, La Salle added, though some Indians might indulge to excess, many did not drink at all, and even those who did drink caused fewer problems than the revelers who crowded into fairs in Brittany each year. To La Salle, the brandy trade was vital: "[T]he health of the colony depends on it." When the king issued a proclamation the following year allowing the trade to continue, it was obvious that alcohol had become a crucial item in the French colonial economy (Munro 1921: 174–79).

Economic necessity was not enough to convince Jesuit missionaries to abandon their quest to end the brandy trade. The Jesuits, arguably the most successful European missionaries in eastern North America, lived among their Native charges; many of the Indians who converted to Catholicism became assiduous opponents of drinking. Some missionaries were so confident that they had the support of local converts that they engaged in acts of ritual humiliation, such as an event known as the *saint pillage* (holy pillage) in which the Jesuits stole the property of drinkers in a gesture intended to humiliate those who craved alcohol. In such pursuits the missionaries sometimes succeeded; Natives in mission communities often chose not to drink (Reverend Father Jacques Bigot to Reverend Father La Chaise, 8 November 1685, in Thwaites 1896–1901, 63:103–5, 115, 119–21, 125–29; Mancall 1995a:145–49).

In English America, where colonization took a very different tack, the colonists passed various laws intended to ban the sale of alcohol to Indians. The first laws emerged even before the trade became well established; as early as the 1630s Puritan authorities in Massachusetts sought to ban the sale of any alcohol to Indians in their so-called Bible Commonwealth. In these colonies, which were allowed to enact their own legislation regarding relations with Native Americans, one legislature after another recognized the dangers of the alcohol trade and tried to eradicate it. When the commerce continued, colonial legislators mimicked their predecessors and enacted law after law in a seemingly futile quest to stop Natives from drinking.[4] North Carolina's legislature attempted to limit the trade but never tried to ban it outright.[5]

As time passed, Native communities adapted to alcohol in ways that made sense at the time. Since alcohol could alter perception, it is perhaps not surprising that some groups adopted it in rituals, especially mourning rites intended to propitiate the spirits of departed members of their communities (Gates 1965:35–36; Long 1922:89; Zeisberger and Sensemann 1768). Colonial observers recorded such uses of alcohol; though they were not trained ethnographers, their accounts reveal emerging cultural acceptance of certain drinking styles. Further, by the mid–eighteenth century there were Natives who became crucial intermediaries in the alcohol trade; many of them were women, whose efforts to transport alcohol into rural communities suggest the emerging economic lure of the commerce for Native Americans (Lawson 1967:232–33; Mancall 1995a:57–61).

Consequences of the Trade

What do the existence of the French clerical campaign and the laws of English America suggest about the use of alcohol as a drug food in the fur trade in eastern North America? First, they reveal the great differences of opinion about race relations that existed among colonists. In New France, where missionary efforts among the Natives were always more important than corresponding efforts in the English colonies, repeated clerical insistence on the dangers of the brandy trade suggested that not everyone involved in the colonization of the St. Lawrence Valley supported the use of brandy as a drug food; even the king, who allowed the trade to continue, ordered that brandy be sold only in French settlements so that the commerce would not destroy Native communities. In English America, the seemingly fruitless legislative campaign to ban the rum trade revealed a deep rift between formal colonial policy, expressed through acts of self-governing legislatures independently trying to establish stable colonies, and the goals of fur traders, whose primary aim was to transport one of the Western Hemisphere's most valuable commodities to Europe.

Second, the creation of new rituals relating to drinking in Native communities suggests that drinking needs to be understood in its cultural context. Natives and colonists alike noted the deleterious effects of drinking binges, but their accounts also suggest a specific drinking style that developed among those who chose to drink. The fact that drinkers were often young men suggests that heavy drinking fit a certain stage of life, but many of those who drank quite possibly stopped drinking at some point and became opponents of the alcohol trade. As such, the documentary record for the seventeenth and eighteenth centuries suggests that consumption patterns in eastern North America developed along lines similar to those among the Navajos; like those Native Americans in the modern-day southwestern United States, the Iroquoian and Algonquian peoples east of the Mississippi River also had discernible "drinking careers" (Kunitz and Levy 1994). Natives who opposed the commerce, like temperance-minded colonists, often failed, but their efforts suggest that alcohol had become integrated into Native communities in ways that the colonists never anticipated.

Given the competing agendas of those who supported the alcohol trade and those who opposed it, which prevailed? According to the documentary record, the answer is obvious: the providers of alcohol emerged victorious. They did so not because of active complicity from colonial officials, though some of these officials (most notably, the superintendent for Indian affairs for the northern colonies, Sir William Johnson) did recognize the economic necessity of maintaining the trade. As he informed the Lords of Trade in 1764, if the liquor trade were eliminated, "the Indians can purchase their cloathing with half the quantity of Skins, which will make them indolent, and lessen the Fur Trade" (Johnson in O'Callaghan and Fernow 1856–87, 7:665). At this moment, when the British still glowed from their victory over France during the Seven Years' War, the dominant ideology was clear: the merchants prevailed because the logic of colonization, at least by the eighteenth century, had shifted in their direction. If the early plans for colonization emphasized the importance of converting Native Americans to European ways and, especially, to Christianity, later colonial plans for Native Americans emphasized the importance of maintaining commercial links to the Indians. In that calculus, the merchants succeeded, regardless of the impact of the alcohol trade on Native Americans. Alcohol thus became a drug food because it encouraged indigenous peoples to use their labor to provide goods for the European market economy.

6

Rum and Ganja

Indenture, Drug Foods, Labor Motivation, and the Evolution of the Modern Sugar Industry in Trinidad

Michael V. Angrosino

The cross-cultural survey of the relationship between the use of drug foods and the rise of the capitalist world market conducted by Jankowiak and Bradburd demonstrated that colonial expansion began without its agents having the means to compel native populations to engage in the amount and intensity of labor that would support the production of goods important to the world market but irrelevant to the local economy. In order to motivate and organize the population, colonial agents fostered chemical dependencies, resulting in social dependencies that tied the labor force to the colonial system.

Jankowiak and Bradburd contend that "the introduction of drug foods was such a common feature of nation-states' economic expansion that it warranted recognition as one of the primary forces employed in the expansion." Drug foods, defined as "pharmacologic agents that alter cortical stimulation, resulting in the modification of mental activity," were introduced as "labor inducers." Substances such as alcohol and tobacco also functioned as "labor enhancers" to the extent that they improved the state of mind and hence the productivity of the workers (Jankowiak and Bradburd 1996:719). Alcohol was a common labor enhancer on tropical plantations in various parts of the world, at least until industrial capitalism overtook agricultural capitalism with its requirement for a relatively more skilled, technologically aware workforce.

Jankowiak and Bradburd deal mostly with situations in which an external colonizing power imposes itself on an indigenous population. This essay accepts the basic connection between the use of drug foods and the expansion of the world market, but it deals with a somewhat different scenario, one in which the workforce in question was itself imported. Moreover, it looks at the evolution of drug food and market interactions within an evolving plantation economy, that of Trinidad in the West Indies, and does not deal with the subsequent shifts occasioned by the rise of the nonagrarian sector.

The Indenture System: Historical Overview

Following the emancipation of the slaves in the British Empire in the 1830s, Caribbean sugar planters lobbied the government to approve a system of indenture whereby bonded workers were recruited in British India and brought to the sugar estates to replace the slaves. The majority of indentured Indians went to Trinidad, British Guiana (now Guyana), and Dutch Guiana (now Suriname). Since the people were recruited specifically as plantation laborers, there was never really a question of the authorities having to "induce" cooperation. The issue in this case is, however, one of a particular labor enhancer favored by the laborers themselves contending with one promoted by the authorities. Ganja (marijuana), which the Indians brought with them, was tolerated (and, to a limited extent, even promoted) as a legitimate "enhancer" as long as sugar production took place within a loose network of independently owned plantations. But rum, a primary product of the centralized, company-dominated mechanized sugar industry that developed late in the nineteenth century, came to be favored by the authorities, who were as interested in creating a captive consumer class as they were in enhancing the labor of those already working under indenture. Concomitant with the official tolerance for rum was the official prohibition of further growing and use of marijuana. The Indians attempted to conflate the two drug foods by incorporating rum into culturally sanctioned ritual situations in which ganja had been the norm. But they were not really prepared for the relatively more disinhibiting effects of rum or for the way in which it served to enmesh them in a cycle of debt and poverty. The evolution of the modern sugar industry in Trinidad is thus mirrored in the contested symbolism of two drug foods, rum and ganja.

The development of a European predilection for sugar took place against a backdrop of overseas colonial expansion and the proliferation of tropical plantations staffed by slave labor (Hutchinson 1957:3; Mintz 1996:19).[1] Sugar plantations in the Caribbean, southern Africa, Asia, and the Pacific serviced an ever-increasing demand for the commodity. The end of slavery in the British Empire therefore created a crisis that had as much to do with food preference as with political and economic concerns. British consumers demanded sugar, but the sugar planters were convinced that they could not supply the demand with free labor. According to Klass, "[I]n colonies where the economy involved the production of staple articles on a large scale for an export market, land and capital were both useless unless a constant and disciplined labor force were available" (1961:7). Eric Williams, the late prime minister of Trinidad and Tobago, noted, "When slavery is adopted, it is not adopted as a choice over free labor; there is no choice at all" (quoted in Klass 1961:7). In effect, "since the requirements of sugar production had in no way changed, obviously the Emancipation Act did away only with slavery, but not with the need of the planters for a slave labor force or its equivalent" (Klass 1961:7; see also Adamson 1972; Sewell 1861; Stinchcombe 1995; Wood 1986).

In the Caribbean, certain territories, such as the relatively large island of Trinidad, had open land to which the emancipated slaves fled. Despite the planters' acute labor shortage, they never seriously considered abandoning the enterprise, for "too much capital had already been invested, and the island represented a fresh frontier of sugar-lands for the planters of the 'old' colonies, as well as for British capitalists" (Brereton 1981:83). The crisis was solved when the powerful forces that depended on the intertwined sugar and slave trades (merchants, refiners, ship owners, insurers, lawyers, grocers) persuaded the British government to introduce an indenture system that transported supposedly "surplus" labor from British India to the Caribbean colonies (Carter 1996:19–61; Laurence 1994; Rogozinski 1992:109; Tinker 1989; Weller 1968; Wolf 1982:368–71).

The indentured laborers were not technically enslaved, inasmuch as they were bonded by contracts of fixed duration. Nevertheless, the conditions of their employment during the term of the contract were virtually indistinguishable from those of slavery (Klass 1961:14–20). Indentured laborers, while not "chattels," were nonetheless defined legally as "unfree humans" who were "put to work in the same way, supervised in the same way by the same kind of overseers, kept in the same kind of quarters on the sugar estates, and given the same kind of food to eat" (Klass 1991:19). In terms of the colonial society, to be a "coolie" was tantamount to being a slave (Wood 1986:159).[2]

The Indian indenture in the Caribbean was a great success in mercantile terms: the sugar industry was saved from immediate disaster, and the plantation system was granted another two generations of life. Although sugarcane was often challenged as a source of sugar in the nineteenth century, it never lost out completely; indeed, the acreage devoted to sugarcane in the last decades of that century was markedly expanded because of the new labor supply (Wolf 1982:333). The indenture was also a demographic success insofar as the Indians by and large were not in a financial position to return to India at the termination of their contracts (Klass 1961:221–22; Look Lai 1993; Maharaj n.d.:14; Newman 1964:27). They remained and formed the basis for a large and distinctive segment of the modern West Indian plural societies of Trinidad, Guyana, and Suriname, where they still represent at least 50 percent of the population. It has been estimated that 1,439,939 Indians were brought to Trinidad alone during the indenture (Brereton 1981:103).

Drug Foods and Labor Motivation

The story of the habituation of the Indians to the world of the sugar industry in Trinidad is one that contrasts a substance new to them, rum, with one with ancient resonance in their culture, marijuana. It would be easy enough to conclude that, living in the midst of a rum-producing industry, the Indians simply gave in to temptation and, abandoning their traditional religious precepts, became enthusiastic consumers of alcohol. The reality, as seen in the historical record as well as in contemporary ethnography, is actually more complex.

The indentured Indians were mostly from the northern part of the subcontinent and were shipped to Trinidad mainly through the port of Calcutta; a much smaller number of South Indians were shipped through the port of Madras. The majority of the laborers were Hindus, with a numerically significant minority of Muslims. Both Hinduism and Islam were (and remain) strongly opposed to alcohol consumption. Nevertheless, virtually every observer of the indenture period remarked on the drunkenness of the Indians, a perceived problem that grew worse as that period wore on; indeed, my own fieldwork among the Indians in Trinidad began nearly three decades ago with a study of the Indian community's response to an ongoing problem of alcoholism that long outlasted the estate system (Angrosino 1974).

Cultivation and use of ganja were long part of Indian culture. Marijuana always had medicinal and even spiritual connotations, as the mildly euphoric state of altered consciousness that it induced was believed to open the user's mind to a level of reality beyond (and superior to) the illusions of the material world. Given its quasi-religious connotations, ganja would not have been thought of as a labor enhancer by the Indians themselves, but they did bring it with them to the West Indies and found that it grew well in Trinidad. In fact, the growing and trading of ganja seem to have been a thriving cottage industry on the margins of the estates, where the Indians came to be more explicit about the virtues of ganja in enhancing their ability to function as plantation laborers. But by the official end of the indenture system (1917), ganja cultivation had been almost completely wiped out on the island, leaving rum as the predominant labor enhancer.

Cannabis sativa is one of the oldest-known multipurpose plants. Indigenous to central Asia, it was used for the making of rope, as medicine, as a dietary supplement, and for religious purposes (e.g., as an ingredient in incense) as well as for its psychoactive properties. It was brought to the New World by Europeans, who were mainly interested in it as a source of hemp fiber and who seem to have been largely unaware of (or at least uninterested in) its potential either as a medicine or as a narcotic. Although the latter uses for the plant had been brought to Africa by Arab traders, there is no evidence that the African slaves brought such practices to the Americas. Indeed, the circumstantial evidence points to the indentured Indians as the source of a fully articulated "ganja complex" in the West Indies (Mahabir 1994:28; Niehoff and Niehoff 1960:52; Rubin and Comitas 1976:16). That complex includes techniques and types of ganja use, critical parts of the popular lexicon related to practices and paraphernalia and to the justificatory ideology that supports ganja use within the society (i.e., that ganja was enjoyed by the gods, who gave it to humans for their enlightenment, a line of reasoning that has more recently been adopted by the Rastafarians) (Rubin and Comitas 1976:38). Cannabis had been a familiar element in the Indian pharmacopoeia since ancient times, cited in traditional texts as effective in sharpening the memory and creating energy and as an elixir that refreshes, stimulates, alleviates fatigue, and creates the capacity for hard work and the ability to concentrate. Despite its association in the West with contexts of recreation and relaxation, these energy-creating and mind-centering properties seem to have been a major part of the Indians' particular cultural experience with the drug. It has been said that for all these reasons, "marijuana-growing and its consumption probably reached its greatest efflorescence" in India (Goode 1969:6). In 1839 W. B. O'Shaughnessy, an Irish physician serving in India, confirmed the therapeutic benefits of cannabis and reported that he had successfully treated with cannabis extract those suffering from epilepsy, rheumatism, tetanus, and rabies (Mahabir 1994:36). Not incidentally, cannabis was also prized because of its capacity to give rise to pleasurable sensations, so that one is "at peace with every body" (Indian Hemp Drugs Commission 1969:192).

In India, marijuana was long associated with the Brahmin (priestly) caste, which has been the most careful of all Hindu groups in its avoidance of alcohol. The Brahmins' distaste for alcohol was pragmatic as well as philosophical; the money that others drank away could be hoarded by Brahmins against a rainy day (Klass 1991:21). The Brahmins preferred to drink bhang, a tea made from cannabis, although smoking the plant (filtered in a water pipe) was not unknown (Elder 1970:67). It is quite likely that by the late nineteenth century ganja smoking was coming to be associated with lower-caste and even criminal elements. Nevertheless, the qualities associated with ganja (the term refers specifically to the smoked form) were still seen by many Indians to be essential elements that supported the value system and lifestyle of those considered paragons of piety in traditional Hindu culture (Carstairs 1966:116). The use of ganja among the indentured Indians in Trinidad was by no means limited to the Brahmins among them, but such use retained a kind of cachet reflecting the prestige and spiritual values of the religious elite. There were other reasons behind the preference for ganja among the indentured laborers, most notably, a price factor. As long as ganja was sold at a lower price than rum, it remained the drug food of choice both for ritual use and as a labor enhancer. In the words of one of Mahabir's informants:

> *ganja is three cent*
> *three cent ganja*
> *e no drunk all a we*
> *dat time rum no selling*
> *whole half bottle is forty cents*
> *nobody no want*
> *dem smoking ganja*
> *singing like hell*
> *eating like hell*
> *eating and singing*
> *ganja come from india an selling*

only sixty dollars license every year
who selling ganja dem no have no shop
e have house.

(1985:58)[3]

The Transformation of Laborers' Preference for Ganja

Two forces worked to end the Indians' preference for ganja. The most obvious was the planter bloc, which needed to create a supplemental market for its own product and did so by making sure that ganja got priced out of the market even as the price of rum was driven down. There were also the missionaries, who served as the planters' unwitting allies. The missionaries ignored the cultural context of ganja use (with its religious connotations and very mellow behavioral consequences) and focused almost entirely on the immorality of the "vile weed" (Martell 1975; Neehall 1958; Sitahal 1967; Turner 1968). They were particularly disturbed by the fact that most use of intoxicants took place on Sunday, the laborers' one day off (Weller 1968:66). The missionaries' bitter campaign against marijuana gave an unintended boost to the planters, who were intent on plying the Indians with rum, in part as a mechanism for tying them in debt to the company store (Weller 1968:66).[4] While the missionaries ultimately came to rue the shift to rum, they were initially more concerned with the deleterious effects of ganja, perhaps because it was an element of an exotic culture for which—unlike "demon rum"—they had no ready-made remedy.

There are unsubstantiated reports that some planters actually used rum as a kind of currency in which they paid the Indians' salaries in lieu of cash, but there is certainly documented evidence that the plantation stores "dispensed rum twenty-four hours a day" (Clarke 1986:13). In the plantation community studied by Jayawardena (1963:52), there were, in addition to the company store, three rum shops just outside the plantation's gates and a fourth about half a mile away. All the shops were known to sell rum even after closing hours, and several establishments without licenses to sell liquor (e.g., grocery stores) were also known to sell rum under the counter. Several entrepreneurial types were in the business of buying caseloads of rum at wholesale prices and then selling individual bottles from their homes at a huge markup.

Official opposition to marijuana ultimately came to rest on the supposedly debilitating aspects of the drug, which led, in later psychoanalytic terms, to an "amotivational syndrome" among habitual users. The Indians, however, thought of ganja as a definite enhancement to motivation, even if that motivation did not always translate into the sort of productivity the planters expected (Rubin and Comitas 1976:156). The 1884 report of the surgeon general of Trinidad noted that "patches of Indian hemp cultivation [could be] observed wherever coolie huts [were] numerous." The surgeon general went on to detail the complaint of a local planter, who charged that the "coolies" had "given up, in great measure, growing vegetables, because hemp was more profitable" (quoted in Mahabir 1994:28). The implication was that the Indians not only were depraved but were earning money apart from the approved plantation system. In other words, ganja did, indeed, make them more efficient laborers; the problem, from the planters' point of view, was that the labor they did under the influence of ganja was not necessarily that of the estates.

The government's first response was to try to cut itself in on the presumed profits, and in 1885 legislation was passed requiring the payment of a $100-per-acre license fee for those wishing to grow marijuana in addition to the $60 license fee noted above for the selling of ganja. It was not until the turn of the twentieth century, when it became clear that this charge would wipe out those profits almost entirely, that official rhetoric switched to a prohibitionist mode. The tax came to be seen as a weapon in the new war against "the weed." The governor of Trinidad claimed that perpetuating the fee was a way to discourage the use of ganja, which he said was a "prolific cause" of violent crimes and insanity. That violence was prevalent among the Indians is not in doubt (Carter 1996:54), but Brereton (1974:32), for one, attributes it to the sexual disparity inherent in the indenture. Relatively few women were brought to the colony during the first decades of the system, so that even minor incidents of male aggression could get out of hand in the absence of the restraints imposed by family obligations (see also Klass 1961:18–19; Samaroo 1982:98; Wood 1986:154). In any case, the governor drew on the authority of the surgeon general, who tended to rely on anecdotal incidents, such as the case of a man who, doubting his wife's fidelity, hacked her to death after smoking ganja and then attacked the estate manager, who had attempted to disarm him (Weller 1968:95). Try as he might, however, the surgeon general was unable to provide statistics to show a correlation between ganja use and violent behavior (Weller 1968:95), although in his zeal to justify his antimarijuana crusade he nonetheless asserted that it was indeed the root cause of crime (Mahabir 1994:29). A British medical inspector, Dr. Comins, went further. He claimed that in his experience, the use of Indian hemp aroused all sorts of dangerous passions, including an "irresistible inclination to kill, regardless of consequences" (Weller 1968:96). K. T. Grant, a founder of the Trinidad mission, claimed that five out of six people executed for murder in Trinidad were non-Christian Indians, presumably inveterate users of ganja (Samaroo 1982:98).

A considerably less lurid picture of crime and violence during the estate period is presented by Trotman (1986), but even so, the authorities' overriding concern was for order in the colony. The image of the Indian Mutiny of 1857 was always in their minds, and they were bound and determined to avoid a repeat among the supposedly unruly compatriots of the mutineers (Wood 1986:154). The missionaries' efforts were designed to play a part in stilling the wilder impulses of the Indians (Samaroo 1982:96), which included their use of marijuana.

Some health reformers may actually have believed these assertions, but the authorities seem to have taken a more cynical view. As late as 1907 the government was tacitly allowing the importation of marijuana into Trinidad to replenish the supplies that had disappeared when the license fees drove local producers out of business. Company stores on the plantations were licensed to sell the imported marijuana, for the planters, notwithstanding their public rhetoric about its links to violence and aggression, seem to have been more concerned with the way it made the laborers docile and dependent. But since it did so in ways that did not make them maximally useful as cane cutters, the planters in the early years of the twentieth century decided to turn to the promotion of the use and sale of rum, the production and distribution of which they controlled and from which they profited directly. Such direct profits inclined them to encourage rum rather than marijuana as a labor enhancer, because from the sale of marijuana they derived only the dubious, indirect benefit of a passive workforce. The link between rum and violence was far more apparent than that between ganja and crime; the planters, however, seem to have been willing to bear with their workers hacking each other to death as long as the agent of their violence was a product they themselves had manufactured and from which they reaped the profits.

The missionaries, for their part, initially bought into the widespread belief that they were part of a general civilizing mission. Grant claimed that "British rule in India has brought order out of chaos, given peace to warring creeds and races, chained human tigers, introduced civilization, established justice, opened wide the doors for all the forces of Christianity to enter" (quoted in

Samaroo 1982:94). His colleague John Morton, perhaps the most revered of the numerous Canadian Presbyterian missionaries, claimed that the Hindu gods were loathsome, Indian women were "wicked, wild and unkempt," and Hindu temples were unworthy of respect (quoted in Samaroo 1982:98). As a result, "in the Caribbean, missionaries worked closely with the government and the planters" (Samaroo 1982:95). Those missionaries whose memoirs have come down to us ultimately came to regret the part they had inadvertently played in turning the Indians into drunkards, but they usually excused themselves on the grounds that alcoholism was not as morally reprehensible as drug addiction and that the Indians were heathens to begin with. In any event, their remorse came long after the fact, when the memoirists were already retired and the damage to the Indians had already been done. Some of the missionaries, however, ultimately realized that they had been used by the cynical planters and hypocritical government officials. Morton, for example, came to the conclusion that "rum sellers contribute tenfold more to the degradation of our rural population than the use of ganja," and he recognized that the effects of ganja were mild compared with those of alcohol. Writing in 1916, Morton noted sadly, "I have never been in a place where rum stares one so constantly in the face as in Trinidad" (quoted in Niehoff and Niehoff 1960:53).

The Indians' basic need was to tune out the wretchedness of life on the estates (Swan 1991:121); a typical function of drug foods is to enhance labor by making otherwise intolerable working conditions bearable. Nevertheless, if marijuana were no longer easy to come by, rum could serve the same purpose as far as the workers were concerned. The Indians' needs persisted, since, even after leaving the estates at the end of the indenture, many of them remained tied to the "latifundial environment of the sugar belt," which meant that even as independent cane farmers they were required to sell their crops through the estate system (Heath 1974:110; see also Klass 1991:23; Singh 1974:53). It would be misleading to conclude that the Indians were the passive victims of the colonial system; they acquiesced in the dissemination of drug foods as a means of labor enhancement and made more or less rational choices about which drug food to use, given the constraints of their circumstances. On the other hand, it would be wrong to ascribe free agency to a group of people living in a condition of legal bondage. The choices they made could only reflect the limited options provided by the colonial authorities, who were able to monopolize both supply and pricing in ways that the Indians never could. The Indians' consequent willingness to substitute rum for ganja was therefore confounded by the fact that the latter had an ancient and quasi-spiritual role in the traditional culture, while rum was entirely a symbol of their new life as dispossessed exiles. Even though the functions of the two substances were the same in the minds of the Indians, the transition from one to the other represented an important cultural surrender to the harsh fact that they could never go home again.

The Evolution of the Modern Caribbean Sugar Industry

The Indian indenture in Trinidad coincided with the transformation of the old sugar estates into modern, capital-intensive mills. The Trinidadian sugar industry, like those analyzed in other parts of the world by Wolf (1982:335), began with the labor-intensive production of a raw commodity, often referred to in the West Indies as *muscovado,* an old Portuguese word for unprocessed sugar (North-Coombes 1991:25). It evolved, however, into a capital-intensive system that was responsible for a larger range of processing tasks associated with preparing sugarcane for the international market. Perhaps the most economically and socially important processing by-product of the new sugar industry was rum. The Indian laborers arrived on the Trinidad plantations just as the estates were transforming themselves into the institutions Wolf terms "factories in the field" (1982:335; see also Hutchinson 1957:5). In Trinidad, this transformation entailed the installation of distilleries for the production of rum as well as mills (known in Trinidad as *usines*) for the production of refined sugar and molasses (Niehoff and Niehoff 1960:54).

The cultivation of sugarcane was associated with a "remarkably stable way of life"; indeed, sugar production persisted long after the crop had ceased to be an automatic moneymaker (Hutchinson 1957:4). Declining sugar prices were the result not only of an oversupply in the world market but perhaps more directly of the end of protectionist import policies in Britain (Wood 1986:159). In the laissez-faire market economy of the later nineteenth century, competition among the various sugar-producing areas intensified, and even the most hidebound planters were moved to experiment with innovative techniques. The indenture itself was one such innovation, and it is not entirely unlikely that the importation of a very large and deliberately unassimilated labor force—clearly an agrarian proletariat rather than slaves, who could be construed as "part of the family"—into a colony like Trinidad hastened the shift from the old paternalistic plantation into the later corporate "factory."

There were, moreover, experiments with new types of machinery and refining techniques with the hope of securing an improved product and consequently a larger share of the world sugar market (Hutchinson 1957:4). It was the introduction of steam-powered machinery that made possible the creation of the large, centralized sugar mill that yielded both larger outputs and higher quality products. Between 1850 and 1897 £2.5 million were invested in Trinidad to facilitate this transformation. The Usine Ste. Madeleine, the traditional economic hub of the region in which I have conducted my own field research, was constructed with an investment of £180,000, and its modern facilities resulted in a reduction of production costs by 50 percent between 1884 and 1984. By 1896 its output amounted to 12,000 tons per year from a total acreage of 10,000 acres. By 1897 almost all of Trinidad's sugar was produced from eleven central factory units, and despite the generally poor market prices at the end of the century, the island's production held up well, and prices were (temporarily) stabilized because of the efficiency of the "central mill" system. By 1900 the "old plantocracy" based on individual landholdings had been almost totally superseded by a company-based system organized around the central mills (Watts 1987:499, 517).

Ganja to Rum: An Interactionist Perspective

The political-economic account of the evolution of the Trinidad sugar industry and of the gradual triumph of rum over ganja as the predominant labor enhancer must be supplemented by a more psychological, interactionist point of view. In time, rum was used for a variety of reasons and in multiple contexts. There are several factors that help explain this shift. First, the desire for a narcotic effect was clearly a factor in the Indian religious milieu; the pressing need for an anesthetic was even more clearly a factor of the miserable conditions on the estates. Second, as Bhana and Bhana (1991) have suggested, the quasi-voluntary nature of the indenture system produced a type of alienation that was even more in need of palliation than that induced by slavery, since it inspired higher expectations and hence resulted in deeper disappointments.

The religious and the psychological-palliative motives have continued in tension with one another. Indeed, despite the sensationalistic accounts of their gross behavior, the Indians themselves (at least in the recollection of their descendants) saw the rum drinking of the estate days as a conscious continuation of the ganja effect, flowing from a need to "bliss out" (to use a modern phrase). Moreover, rum became a ceremonial item in the developing sociocultural system known as *mati,* "a relationship between persons of relatively equal social status which should be characterized by amity, respect, and consideration for the interests and prestige of each" (Jayawardena 1963:49). This relationship is typically affirmed by the sharing of a narcotic, which also helps redefine loyalties and networks of cooperation and competition that, to some extent, replace the caste system that had been disrupted by the "crossing of dark water" (Jayawardena 1963:51–52; see also Yawney 1969:37). In village India, marijuana was usually ingested in the form of bhang or as ganja smoked in a water pipe. These forms were highly significant in light of norms of purity and pollution relating to caste. Only men of equivalent status would be able to drink from a common cup or share the stem of the water pipe, so the very act of sharing took on religious as well as social overtones. Even after the general dissolution of caste following the crossing of dark water, Indians interpreted the act of getting together to share ganja as more than a simple act of letting off steam. Ganja still had medicinal uses and was prized because it brought about a general sense of well-being. As one of Mahabir's informants put it:

> smoke ganja
> all e sickness done
> long time all a dem sit down
> smoking
> no fever
> no cough have
> no courthouse.

(1985:104)[5]

In Trinidad, ganja was smoked in a chillum, or "smoking pipe," rather than in a hookah, or water pipe (Mahabir 1985:104). On the estates, caste no longer determined who shared a pipe with whom, but the ties that bound certain of the laborers together (as distinct from other "crews") inherited a quasi-religious connotation. When someone who is presumed to have the same status as the other members of a group is invited to share in this ritual of conviviality, it is considered an offense of the highest order for him to refuse. In Trinidad, such a man will be scornfully referred to as "too social." According to my informants, an exception would be made if the man who refused were known to have taken a vow to lead an ascetic life, but such an exception only made sense once rum had become the engine of conviviality; in the days when ganja prevailed, even a sadhu (holy man) would not have disdained participation.

113

Michael V. Angrosino

The Indians seem to have taken pains to invest rum with the same sort of spiritual cachet that was attached to ganja, hence the highly ritualized aspect of plantation drinking sessions associated with the mati complex, the classic definition of which is provided by Jayawardena for British Guiana. Jayawardena describes the sessions as "communions" because they "reaffirm the bonds of the group" (1963:51). The men sit around a table set with numerous bottles of rum as well as a jug of water. Each man has a "snap glass," equivalent in size to a standard shot glass. One man opens the proceedings by striking the base of a rum bottle and then pouring out a few drops on the floor "for the spirits." The others wash out their glasses with water from the jug—an act that seems to be not so much an actual cleansing of the glasses as a survival of the old Hindu practice of ritual purification. The snap glasses are then filled, and each man swallows the rum in a single gulp. A water chaser is then poured out and similarly gulped down. (My Trinidadian informants affirmed that it would be considered very bad form—almost "too social"—to sip rather than gulp.) The glasses are filled, raised, emptied, and set back on the table more or less in unison. As many rounds follow in similar fashion until all the bottles are emptied. Conversation may occur during the drinking, but it is rare for the content of the talk to be consequential; the important communication has to do with the sharing of the drink, not the substance of the discourse.

Drinking sessions as an expression of mati can be held at any time—there need not be an "occasion" to celebrate. But certain events are always associated with a session such as the one described by Jayawardena. In Trinidad, the night-long wake preceding a funeral is one such ritual occasion, although by far the most important one has been associated with the formalization of a betrothal (a situation now in flux given the increasing popularity of marriage by personal choice). In India, the latter ceremony was traditionally a time for the sharing of the hookah, so that the use of the drinking ritual in the West Indies seems a clear attempt to clothe the new drug—the symbol of the new economic order and the very substance decried as a wicked abomination by pious Hindus and Muslims—with the trappings of traditional religiosity.

The socioreligious character of rum drinking among plantation laborers is also ironically linked to the labor-enhancing goals of the authorities, even though the latter would have scoffed at the notion that drinking rum could be a spiritual exercise. The fact is, however, that ritualized conviviality that maintained the bonds of mati also served to siphon off excess wealth that might otherwise be used for capital improvements in the workers' lives. "The emphasis on spending thus performs a double function—reaffirming the bonds of mati and inhibiting status differentiation" (Jayawardena 1963:52). In sum, every man who participated in the ritual remained equal to every other man, to the extent that all were spending their cash on maintaining the round of drinking parties and not on improving their homes or saving or investing their earnings. As a result, all remained stuck in poverty. Even if they were not literally in debt to the company store (although they often were), they had to be ready and able to work at full throttle in order to earn enough just to keep pace with the demands of the conviviality system. Indeed, the drinking bouts were a way of imposing limits on any tendencies the men may have had to get out of hand and be unfit for work—the plight of the solitary drinker. One of Mahabir's informants insisted:

> dat time have good rum bhai
> good rum
> an Saturday we taking
> Sunday we eh want
> so Monday we turn out to wuk
> we eh drunk
> we eh drunk.

(1985:178)[6]

In spite of such assertions, it is clear from my own research (Angrosino 1974) as well as that of Yawney (1969) that consumption of alcohol rapidly got out of hand and had behavioral and psychological consequences far more serious than any that had been associated with marijuana. The image of the drunken, machete-wielding cane cutter is just as pervasive—and probably closer to the truth—than that of the ganja-fueled man of violence. The enduring problem of alcohol abuse in Trinidad is the long-term result of the planters having won the economic battle to supplant ganja with rum. The problem has marked the Indian community in Trinidad for decades beyond the end of the indenture and the end of the traditional plantation system.

Conclusion

Ganja and rum can both be highly effective labor enhancers in the strictly pharmacological sense. But in the case of the indentured Indians in the West Indies, the choice of one or the other was determined by numerous subtle factors of cultural expectation and economic calculation that did not always result in the kinds of enhancement that might have been maximally effective in the context of the evolving sugar plantations. Ganja was desirable from the Indian cultural standpoint because of its links to ancient spiritual traditions. It helped a displaced and oppressed people think of themselves as heirs of a special and desirable past, but in doing so it seemed to have encouraged them to turn their productive labor to activities that were personally profitable (i.e., growing marijuana) rather than ones that contributed to the economic success of the plantations. Alcohol, by contrast, made for a less disciplined workforce. The production and distribution of rum were controlled by the planters and not by the laborers, who nonetheless attempted to mitigate some of the worst aspects of alcoholic indiscipline by integrating rum into a traditional ceremonial complex, a process that had only marginal success. As such, use of rum mainly served to tie the Indians in a cycle of debt and other obligations to the estates—a kind of enforced indenturing of their labor that long outlasted the official indenture system itself.

Exploited and oppressed people would seem to have a fundamental psychological need to compensate for their misery by relying on resources (including drug foods) that either chemically or by means of spiritual, historical, or cultural resonance made them feel better about themselves. But as this case study demonstrates, when two such drug foods are equally available as labor enhancers, the psychological needs are cross-cut by political and economic exigencies. In this case, the labor enhancer that profited the elite, who not only got an enhanced labor force but also made money on the production and distribution of the enhancer, won out over the one that could be made available through the initiative of the laborers themselves. As the Trinidad sugar industry evolved into a more capitalist mode, the profit motive of the owners came to color all decisions about the disposition of its workforce.

7

Inside the Windhoek Lager

Liquor and Lust in Namibia

Robert Gordon

In Namibia before the creation of the colonial state, most indigenes had reasonably free access to a number of drug foods, including tobacco, cannabis, alcohol in the form of several home-brewed beers, and a large variety of local teas and coffees. With the expansion of the industrial capitalist system, indigenous drug foods were rapidly replaced by manufactured goods. This was policy at least during the initial phases of colonialism. As Gen. Lothar von Trotha, one of the more notorious German generals involved in Namibia, put it, "[C]onquered the colonies have to be, nothing of that can be withdrawn. The natives have to give way... [e]ither by the bullet or via (the Christian) mission through brandy" (Pool 1991:38). This essay explores how one of these drug foods, beer, assumed a preeminent position in the making of modern Namibia both as a means of inducing the European subalterns of empire to work in the colonial project and later, ironically, as a symbol of Namibian national identity.

In particular, I examine two integrally connected features of the colonial scene: how beer would come to symbolize Namibian identity for so many local people and how the settler populace promoted a dominant-nationalist ideology through developing a specific taste during the colonial era using a logic of practice that is today distinctly Namibian. To understand this, in addition to looking at the politics of beer production and consumption, one also needs a longer historical perspective in which to locate the genesis of this apparently arbitrary association. It was the application of sumptuary laws to the indigenous populace that served to stimulate the demand for liquor and later to propel Namibia to its current high-use profile. Eventually, ordinary Namibians appropriated Namibian beer as an icon of what they perceive Namibia to be.[1] This is epitomized in the following tale:

> Shortly after Independence, Namibian urban-based intellectuals launched a debate on what should be done with colonial memorials. Perhaps the most prominent of these was the "Reiter-Standbild," a heroic statue of a German trooper astride a horse and located on a prominent hill overlooking Windhoek, the capital. Tapscott thought he would raise this issue as well, while doing fieldwork in an isolated rural area. To his surprise the issue failed to ignite argument. Why, his informant queried, didn't the statue belong to Namibia Breweries? And if not, why not just sell it to them he pragmatically suggested? It is not difficult to see how or why he saw the issue this way. Namibia is "beer-country" and by far the best-selling beer at that time, Windhoek Beer, had a logo fashioned after the "Reiter-Standbild." (Tapscott 1990)

Yet Namibia was not always "beer country." Quite the contrary: until 1967 by far the most common criminal offense for which black Namibians were convicted was violation of the Liquor Laws, not of the dreaded Pass Laws or the Masters and Servants Proclamation, the ostensible building blocks of apartheid-style colonialism (Gordon 1998).

This vignette illustrates the merits of unintended consequences. It foregrounds the fact that the spread of capitalism is decidedly heterogeneous. This essay suggests on the basis of the Namibian experience that drug foods were important not only for incorporating or seducing the indigenes but also for inducing the clerks, orderlies, and police sergeants to go about their work.

The story also provides an opening to discuss the use of consumable commodities in the creation of a nation. Several scholars have recently examined this theme. Guy (2002), for example, has looked at the role of wine in the making of French identity in the late nineteenth century, while Penfold (2002) has examined the role of Tim Horton Donuts as a Canadian national marker. Wilk (2002) has looked at the origins of "Belizean Food." Despite the large amount written on this topic, we still do not have satisfactory answers to what exactly makes a nation. Anderson's *Imagined Communities* and Hobsbawm and Ranger's *Invention of Tradition* have been classic starting points for such analyses, but frequently work in this genre has denied agency to the underdogs, the formerly colonized who are treated insultingly as simply reacting externally to the schemes of Machiavellian manipulators who run the black box of self-interested nationalism. Much nationalism is indeed planned and is the result of manipulation; how could anyone who lived in South Africa during the sixties not realize this? Namibia has certainly seen its share of cultural coaxing with textbooks like *Namibia: Birth of a Nation* (Breytenbach 1989; Kinnock 1989) coupled to the almost constant press portrayal of President Sam Nujoma as the father of the country, but nationalism—that feeling of identity with a larger entity frequently encompassed by the nation-state—is also a grassroots effort by people who identify with it for a number of reasons the elite do not anticipate. Beer being the major marker of nationalism is not something the state elites would like to promote, although, as will be shown, they have manipulated the local brewing company. Rather, it is a populist naming and capturing of a symbolic national marker.

I want to approach this nation symbol by developing a social analysis of taste using Bourdieu's notions of habitus and logic of practice.[2] Bourdieu argues that taste is not an idiosyncratic thing but rather is socially patterned and serves as a mechanism whereby symbolic resources are distributed. Indeed, the example he cites is how elite French wine is intertwined with "French" culture (Bourdieu 1984:53). Such a stance allows one to examine the social conditions that give rise to such acquisitions but also allows some space for individual agency.

Namibia became independent in 1990 following a long struggle between South Africa and most of its black inhabitants, who were supported by the United Nations and many allies. The struggle's central characteristic was a low-intensity guerrilla war reaching back to the late sixties as the Southwest African People's Organization sought to overthrow what it termed the "illegal racist regime." When independence came it came swiftly; many factors contributed to this change, including, most important, the collapse of the East-West rivalry and South Africa's precarious international financial debts.

The Southwest African People's Organization won the UN-supervised elections, and reconciliation became the cornerstone of its policies. In addition to a new name, a new flag and currency were introduced, and the new regime set about fostering a new national pride in being Namibian. Every event that could be used to nurture national pride was manipulated by the state-controlling elite. When a white Namibian, Michelle MacLean, won the Miss Universe competition she became a national heroine overnight and was treated to a personal welcome

119

by the president; she even had a Windhoek street named after her. Sprinter Frank Fredericks's international prominence also earned plaudits and a Windhoek street name.

Nationalism is undoubtedly an ideology of control by the elite, who need to shape the population within their territory. In the Namibian case, because of long historical domination by South Africa, nationalism was defined primarily in terms of opposition toward its former occupier. And while state elites tried to manipulate various cultural forms for this purpose, local entrepreneurs were also quick off the mark, for example, marketing Namibia's heritage through the construction of a national past with acts of preservation and conservation (Fairweather 2002). Commercial interests also engaged in objectification by promoting tourism, perhaps most strikingly in the case of the marketing of Bushmen (Garland and Gordon 1999). Virtually any commodity can, under certain conditions, function as a medium for objectifying a nation, like Namibian biltong (jerked meat) sold in South Africa. But while expatriates and tourists emphasize the importance of the country's natural heritage and can afford the pleasures of leisure travel and the expense of biltong, it is beer, which is relatively inexpensive and readily available to the masses, that most Namibians argue is distinctly Namibian. Through the consumption of Namibian beer, objectified and commodified, drinkers are promised nothing less than the possibility of national personification, the appropriation of qualities deemed essentially Namibian as attributes of personal taste.

Commodifying Identity

In a country basically dependent upon mining, some agriculture and fishing, and very little manufacturing, breweries are one of the most developed sectors of light manufacturing, and they became an important focus of marketing and advertising after the Second World War. Over the years, Namibia (originally South West) Breweries, which started in 1920 when four local breweries amalgamated, has established a near monopoly position. Most of its interests and investments are in Namibia.[3] It is now a frothy business. When South African Breweries (SAB), then the fourth largest breweries group in the world, with annual profits more than twice the GNP of Namibia, tried to move into the country after independence, Namibia Breweries portrayed itself as the local David fighting Goliath and abetted the definition of national identity in terms of opposition to South African domination, both political and economic.[4] Identity is an account of oneself and others in a relationship of reciprocity and mutual recognition. Indeed, there were very few issues elites could grab to generate nationalism except political and cultural domination by South Africa, but even here border issues, so common and effective in other situations, were quickly neutralized in the Namibian situation when South Africa allowed the contested enclave of Walvis Bay to be ceded to Namibia (many locals referred to this event as a "birthday gift").

Brewing is highly profitable too. After successfully petitioning the government not to allow SAB to set up a plant in Namibia on the grounds that it would endanger local industry and jobs, Namibia Breweries reported an almost 40 percent increase in production to 735,000 hectoliters, despite a generally poor economic climate (*Namibian,* 11 June 1997). The steady increase in production, out of all proportion to population demographics, can be seen from the fact that in 1982 beer production amounted to 350,000 hectoliters, of which 90 percent was consumed by blacks (Kube 1985). A significant factor in the dramatic rise in profits must also be attributed to beer exports to South Africa, a successful counterpenetration strategy in a commodity war during which SAB tried to undermine Namibia Breweries' monopoly by exporting lower-priced beer to Namibia. SAB's ploy of offering a nonreturnable bottle led to it being accused of dumping bottles on the Namibian market and contributing to pollution. After SAB won the bid to sponsor the local national soccer team, the Brave Warriors, business baron Werner List, Namibia Breweries' chief stockholder, in a symbolically potent gesture given the land crisis, donated 21,000 hectares, or six farms, to the nation on President Nujoma's birthday in the hope that it would be used by the university (*Namibian,* 13 May 1997, 26 June 1997, 3 July 1997).

The fact that during the long guerrilla war SAB had had the exclusive contract to provide the occupying South African defense force with beer was also made known. Politicians shrewdly played off this rivalry: when the president gave his annual birthday party, for example, Namibia Breweries was expected to provide free beer. But SAB came back with a new offer: local (mostly Owambo) shareholders would hold a 51 percent interest in a proposed N$100 million brewery in Ovamboland. Trade and Industry Minister Hidepo Hamutenya claimed this new proposal had an almost zero chance of success: "'We have a company [Namibia Breweries] that is Namibian, that pays tax, and is the largest manufacturing plant employing over 700 Namibians. We cannot let it be overrun by SAB as has been the case in other African countries where SAB has set up breweries,' Hamutenya said. The Government viewed the majority share-holding offer as camouflage" (*Namibian,* 22 July 1997). Later, Namibia Breweries announced that it was funding a development center to help entrepreneurs and then followed that up with the announcement that it was going to pump N$4 million into the Oshakati sports stadium in Owambo as part of its N$5 million Development Trust Fund in northern Namibia (*Namibian,* 25 July 1997, 28 July 1997). But it was more than simply a question of ambitious politicians playing the breweries off against each other. Nationalism is more than outward identity with symbols and products. To understand the meaning and emotions behind such identities one needs to take a chronological and sociocultural "vertical slice" of Namibian society and examine the role that commodities, in particular, liquor, played in the creation and dialectical maintenance of the entity currently known as Namibia.

Most studies on the history of alcohol and other drug foods in the region have focused on its impact on the colonized, its use to entice and control the colonized, and how the colonized used intoxication as a site of resistance (Crush and Ambler 1992). While this is an important focus, one needs to go further: to comprehend how the colonized variously interpreted alcohol. One also needs to examine the use and cultural value of liquor by the settlers. Such a stance also permits one to highlight the role of sumptuary laws in trying to regulate liquor consumption. This is important, because if there is one question that needs to be asked, it is why the state or the administrators of Namibia undertook such a gargantuan effort to prosecute indigenes for statutory liquor offenses. By far the largest single category in the crime statistics, certainly in the fifties, was for illegal liquor possession, use, or brewing by blacks. Yet, as I will show, settler drinking was, to say the least, not immoderate.

The Work of State Making

Bourdieu's notion of habitus forcefully directs attention to the fact that taste is the product of a long history in which the state plays a major part. There is a certain irony here in that one could argue that alcohol played a crucial role in creating the colonial state of Southwest Africa. The expansion of German trade to Africa was closely linked to Prussian potatoes from which was produced poor-quality liquor. Changes in European import laws meant that a new market had to be found for this readily transportable commodity. One of the places Hamburg export merchants concentrated on was West Africa, where they successfully competed against British firms (Ambler, this volume). So influential did these merchants become that they persuaded the Hamburg Senate to conclude friendship, trade, and shipping treaties with Liberia in 1855. Liquor headed the list of exports to Africa and in 1884 accounted for about 64 percent of the weight of Hamburg exports to West Africa (Stöcker 1986:31). Motivated by a desire for markets and partly inspired by the book *Bedarf Deutschland der Kolonien?* (Does Germany need colonies?), written by F. Fabri, inspector for the Rhenish Mission Society, German merchants began to look to acquire real estate in Africa.

In some versions of the origin myth of the establishment of Namibia as a *Schutzgebiet* (protectorate) in 1884, the rationale was to control a liquor trade that was fueling large-scale cattle theft and war. Ironically, the colonial state exacerbated the situation. According to the Reverend Irle, a long-time resident, the brandy trade only really took off in Hereroland after 1885 (Pool 1991). The government was forced to act, but its proclamations were rarely successfully or forcefully implemented. While the sale of liquor to indigenes was officially prohibited, masters were still allowed to supply their servants with tots as part of their food rations.

But it is settler consumption that is striking during this period. Discussing unsuccessful horticultural smallholders, Clara Brockmann suggests that many failed not only because of "inactivity" and "stubbornness" but by "playing the great gentleman" and "drinking themselves to ruin by buying rounds of champagne" (1912:171). Shortly after diamonds were discovered in Lüderitzbucht, prospector Fred Cornell visited the mines and described how "the first thing that struck me was the enormous number of empty bottles that lay piled and scattered about in all directions—principally beer bottles" (1986:9).

Official figures substantiate Cornell's rather vivid imagery. In 1903, of the 167 firms and companies licensed in Southwest Africa, some 53 were exclusively or mainly concerned with the alcohol trade. By 1903 there was one commercial drinking establishment for every seventy-eight Europeans. Windhoek, with a population of five hundred Europeans, had fourteen public bars—approximately one bar for every forty-one settlers! By 1913 the territory boasted four breweries, two distilleries, nine soda water factories, and three *weiss Bier* (white beer) breweries. The largest industry after the government was by far hotels, which numbered some 121 establishments employing 247 whites and 537 coloreds. Just over a quarter of all employees were to be found working at hotels; this category included a third of all whites and coloreds (Foreign Office

1969:82). There was some criticism of excessive settler alcohol consumption, especially from the so-called moral purity movements in Germany (*Windhoek-Nachrichten,* 28 October 1908, 17 April 1909). A Dr. Warneck, for example, complained that beer consumption in the territory was 50 percent higher than in Germany (quoted in Walther 1998:148). Others noted complaints that farmers would consume champagne for any slight occasion despite paying twenty marks a bottle. They drank it like soda water and called it Farmer Weisse (Mamozai 1989:147–48). Dr. H. F. B. Walker described his part in the 1915 campaign against the Germans in Southwest Africa:

> I believe the Germans here are heavy drinkers, although I must say that since I have been in Windhoek I have never seen one the worse for liquor. But there is very conclusive indirect evidence to show that they drink a lot. A small place like Swakopmund had over thirty hotels and beer shops. Breweries and distilleries abound; I don't think it is an exaggeration to say that it would not be safe to walk anywhere in the country with bare feet, because you would cut yourself with broken glass. On the mountain-tops, in the desert or bush, you find bottles; you see buildings and walls made of bottles and mud; garden paths and beds are ornamented with them; and where German troops have camped you see regular pyramids of them. Whenever we captured their convoys we found quantities of liquor, chiefly rum of good quality. (1917: 136–37)

Oral history, liquor import statistics, and travelers' accounts support the notion that drinking was and still is a major pastime among settlers. This should not surprise the reader, given the fact that, along with sparse distribution, male settlers outnumbered females by about two to one. For this group, drinking was the major leisure activity.[5]

After defeating the Germans in the territory in 1915, the South Africans were awarded Southwest Africa as a "C" class mandate by the League of Nations in 1920. Article 3 of the covenant specifically stated that "the supply of intoxicating spirits and beverages to the natives shall be prohibited." Such a prohibition was inevitable given the international climate exemplified by the Convention of Saint Germain Relating to the Liquor Traffic in Africa signed in September 1919 by, among others, the United States, Belgium, France, Italy, Japan, Portugal, and Great Britain. It prohibited the import of trade spirits and distilled beverages to all of Africa except North and South Africa.[6] One of the first ordinances the South Africans, sensitive to these issues, passed (no.

14/1915) regulated the sale of intoxicating liquors by providing a licensing structure. Later this was consolidated into the Liquor Licenses Proclamation (no. 6/1920). In many ways a remarkable document, this long piece of legislation provides a graphic formal ethnography of how the state conceptualized liquor consumption. The proclamation made it illegal for indigenes to purchase or carry European liquor with more than 2 percent alcohol.[7] So seriously was this restriction taken that violations of the proclamation, illicit diamond buying, and immorality were the only cases in which the state condoned entrapment.

There was a major loophole in the mandate convention: indigenes were not prohibited from making and consuming traditional alcoholic beverages of which they were regular users (Siiskonen 1994:79). One of the earliest examples of martial law prohibited the brewing of beer (National Archives of Namibia 1915), but, since it was in conflict with the mandate, this legislation was allowed to lapse, causing much anger on the part of settlers. An editorial entitled "Native Trouble" in the *Windhoek Advertiser* expressed settlers' serious concerns:

> [T]he local location contains some 5,000 natives, and we are not over-stating the case when we say that they are almost entirely out of control. Every week-end numbers of natives are in a state of hopeless intoxication, and the quantity of beer that is being brewed must be considerable. Domestic servants are frequently absent from work and take part in orgies of drunkenness that are now prevalent. The authority of the Municipal Location Superintendent is being deliberately flouted in every direction. The natives are now setting their faces against the payment of the hut tax and have practically set the Municipality at defiance.... Today they can be brought to their senses by the use of the business end of a police truncheon; in another month or two it may require the use of machine guns. (13 December 1924)

But even as officials were engaged in a discourse of control, indigenes were engaged in subverting their efforts. By early 1926 the local brew on the diamond fields was *khali,* made of peas and yeast. Khali first came into prominence in the South African gold mines, where miners, mostly Mozambican, used Lyle's Golden Syrup as the base. Within two decades khali (or *kari,* as it was known locally) had become the beverage of choice for indigenes throughout the territory.[8] Inevitably, kari brewing was a female activity and was usually associated with a drinking place known as a shebeen, a word of Irish origin and popular in South Africa.

Eradicating kari became a major state activity. A survey of crime statistics for Windhoek shows that since 1937 liquor cases have exceeded all other cases often by as much as 100 percent. By 1950 they accounted for 57.6 percent of all cases and 89.4 percent of all fines imposed on natives. So why were liquor law infringements the focus for state and indigene interaction? Was the state simply enthusiastically fulfilling its obligations to Article 3 of the League of Nations mandate? From a materialist perspective the answer is obvious. By far the greatest shortcoming of native labor was absenteeism, which, according to Gunther Wagner, the government ethnologist, had reached "disastrous proportions," especially after long weekends. On Saturdays and Mondays absenteeism rates would soar to between 20 and 50 percent, and during longer vacations, as in the break between Christmas and New Year's Day, only 30 to 50 percent of workers would return on time. Large employers like the railways were especially vulnerable to problems of absenteeism, and workers would lose an average of 25 percent of their pay because of absenteeism. "The worst days are from Saturday to Wednesday. On Thursday and Friday the men begin to recuperate from the effects of their alcoholic excesses during the previous weekend" (Wagner n.d.). To deal with the absenteeism problem, most firms hired 20 to 30 percent more workers than they needed.

Settler Development Discourse(s)

How did settlers view alcohol and its indigenous consumption? From the very beginnings of colonialism, influential settlers have been concerned about the "crisis in drinking." Indeed, if there is one thing that has been consistent, it is this concern, which stretches back to Capt. James Alexander's explorations during the 1830s and missionary Hugo Hahn's precolonial crusade.

Blacks were generally viewed by all influential segments of the settler population as incapable of drinking alcohol responsibly, and irresponsibility was seen to cause a vicious spiral of problems: "Natives are inclined to drink to excess, which gives rise to riotous behaviour and a craving for meat, which leads to stock thefts," the Windhoek magistrate argued (National Archives of Namibia 1925). Urban areas, and Windhoek in particular, were seen by settlers as lures of vice and decadence for Africans. Farmers complained of how normally reliable boys became recalcitrant once they visited the metropolis. "Windhoekitis," an anonymous author complained, consisted of three activities: drink, gambling, and prostitution. The former two were relatively new and had been introduced in the 1920s. The practice had become to get drunk at least once a week, and this practice was spreading all over the country from Windhoek.

Drinking, the administration believed, was caused by idleness, and the best cure for that was work. As the administrator informed the League of Nations, "Civilization will never be developed on idleness[,] and education of the native does not consist of teaching him the alphabet or the [B]ible only.... Left to himself he will simply sit in the sun and dream about women and cattle. A good harvest results in liberal brewing of beer, heavy drinking and tribal disorders. Work brings him in contact with civilization and therefor[e] necessarily assist[s] the process of civilizing him" (South West Africa 1927:98). While the settlers in Namibia were renowned for their factionalism, there was a unique homogeneity with regard to this development ideology that was consistently maintained.[9] A more direct consequence of this ideology was that native drinking provided an important justification for paying low wages. Indigenes were believed to be target workers par excellence. They were perceived to be incapable of saving money. Thus local experts believed that "absenteeism is worst after major holidays when people have extra money from bonuses, etc[.] to spend on drink." Wagner's considered conclusion was that "[h]igh wages, weekly bonuses, paid leave and other amenities such as warm meals, shower baths, working clothes, radio entertainment during working hours, etc[.] evidently are no incentive to regular working habits. Experience seems to point in the opposite direction" (n.d.:paragraphs 555, 565). The basic problem was perceived to be one of lack of discipline. Civilization was near universally held to be about self-control. Indigenes lacked self-control, and thus sumptuary laws had to be passed for their own good. A corollary was that laws formed the basis of civilization. Laws, especially of the sumptuary variety, were there to control behavior.

Many colonial laws, I have argued elsewhere (Gordon 1998), served to anesthetize the fears and insecurities of settlers by shackling the colonial imagination and its wilder fantasies. The laws created the illusion of control, even though they were in reality largely unenforceable. A major factor in exacerbating the fears of settlers was the unpredictable behavior of drunken indigenes. One can begin to understand the enthusiasm with which the colonial police force engaged in its notorious "liquor raids." On the other hand, alcohol was essential for settling settlers. Each town and every little hamlet had its club or pub in the local hotel that served as a social center where settlers of all social strata could congregate.[10] Drinking places were important nodes of social information and control. It is difficult to gauge how successfully the liquor infrastructure described in the Liquor Licenses Proclamation worked, but inferences from fragmentary data certainly substantiate the settlers' self-image of being hard drinkers.

Laws regulating liquor were very effective status markers. They differentiated blacks from whites because they imposed their presence not only into public places but private ones as well. Drinking was, after all, the major leisure-time activity. The enthusiastic prosecution for liquor offenses perhaps led to the failure of officially sanctioned and marketed African beer brewed from sorghum or millet. The point that needs to be made is so obvious that it is frequently overlooked. It was first made by Montaigne: "To say that none but princes shall eat turbot, or shall be allowed to wear velvet and gold braid, and to forbid them to the people, what else is this but to give prestige to these things and to increase everyone's desire to enjoy them?" (quoted in Hunt 1996:102). Certainly, tales of the genius of local people in circumventing the liquor laws are still very much common currency and are ever available as a topic of discussion in the black-dominated bars and shebeens of contemporary Namibia. But there is another item that also needs to be discussed, and this is the role of drinking in the settler segment of the nascent Namibian society.

Distinguishing Settler Community

One of the most significant (non)events in Namibian history was the activity of the Commission of Enquiry into the Sale of Liquor and Desecration of Sundays. It symbolizes an important milestone in Namibian identity and also illustrates the way contradictory dialectics work.

In 1948 the Nationalists, with their slogan of apartheid, won the elections in South Africa and, riding on the vote of disillusioned German speakers, managed to procure a small majority in Namibia among the settler electorate. Emboldened by these electoral successes, some Afrikaner clergy submitted a memorandum to the administrator on behalf of the Joint Committee for Fighting Social Evil. They claimed to represent some seventeen congregations consisting of 22,000 Afrikaner souls, 12,000 of whom were adults, and they wanted Sunday sports banned and the liquor legislation drastically changed. Drinking, they claimed, led to "the disintegration of married life; the destruction of a happy household life, which is the essential source for a healthy and contented nation in the future; the neglect of the child...; the lowering of the nation's morality; and the weakening of public morality" (National Archives of Namibia 1950, my translation). In particular, they wanted hotel bars closed on Sundays, weekday bar hours restricted, and women banned from entering bars. The age for male drinking was to be raised to twenty-one. In sum, they wanted the liquor laws to be synchronized with those in force in South Africa. This delegation represented influential members in Afrikaner cultural politics, and the administrator was forced to deal with them in a diplomatic way, although he knew the English and German settler segments would see such draconian legislation as an infringement of their rights. Emboldened, the Afrikaans Church delegation now claimed to represent 55 percent of the European population and was critical of the administrator favoring the politically expedient principle of seeking the support of the liberal part of the population as represented by the other so-called Christian Churches. The administrator shifted the debate by appointing a Commission of Enquiry into the Sale of Liquor and Desecration of Sundays to investigate the issue and promised that if all the churches in the territory wanted change, he would undertake such steps.

The commission was chaired by a retired South African chief magistrate, J. F. Enslin, and consisted of four clergy, two representing the Afrikaans Church (both, incidentally, parties to the original complaint), one from the "English" Church, and one representing the German Lutherans. In addition to the clergy, the following people served on the commission: the deputy commissioner of the police; Mrs. Bell of the municipalities; Mr. Meinert, scion of a well-established German family, representing the sports teams; and Mr. Jaap Snyman, rising star in the National Party and later mayor of Windhoek, representing the hotel industry and the bottle store owners. The commission produced two documents: an official report signed by all members of the commission that is surprisingly sympathetic to the Afrikaans Church petition and a confidential report by the commission chair to the administrator that is highly critical of the attempt to impose the new moral legislation. In mid-1953 the commission toured the white urban centers, but despite widespread publicity, very few settlers availed themselves of the opportunity to give evidence. In his confidential report to the administrator, the chair complained bitterly that the public as a whole thoroughly ignored the commission. The 23,000 members of the Afrikaans Church shone by their absence. All the church's witnesses were clergy. A number of church councils sent memoranda with almost identical wordings. Some church elders didn't even know about the contents of the memoranda sent on their behalf. The chair's impression was that the Afrikaner public was "cold and

Robert Gordon

unfeeling toward this predikant agitation.... A medieval witch-hunt threatens the territory. Religion—our religion—must be maintained with raw violence" (National Archives of Namibia 1950:paragraph 31, my translation).

All in all, some thirty-six memoranda were received. Perhaps the most influential memorandum was that of the German Lutheran Church, which was included as an appendix to the report. It accused the Afrikaans Church of feeling incapable of stopping "degeneration" and thus seeking government intervention, but the state had no right to take such action because drinking and Sunday sports were matters of individual choice, and the way of life of a large section of the community would be threatened. Legislation would widen the gap between European groups: "A new nation has to be built in South West Africa with its own way of life and tradition. Such a nation cannot be built as the result of legislation, it will have to evolve." The commission voted to retain the status quo ante, with the two Afrikaans clergy being outvoted. Its rationale was, first of all, that the territory suffered from the tyranny of distance. It did not make sense to have people travel great distances and then expect them to spend only Saturday participating in sports, and travelers were entitled to a drink after a long journey. Second, the commission argued, settlers in the territory had developed a distinctive culture:

> It is difficult for a person coming from the Union to adapt to local circumstances. Words and expressions like *kroë* (taverns, bars), which a civilized person does not enter if he can avoid it, "women in bars," and so on, are repulsive. Circumstances here are, however, different from those in the Union. The national drink of the German speakers was and is beer, which in its light form is not the cause of much drunkenness. Bars as found in the Union hardly exist here. The so-called taverns, especially in the rural areas, are congregation places for people; they are combination meeting place, café, and restaurant. Witnesses used the expression "bar-lounges" a lot. (National Archives of Namibia 1950:paragraph 31, my translation)

The major distinction between South African and territory drinking practices concerned women in drinking places. The Afrikaans clergy argued strongly for women to be banned from such places on the grounds that they were "emotional and more susceptible to wrong influences. She is a stimulus for a drunken man, and her presence promotes prostitution. A liquor establishment is no place for the shaping of a future mother" (National Archives of Namibia 1950:paragraph 31, my translation). Others pointed out that bars were not

130

really bars but rather "bar lounges" and that ladies' bars did not exist in the territory. Many clubs did not discriminate against female members, and besides, the National Council of Women strongly opposed the ban.

The final report in 1952 contained some minor proposals to alter the system of liquor licensing, but despite repeated requests from the Dutch Reformed Church Ring to enact these proposals, the administrator was able successfully to avoid doing so by claiming that they were impractical.

By the early fifties, then, local German beer was firmly entrenched and hailed as the national beverage for settlers, and the price controller was instructed to maintain its low price. Its paltry alcohol content of 3 percent led to it being viewed as a wholesome, nourishing "family drink" that even teenagers (but not indigenes) could partake of. Distinctive drinking rituals emerged. Beer should not be drunk off the shelf: to drink it properly it had to be served ice cold and with a full head, and it was often accompanied by a chaser of cognac or brandy, especially in winter. Since there were no formal controls at the border, settlers returning to the territory would celebrate this crossing by symbolically ordering a cold Southwest beer.[11] This trend was already developing before the Second World War. In 1936 a Swedish lady traveled to Namibia and, after landing in Walvis Bay, met an Anglican parson and asked him how he survived in such a godforsaken place: "Oh there are compensations! Beer for instance. The Germans over there in Swakopmund make the best beer in Africa. And we are rather a thirsty lot here!" (Oldevig 1948:16)—this despite the fact that the English and German sectors of the settler population were bitterly divided by the rise of Nazism in the territory. Back in Sweden, the lady reflected: "I think that the chief impression he gave was of a fantastic dry and hot place, where God in His bounty had given mankind an excellent German beer with which to quench its thirst, and in addition in His wisdom, He had ordained that the beer could always be served cold, since the very dry air created such intense evaporation for an old wet sock wrapped around the bottle that it was easily reduced to the right temperature" (Oldevig 1948:19). Her impressions were bolstered in the postwar period by other ecclesiastical travelers (Haythornthwaite 1956).

Locally produced beer rapidly established a solid niche for itself, first because of the cost of transporting foreign beer into the country and second because of its much advertised higher quality. Settlers had to pay more for it, but they could afford to, since it was estimated that the per capita income of the 60,000 settlers was some two and a half times that of their South African compatriots (see the *South West Africa Guide* published in 1960 in Windhoek). "Das echte Südwester-Bier" [the genuine Southwest beer] became a settler catchword. A Windhoek Beer advertisement in a fifties travel guide, *Arrive in Windhoek,* captured the ambience well when it proudly and accurately proclaimed: "Windhoek Beer has become a household expression. The factory building stands in Windhoek as a symbol of security. 'Let's discuss things over a glass of Windhoek Beer.' This remark is always heard when a big business deal is in the air."

Starting in the fifties and continuing to the present, local breweries have become major advertisers and sponsors of local community events, both sporting and cultural, and can always be counted upon to take out full-page advertisements in any annual or publication promoting the territory. White Namibians had clearly appropriated Windhoek Beer and Hansa Beer as their icons of national identity. Beer embodied their identity.

For many years Windhoek Beer ads promoted the self-definition of the settlers rather than the subjugation of the others. The colonized "eavesdropped, fascinated by the phantasmagoria" of the beer (Richards 1990:7). The consumer economy as epitomized in advertisements had yet to reach the native people. The cultural forms of consumerism thus came into being well before the consumer economy did. And when it came, it came with a vengeance. A study in the late eighties of Owambo, the most densely populated part of the country, described the region as having an "alcohol-driven economy." Twenty percent of all formal businesses there were liquor outlets. It was estimated that there was one shop selling liquor for every one hundred people, excluding formal bars and private homes as places of liquor consumption (Tapscott 1990).[12]

Conclusion

Following in a long tradition of anthropologists, I have suggested that the use of commodity items like beer has been at least partly structured by their symbolic dimension. In Namibia the production, exchange, and consumption of beer are structured by the perceived expression of beer's symbolic aspects. Consumerist forces provide resources not only to fashion a new national culture but also to provide resources for people who cannot imagine themselves as part of the national community. Ontologically, capitalism and nationalism interpenetrate and reinforce one another, especially when they combine to form a potent brew. Namibia is a fine example of how a country's association with certain commodities objectifies the nation in such a way as to imbue it with the properties of capitalist commodities. "When linked and likened to a commodity, the nation appears to be 'objective' rather than socially constituted; it appears as primordial rather than historical; it appears as 'necessary' rather than contingent; and it appears as a unified, autonomous reality" (Foster 1996:20). This does not mean that Namibian social life was homogenized by the commodity; rather, "the commodity was the coordinating frame within which very different forms of social life—economic, political, cultural, psychological, literary— were grouped" (Richards 1990:14). In Baudrillard's words, "consumer objects are like hysterical symptoms; they are best understood not as a response to a specific need or problem but as a network of floating signifiers that are inexhaustible in their ability to incite desire" (Poster 1988:17). In this case, the "floating signifiers" have gotten entangled in the complex that makes beer not only nourishing but tasty as well. Beer also provides a way for Namibia to successfully distinguish itself from its dominating South African neighbor. Certainly outsiders, especially South Africans, associate Namibia with good Windhoek Beer.[13] Clearly, in Namibia the fundamental imperatives of capitalism have become wrapped up with certain types of cultural forms that at the same time are virtually indistinguishable from economic forms.

More important, Namibia Breweries, which follows a sixteenth-century *Reinheitsgebot* (purity edict), has been marketing its beers as being purer and of better quality than those of its South African rival, Castle and Lion. Indeed, Namibia Breweries has been remarkably successful in counterpenetrating the upscale South African market, and this marketing of quality has important consequences. No matter how hard SAB tries, and no matter how many bribes it offers and how many shady practices it engages in (like encouraging the urban legend that Windhoek Beer is brewed with sewer water), it will find it hard to eat into Namibia Breweries' market stronghold, because in Namibia shared mass consumption practices provided, and still provide, Namibians with the means not only to demarcate a shared common sense but also to anchor the imagined national community in daily practice (Foster 1991:250). Such strategies simply serve to underline the belief that SAB (and, by implication, South Africa) is simply trying to use its clout to dominate Namibia economically and culturally. Local Namibians can cite no better example of their distinction vis-à-vis South African domination than the fact that they drink local beer that is not ordinary but indeed superior to South African brews. In this regard, Bourdieu's notion of habitus is crucial. Habitus is evident in taken-for-granted preferences in taste and is more than simply knowledge or even competence. It is inscribed in an individual's body and ways of drinking, operating according to a logic of practice that is organized by a system of classification. It operates below the level of individual consciousness.

The type of nationalism emerging in Namibia is decidedly multilayered and heterogeneous. For nationalism to succeed it must have a capacity for personalization, and this is what beer drinking provides. But it does so using two entirely different fantasy paradigms. For those associated with the white settler legacy, drinking is a means of cementing social ties as portrayed so strikingly in the beer ads. For those associated with the colonized legacy, drinking reinforces the fantasy associated with heroic resistance to one of the most irksome aspects of colonialism: constant illicit liquor raids by the colonial police forces and how local people subverted these raids. It needs to be emphasized that nationalism is not simply a matter of symbols that can be manipulated by elites. Indeed, some of their efforts at social engineering have failed dismally (for example, most people still prefer to refer to their currency and coinage as South African rands and cents rather than as Namibian dollars and cents). At the same time, one should not take the rituals and camaraderie of beer drinking too far: the notion that consumption shapes identity is decidedly ethnocentric. Concepts of selfhood and personhood are parochial and hardly central concerns in Namibia. How this interest in luxury consumables like beer was "naturalized" is an epic in marketing and desire. And this focus on desire and addiction raises troubling questions about much of the literature on the "invention of tradition," which assumes reasonably free agency. Beer consumption is now a marker of social achievement and thus part of everyday life. People now consume stories through the media, whereas previously they could only dream and fantasize. High consumption is now a marker of social status. Namibia Breweries has achieved the unique distinction of placing its product in the "populuxe" category. It is for this reason that the chances of it being displaced by South African Breweries is unlikely, but, then again, anthropologists have been wrong before.

Acknowledgments

My thanks to Josh Forrest, Udo Krautwurst, David Simon, Padriag Carmody, and Dag Henrichsen for advice and assistance of various sorts. Hans Bothma kindly vetted this paper and added to its value by recounting reminiscences of his own.

8

Alcohol as a Direct
and Indirect
Labor Enhancer

in the Mixed Economy of the BaTswana, 1800–1900

David N. Suggs and Stacy A. Lewis

There is a growing literature on alcohol use in sub-Saharan Africa that addresses the social, political, and economic value of alcohol consumption in particular locations (see, e.g., Colson and Scudder 1988; Karp 1980; Haggblade 1983, 1984). Suggs (1996, 1998) has contributed to that body of research, focusing largely on the BaKgatla of Botswana and exploring current social constructions of age and gender in alcohol use under the influence of a cash economy as well as their relation to remembered "pasts." This essay draws from that work and explores the idea that one might usefully think of alcohol consumption in the mixed economy of the nineteenth-century BaTswana as a labor incentive. One must exercise caution in doing so and recognize that this idea calls for an understanding of an "incentive" largely distinct from the use of alcohol in the interests of colonial expansion; that is, it was an incentive that supported values other than those of the later cash economy, values that were in many ways inimical to colonial interests. But the prior association—symbolically and structurally—of alcohol with production and authority made the European provision of alcohol as a labor incentive for capitalist production seem reasonable and familiar to local populations, even if the interests of the employers did not, in fact, correspond to their own.

We think there is no question that one *can* think of alcohol as a labor incentive in the mixed economy. Indeed, a number of authors have profitably (if implicitly) done so in a variety of contexts (see, e.g., Karp 1980; Dietler 1990; Dove 1988). The routine consumption of alcohol by BaTswana men following collective agricultural labor is well documented (Haggblade 1983, 1984; Molamu 1989; Suggs 1996). Suggs's (1998) research on the construction of masculinity in alcohol consumption shows that from the oldest to the youngest of men, routine alcohol consumption today is perceived as a reward for responsible labor in both the collective agricultural context and the rationalized cash economy. Rewards, in general, are commonly discussed as incentives to further responsibly productive labor.

But, as Colson and Scudder (1988) have argued, it seems obvious to us that the integration of beer into the *cash* economy makes of it something wholly other than it was before. Whereas formerly beer as an agricultural product was a "special food" to be shared in the creation of community (Karp 1980; Suggs 1996, 1998), beer as a commodity is marketed as a drink to be drunk for the sake of individual drinking. Whereas formerly people drank as an expression of community, in a cash context drinking communities are themselves formed in acts of common individual purchase (Adler 1991). In short, what was symbolic of community cooperation and productivity is likely to become symbolic of self-achievement and individual productivity, even if consumed in groups. Where such a shift occurs, it will, in turn, obviously encourage changes in the cultural meaning of drinking as a labor incentive. So the question that interests us is not whether alcohol *can* be considered as a labor incentive in the mixed agricultural economy but whether it is *useful* to consider it as a labor incentive in that context and, if it is useful, in what sense might it be so?

It seems to us that the answer to that question hinges, in part, on the relationship between two central issues: why the BaTswana were brewing and for whom they were laboring and brewing. Were they brewing in response to demands of the chief or as an expression of the productive solidarity of kin or both? This essay argues that the Comaroffs' (1997) work on the authority of chiefs and the structure of traditional courts is relevant to answering that question, as is Haggblade's (1984) work on the economics of brewing. As a symbol, did alcohol most fully represent the family and its patrilineal, gerontocratic structure in domestic economy or the chiefdom and its patrilineal, gerontocratic power in political economy or both? We suggest that Colson and Scudder's (1988) and Haggblade's (1984) interpretations of the impact of seasonality on alcohol production and consumption are relevant to answering that question. Then, we suggest what we think is a reasonable context for viewing alcohol as a labor incentive in the mixed economy of the precolonial BaTswana and explore how that would influence the use of alcohol as a labor incentive for colonial interests. Like the editors of this volume, we believe it is likely that the physiological effects of alcohol contributed to the potency of the symbol and should not be discounted, but our work focuses on the political and economic values of alcohol distribution and consumption. Throughout the essay we explore the role of alcohol in the mixed economy of nineteenth-century Botswana, arguing that initially alcohol was a "key symbol" that, through its production and consumption, gave power to the notion of the group, making it manifest as a "statement of essential sociability" (Karp 1980) and revealing it to be a structural, systematic incentive to laboring with mutual purpose. We argue that in the colonial period, this "managed accomplishment" (Karp 1980) of sociability was used to legitimate the multiethnic association with nonkin labor that characterized colonial production.

Alcohol in the Agricultural Economy

We believe that the connection of the seasonally bound collective production and consumption of alcohol shows that drink was more than just a labor incentive, even as it was one.[1] The symbolic value of beer would certainly have encompassed the political economy of the chiefdom, but for the numerically greater commoners alcohol primarily represented the domestic economy, the local productivity of patrilines (or, at least, wards with a patrilineal core), and the control of that family and its productivity by senior males. Household- and kin-structured authority was most salient in an act of consumption. That logic extended to chiefly consumption and redistribution as an amplification of the logic of kinship in the political economy, where the chief was theoretically in power because of his place as the senior male in a patrilineal clan core. So if beer was brewed among the BaKgatla, as it was among most people in southern Africa, *as an incentive for relations to engage in labor parties, it simultaneously (and, perhaps, more fully) symbolized the kin who were laboring and the productivity of the laboring group itself.* The drinking group was, as Suggs (1996) has suggested elsewhere based on Karp's (1980) work among the Itesu, a "managed accomplishment" or a structural "statement of essential sociability," something far more, then, than *just* a labor incentive, even if it was one.

This point is seemingly echoed in Schapera's (1960, 1966) writings about the BaTswana in the first half of the twentieth century. Schapera noted the ceremonial value of alcohol in ancestral veneration as well as its social value in the bonding of patrilineal groups. It was much prized as a food item, a drink that, when shared, cemented marriages between patrilineages and rewarded labor cooperation within patrilineages. In this sense, alcohol was a symbol of the social wealth that derives from common descent and family membership. Distributed in quantity according to age and social rank (Haggblade 1984), beer was also a privilege of the esteemed. It was in this sense a symbolic indication of social wealth acquired via seniority. Produced by women, it was consumed primarily by men. Thus, it represented not only the power of women's productive and reproductive capabilities but also the power of senior males in the control and distribution of life's blessings. Colson and Scudder note that alcohol, "even more than food[,]...represented the basic reciprocities of social life.... [It was] a 'key symbol' linking almost everything that...people thought important" (1988:65).

In the mixed economy, the brewing of beer was an inexpensive way to diversify the diet: traditional sorghum brews are not filtered and are quite nutritious as a food item. Even so, like Haggblade (1984) and Colson and Scudder (1988), we think it is reasonable to suggest that brewing—and, consequently, drinking—followed a feast-or-famine pattern of sorts. That is, when the harvest was coming in and grain was plentiful, people brewed in plenty. Later in the year, when grain was less readily available, beer brewing also became less common. This seasonality, then, established a pattern of fairly routine drinking at one point in the year and of relatively little drinking at other points.

Ambler (1987) has appropriately questioned the blanket relevance of such agricultural seasonality to the availability of alcohol in precolonial patterns of consumption in sub-Saharan Africa. At the least, his argument suggests that the seasonality of consumption should be demonstrated rather than simply assumed. Like Ambler, we think well-established trade networks in southern Africa could be utilized in the off-season to acquire grains with which to brew. Also, it is evident that some chiefs and others of renown could demand the preparation of beer almost continuously. But Ambler's general conclusion that "local leaders must have had substantial supplies of alcohol on hand most of the time" (1987:11) has a primarily cautionary value in the particular context of the BaKgatla, among whom a number of considerations make the seasonal availability argument more broadly and culturally salient. Given the centrality of seasonal availability to our understanding of kin-based and patriarchal control of labor in the precolonial period (Ambler 1987:11) and its relationship to defining "incentive" in that context, we will follow Ambler's lead and try to demonstrate (rather than merely assume) its validity.

First, given the brisk pace of spoilage in sorghum beer, "substantial supplies" would be substantially wasted if stocked. Thus, while we do not doubt that such supplies could be produced in the worst of times, they would almost certainly have to be redistributed fairly widely over the very few days—literally—during which they could be consumed. Of course, Ambler's point is, in part, exactly that potentials for abuse are better understood as "abuses of power," since they would be limited to those members of the immediate royalty and their principal patrons. But the BaKgatla have demonstrated historically their intolerance of inordinate abuses of power in their willful migration from Kruger's territory in South Africa and in their later support for the Colonial Office's banishment of Chief Molefi for a wide range of socially detrimental actions, one of which was continuous drunkenness (Schapera 1980).

In fact, one of the points of the Comaroffs' (1997) recent reconsideration of the chieftaincy and the *kgotla* (traditional court or forum) system is the way that ideas of good government interacted with the structure of primogeniture to make the chieftaincy an institution of power while holding chiefs accountable in behavioral terms. That is, they argue that among the BaTswana "the ideology of good government paid less attention to the content of public affairs than to the means by which they were managed" (Comaroff and Comaroff 1997: 130).[2] Thus, if authority was unquestionably vested in the chieftaincy, it was not unquestionably vested in any given human serving as chief. The BaTswana chiefdoms emphasized the "participatory, consultative aspect of the public sphere" (Comaroff and Comaroff 1997:131). In the words of one MoTswana at a chief's installation, "A chief can only be judged by what he does.... If we can not see you in the court we shall draw away from you. And if we do, will you still call yourself chief?" (Comaroff 1975:145). The point, then, is that it is unlikely that a MoTswana chief could command continuous beer production for his own aggrandizement (or for the sake of political patronage) at the expense of general social welfare without calling into question his legitimacy as a ruler. Occasional abuses of that order might be tolerated; routine ones would result in the loss of legitimacy.

For example, Chief Molefi came to installation in 1929 among the BaKgatla. Schapera (1980) notes that he began his reign as a relatively young man at the insistence of the people. Yet in a relatively short time Molefi proved himself less than worthy of the trust and respect that the office of chief demands. That is, "Molefi, although of attractive personality and good intelligence, was addicted to drink [and] tended also to absent himself frequently from his tribal duties at Mochudi" (Schapera 1980:25). By 1934, his increasing drunkenness and misuse of the chiefdom's funds resulted in a sense of crisis. At a *kgotla* meeting called to discuss the situation, Molefi was "publicly censured for his drunkenness and irresponsible conduct" (Schapera 1980:25). A year later, the population of Mochudi by and large welcomed (indeed, many had encouraged) the Colonial Office's decision to remove him from the chieftaincy and replace him with the more capable Mmusi. While the Colonial Office's involvement in this case is far from insignificant, the Comaroffs' (1997) work suggests that the result would have been effectively the same in the precolonial context.

Second, given that collective agricultural labor formed a focal point for alcohol consumption among the commoners, the off-season would still present fewer opportunities for their consumption regardless of royalty's potential abuses. When the agricultural season began, families would leave the village and move to their fields to live in "lands houses"; when the season ended, they would return to the village and their houses there. It was at the lands houses that the agricultural labor occurred, and it was there that work parties would drink after the completion of their labor. So while an occasional despotic ward head or chief might demand the brewing of beer from stored grains in the village during the off-season for his own aggrandizement, for most commoners the movement away from the lands houses for the off-season removed the primary context for socially approved public consumption of a recurrent character: that of the labor party.

Of course, upon return to the town there would be weddings and other similarly ceremonial opportunities during which to consume alcohol. But as the season progressed so too would the weddings decline in frequency as the supplies required to feed and please guests dwindled. If it was not so for those with royal standing, it would have been so for the far numerically greater commoners. In short, *the agricultural season was a primary venue for public consumption for the nonroyal majority (at least), a venue that clearly provided opportunities for and linked approved alcohol consumption with responsible production and cooperative integrity.*

Third, to the extent that trade networks could have been utilized in the event of a poor agricultural year or in the quest for continuous chiefly beer production, the commoners' resources would be relatively limited. That the chief might bring the group's resources to bear on the acquisition of further foodstuffs is possible. Yet the issues of accountability and legitimacy that the Comaroffs discuss would seem to limit the ability of BaKgatla chiefs to act in ways that would be perceived as regular abuses for personal or even familial aggrandizement (we will return to this issue below). For the commoners, such exchanges in lean years would follow the economic patterns of reciprocity more closely than those of royalty's more redistributive patterns. As such, issues of familial need would likely outweigh those of individual desire. The elderly with whom Suggs has spoken tell him of their parents first relying on kin networks beyond the immediate lineage and on affinal ties for support.

Fourth, if the BaTswana had given women greater access to alcohol (as Ambler importantly notes many groups did), then brewing at any time of the year would be more reasonable. But the BaKgatla did, indeed, limit women's access to alcohol, reserving only to women of elder standing a right to drink in areas out of public view smaller quantities than the men, who drank in public (Suggs 1996). Continuous brewing late in the agricultural cycle or during times of extended drought (such as those recurrently experienced in eastern Botswana) would be an impractical denial of food resources to the women, who were the primary food producers, and to the children, who would care for the women in the future. Of course, there have been societies that effect such denials, and we do not doubt that occasional abusive husbands and patriarchs existed who could, indeed, have engaged in that level of self-aggrandizement among the BaTswana. But we have found no historical or ethnographic evidence of its institutionalization among the BaKgatla, nor are we aware of any physical anthropological data on the nutrition of Iron Age populations of the immediate region that would indicate it is a particularly plausible interpretation.

Finally, we believe that there is historical evidence that the BaTswana (or at least some of the BaTswana) were acutely aware of the difference in the potential effect of the "continuous" supply of alcohol in a market economy *specifically in contrast to* the seasonal production of beer in the agricultural economy. That is, given the way that alcohol consumption is and was intimately tied to the construction of adult masculinity (Suggs 1998), laws limiting the availability of trade alcohol would be initially interpreted by most men as an attempt to regulate the expression of patriarchy, as an attempt to question their control of women and resources. After all, the symbolic value of consumption emphasized masculinity and seniority. Yet Chief Khama III of the Bamangwato wrote often and forcefully against European traders being allowed to establish canteens in his chiefdom. Writing to Sir Sydney Shippard, administrator and deputy commissioner of British Bechuanaland, Khama (1888) expressed the concerns of a leader newly converted to Christianity: "Lobengula never gives me a sleepless night. But to fight against drink is to fight against demons and not against men. I dread the white man's drink more than all the assegais of the Matabele which kill men's bodies, and it is quickly over, but drink puts devils into men and destroys both their souls and their bodies forever. It's [sic] wounds never heal."[3]

Khama's commitment to Christianity is evident in his concern for the souls of his people. Yet that concern is only real in a market context that allows for continuous and perhaps unrestrained use (i.e., abuse). That is, the traditional, seasonal availability of alcohol in the agricultural economy would mitigate against abuse being a common problem, as would the attendant social structure of availability. Khama wisely recognized that the traditional social controls embedded in patriarchal and gerontocratic structures as well as in seasonal agricultural availability would be relatively meaningless in a context of continuous availability under the rules of market exchange. He must have also recognized that while the tradition of drinking promoted communal productivity, the "new" opportunities promoted individual consumption.[4] While the agricultural context affirmed the control of juniors by elders and ultimately commoners by royals, the new opportunities would have undermined the structure of that authority.[5] Accordingly, one can understand why Khama III enacted laws against drinking, "withstanding [his] people at the risk of [his] life" (1888), a risk engendered among the BaTswana—literally—by the challenge it presented to masculine privilege. In the agricultural economy of the precolonial years, alcohol had been a diffuse emblem of royal authority, but the market economy and its presentation of alcohol as a commodity challenged that authority, a challenge made all the more real given the greater symbolic value of alcohol use as an emblem of masculinity in general and as a representation of male productivity in labor.

What Type of Incentive for Whom?

A further and interesting twist now has to be considered in a discussion of just what the incentive of alcohol entailed and for whom it served. When we speak of a tot of wine as a labor incentive for agricultural workers on nineteenth-century South African farms (see Pan 1975; Scully 1992), the laborers themselves got the wine. Yet in the agricultural context of the BaTswana, the alcohol incentive was consumed by seniors (as the broadest category) and by males primarily, while it was the women and the junior men who did the bulk of the work. Given that the people who comprised the principal labor force had either no access (the young women) or more limited access (the young men), to whom and what would the incentive refer?

The key to resolving this issue is the recognition that labor and productivity were socially constructed in terms other than those constructed with the logic of a rationalized cash economy. While capitalist interests eventually produced incentives for individual labor excellence via individual labor rewards, the mixed economy constructed alcohol as an incentive to the cooperative labor of patrilineal groups—to the solidarity of kin as productive units. In the nineteenth-century context, alcohol represented a structural, systematic incentive to laboring with mutual purpose rather than a direct personal incentive to individual labor excellence. As Karp puts it, "Beer is not *the item exchanged for labor* in communal forms of cooperation.... The beer party is instead *the vehicle through which cooperation is achieved*" (1980:88, emphasis added).[6] Of course, among the young men it was in some measure a direct reward for labor, but the structure of distribution from senior males to junior would mirror most closely the management of their labor by senior men. Furthermore, the extension of rights to consumption did not link the amount of personal labor performed by any young man to the volume of personal consumption.

As Suggs (1998) notes, even today in the bars of Botswana, where beer is purchased by individuals for individual consumption, the men will tell you, "We have always come together as men at the end of a day's work." And, given the relatively moderate amount that they drink on a given evening, we are inclined to agree when they say that their purpose is the common association with similarly productive peers. That is, even if they buy their beer individually, they seek to consume it as a statement of group identity, an even more "managed accomplishment" centering around gender, class, and cash success rather than kinship and collective distribution.

If change is recognized in the class structure of consumption and the individual purchase of drink, continuity is constructed around that notion that men have "always" consumed alcohol together in groups following labor. For our purposes of examining the notion of incentive, the point is that the mixed agricultural context would be best presented as one that provided alcohol as a direct incentive for collective labor, since that is the primary avenue for alcohol production and consumption, and as an indirect incentive for individual male participation in productivity, since the women did the bulk of the work, and distribution in quantity was tied not to individual labor output but to seniority within the group.

For the seniors who called others to the consumption of alcohol at the end of a day's labor, the structure and act of drinking would have been seen first as a legitimation of gerontocracy, of the *control* of labor by senior men (and to a lesser degree by senior women). But the consumption was an incentive for them as well—an incentive to excellence in labor management. As household heads, segment heads, lineage heads, and/or ward heads, they fell under much of the same expectations in matters domestic as the chief did in matters extradomestic. Restated, while the authority of seniors was unquestioned, the particular household heads were, in the Comaroffs' words of reference to chiefs, "merely human" (1997:130). The legitimacy of their control of alcohol (or any other product of the mixed economy) lay in their ability to effectively command the support and direct the cooperation of family members beneath them. Like chiefs, they were expected to be firm but even-handed in the control and redistribution of the group's wealth. To the extent that there was beer in plenty during the seasonal window of opportunity, their control and distribution of it would legitimate their ability to effectively look after the interests of the patriline. Seasonal fluctuations might present varying yields over a long period of time, but consistent underproduction, uneven distribution, or personal aggrandizement likely would have been received with the same reactionary spirit as abuses of the chief.

As with the deposing of chiefs, genealogies could be relatively easily manipulated to support the claims to authority of more effective familial managers. Indeed, given the ward structure of the BaTswana, the manipulation of genealogies would be even more readily achieved at the local level than at that of the polity. In short, the ability to distribute "enough" beer to the junior men (and to the senior women who most directly controlled the work of the family's junior women) would be a strong incentive to managerial excellence in the productive realm.

With regard to young women (again, the primary producers of the grain and the principal brewers of beer but the only adult population denied access to its consumption), we cannot imagine alcohol serving as an incentive in any way that does not stretch the fabric of "indirect incentive" beyond the bounds of realistic analytical utility. The provision of alcohol would certainly affirm their productivity as women, but the structure of distribution and consumption would credit the control of that labor by men and elders with the greater public import. Similarly, while the right of senior women to drink out of public sight could be seen as some incentive to feminine managerial excellence, the very character of the allowance—*it being out of public sight*—would suggest that the incentive would be understood as the realization of the goals of the elders rather than women per se.

Implications for the Expansion of European Interests

What this scenario suggests is the ongoing significance of the symbolic values— patriarchal and gerontocratic communal values—surrounding the consumption of alcohol, values that initially would be brought to bear on any drinking in the cash context. Ambler and Crush note that while many Africans "came to regard alcohol as a source of social decay... for most Africans moving into southern Africa's towns and labor camps the preparation and consumption of alcoholic drinks represented a continuity in social and ritual life between the country- side and the town" (1992:3). It is unlikely that the Tswana were long mystified by the differences between countryside and town, between an agricultural econ- omy and a cash economy, or between the interests of chiefdom and state. As people took up drinking under the new circumstances, either they would have seen possibilities for the opportunistic rejection and/or reinvention of agricul- tural traditions or they would have found opportunities for the maintenance of those traditions, in either case based to some extent on the control of resources. Regardless, our point is that their recognition of differing incentives— and their motivations for participating in colonial enterprise—would be based on their understanding of "tradition," either as new opportunities presented themselves in contrast to it or in relative conformity with it.

Constructing Continuity in Change

Recall that the agricultural context gave to those who controlled labor the right of distribution of alcohol to workers at the completion of the day. In that sense, an employer's provision of beer or wine as partial payment for labor in the cash economy would be a familiar equation of authority and distribution. Clearly, laborers were surely aware that managers were not trying to act like senior kinsmen, but they were still those who controlled labor. As such, the provision of alcohol by those managers would seem less an act of labor exploitation (payment "on the cheap") than a symbolic legitimation of their directive right to control groups of laborers. Additionally, since masculinity was measured in large part by control of resources (Suggs 1998), the symbolic value of alcohol associated with resource control and distribution would heighten their status as "big men."

Similarly, we have noted that the elders had greater access to alcohol for their own consumption, an access that reflected their competence in decision making as well as their seniority. As young men had access to alcohol by right of masculinity and labor, so elders had greater access by right of greater masculinity and control of labor. In that sense, labor managers in the cash economy having greater access to alcohol would not seem so much a discriminatory class practice as it would a legitimation of their authority in decision making and distribution of resources in line with traditional privilege. Of course, the later colonial imposition of restrictive laws (see Ambler and Crush 1992) concerning African access to alcoholic beverages would be interpreted as a threat to these perceived continuities in masculinity as well as draconian attacks on African men's status as adults.

Most significantly, we have emphasized the fact that groups of men have "always" (by tradition) gathered together to drink upon the completion of labor. Surely in the context of the multiethnic workforce of southern African colonial enterprises, such a tradition would give to a laboring group with obvious differences a feeling of legitimate association and common identity. It would give the feel of the managed accomplishment—the statement of human relation among laborers—rather than the outrage of control and exploitation engendered by colonial cost management (i.e., the *payment* in tots and beer). If the colonials saw that provision as cost cutting and simultaneously as an incentive to further labor, the drinkers might well have seen it as an incentive to further social relations, as a means to community formation. That is, multiethnic association with nonkin in labor would be legitimated as seemingly cooperative by common consumption of alcohol. As Moodie suggests concerning life in mining compounds, "Whatever the informal networks on the compound—and boundaries were fluid, not fixed—drinking was an integral component. For most miners, consumption of alcohol was indispensable to compound social life" (1992:169). Even in the mines, then, mutual beer drinking still served, as Karp (1980) put it in the agricultural context of the Iteso, as "the vehicle through which cooperation is achieved."[7]

While several authors have noted the provision of tots of wine in agriculture or of beer in mines as payment, others have also asked whether such provision would potentially increase the authority of young men at home. For example, Akyeampong (1996) and Colson and Scudder (1988) suggest how young men in emergent cash economies found opportunities for escaping the control of elders in alcohol use in Ghana and Zambia, respectively. This issue begs for archival work in Botswana. But even in the absence of such data, we believe that alcohol in the cash context likely presented such opportunities for young adult men. It is interesting to note that while their access to alcohol in the cash economy presents a discontinuity in terms of traditions of distribution by elders, still the young men could construct their unfettered access to alcohol as continuity via the tradition of men drinking together upon the completion of labor as a right inherent in masculinity. If the elders could decry the loss of their authority in controlling access of younger men to drink, the younger could—and did—justify their drinking by appeal to the "traditional" rights of men. It may well be that Khama's will to limit the presence of liquor traders in his territory reflects not only his awareness of the potential for greater abuse in continuous availability but also the challenge to senior authority presented by a cash-based access to alcohol. Given the need for greater archival work exploring how the chiefs of the nineteenth century may have sought to manipulate the symbols of authority in alcohol and its distribution, we present that idea cautiously. Yet even today the elders claim a degradation of their status as senior men in the presence of younger ones at the bar. As one elder phrased it in 1992, "Men used to be men. Today, these young chaps think they are just men, too." Indeed they do. As the older men see the attendance at bars as a statement of mature masculinity achieved by age and experience, the younger men see public drinking as a statement of mature masculinity achieved in the control of resources (Suggs 1998). Both the elders and the young men appeal to tradition, but the relevance of which tradition is emphasized emerges in each group's negotiation of the locus of authority in the cash economy.

Like the continuities between town and country noted above, the discontinuities are made meaningful by legitimation via the weight of tradition. Whether the traditions are those of all men creating productive communities and reaffirming masculine solidarity in drinking groups or those emphasized by the young men in support of their newfound autonomy and rejection of social seniority, the symbolic value of drinking in the mixed economy favored the easy use of alcohol by employers in the cash economy. Clearly, the context of drinking in the mixed economy promoted kin-based group identities, cooperation, and redistribution. Those values are just as clearly counterproductive to the interests of businessmen in a market economy. Yet the association of alcohol with production and authority in the mixed economy lent a legitimacy to its use in the recruitment of and payment for labor in the cash economy. In that realization one can see how an examination of alcohol as a labor incentive in the mixed economy, even if it is a more diffuse conceptualization of incentive, can illuminate the ease with which the colonial uses of alcohol were achieved.

9

Coca as Symbol and Labor Enhancer in the Andes

A Historical Overview

Vicki Cassman, Larry Cartmell, and Eliana Belmonte

Coca consumption in the Andes is associated with a very rich and well-integrated tradition that serves both spiritual and biological needs. Coca leaves, which are sucked, chewed, made into tea, sacrificed, and used as offerings and as currency, were in common use before the Spanish Conquest. The physiological effectiveness and symbolic importance of coca continue to this day.[1] However, coca has been portrayed as having mostly a symbolic nature in prehistory. In this essay, we challenge this portrait of limited access with new evidence of coca's prehistoric functional uses, and we examine the changing status of coca use during the colonial period.

It has been well documented that coca consumption by the indigenous population increased as the Spanish demanded greater labor output from a smaller population of indigenous people (Klein 1996:23). But what were the circumstances under which this increase occurred? And comparatively, how was coca used before the Spanish arrival? We conclude that coca was regularly used by a large portion of the precontact population for both functional and symbolic uses, and its use as a labor enhancer during the postconquest period dramatically increased compared to preconquest usage, though its symbolic nature continued to be important too. Evidence for this conclusion includes the greater area of coca under production, the greater demands for labor and taxes on fewer people, and the protectionist policies for Spanish coca producers, who supplied a vital product that ensured economic productivity for the viceroyalty. In sum, although the Spanish did not introduce the use of coca in work situations, they quickly saw its advantages and encouraged its consumption in newly introduced work settings and in newly introduced slave populations.

Preconquest Use of Coca

Coca, religion, and ritual were closely linked and formed an integral part of Inka society (ca. 1400–1532).[2] We know this from detailed ethnohistoric accounts. Chroniclers report that both coca and *chicha,* an alcoholic drink often made from corn, were essential to many tasks and used in almost every ritual. Coca was given as a sacrifice to the sun, sea, earth, and many other *huacas,* or sacred or supernatural things. According to the Huarochirí manuscript (Salomon and Urioste 1991:45), a colonial record of religious traditions written in an indigenous Andean language, the ancients, when undertaking anything difficult, used to throw coca leaves to the ground for the huaca they called Vira Cocha, an Inka-promoted trickster deity. Mortuary rituals are also described in the Huarochirí manuscript (Salomon and Urioste 1991:73); these include offering to the dead and mummified remains of a relative the sacrifice of a small llama, or, if llamas were unavailable, coca in large skin bags. In the Huarochirí manuscript coca is described as being in abundance, but Fray José de Acosta wrote in the 1570s that coca cultivation was difficult and that during the time of the Inkas commoners needed special permission to use coca because of its association with elite status (Mortimer 1996). The Inkas imported coca from the lowland Yungas valleys of Bolivia into Cuzco, the highland capital of the empire. The distance and cost of importing the substance enabled the royal Inkas to more effectively control its usage.[3]

This latter conventional literary perception of limited prehistoric coca use draws on assumptions from ethnohistoric literature. Hemming (1970) states that common Inka people were forbidden strong alcohol and coca chewing. The perception of limited coca chewing is common in texts that describe the Inkas and prehistoric periods (Hemming 1970:367; Kendall 1973:141; Klein 1996:23; McElroy and Townsend 1985; Marett 1969:57; Starn, Degregori, and Kirk 1995:385) and appears to be based on ethnohistoric accounts by Acosta (Mortimer 1996) and Cieza de León (1959:261). Murra (1986:50), in his study of early archival documents, and Allen (1988:220) assert that there were far fewer Inka restrictions on coca usage than the chroniclers would lead us to believe.

Evidently, coca use extends back to 3000 B.C. (Schultes 1987:223; Plowman 1984, 1986). Though there are obviously no written records pertaining to pre-Inka coca use, there is now substantial archaeological evidence for its pervasive and generalized use hundreds of years before the Inkas. Coca was a common item in the pre-Inka (A.D. 900–1400) mortuary assemblages in Arica, northern Chile.[4] The grave goods of these Arican individuals often included a bag, also known as a *chus'pa* (ornate bag) or *talega* (plain bag) in the Aymara language. This bag, which still holds an important place in the lives of modern descendants of the Inkas, was either for carrying daily supplies or for ritual use and was often filled with coca leaves and small cigar-shaped cakes of dry white alkaline ash paste (Belmonte et al. 1998; Gundermann and Gonzalez 1989). Such offerings, as well as others of food, were either personal items of the deceased, especially when found inside the mummy bundle, or presumably a gift from mourners when found outside the mummy bundle. We know from ethnographic analogy that in the mortuary context these bags and their contents were symbolically meant to serve the deceased on the journey to and in the afterlife. In some cases a coca-leaf quid has been found in the mouth of a mummy: a twelve-year-old girl who died from an advanced case of tuberculosis had a coca-leaf quid in her mouth when she was buried (Arriaza et al. 1995:39). Most likely, the quid was meant to help alleviate the obvious physical pain she had endured during her life and that she might possibly continue to endure in death.

Coca usage, however, had a material as well as spiritual component. Prior to conquest, coca was not only a sacred substance, it was also used as a stimulant, hunger suppressant, and medicine. In their crosscultural study, Jankowiak and Bradburd (1996) found that hunters and gatherers seldom used drug foods as labor enhancers. However, they did find a correlation between the rise of horticulture or simple farming and the use of drug foods as a labor enhancer. Archaeological research on early Andean societies lends further support to their findings. In a study of prehistoric Arican people by Cartmell et al. (1991), coca metabolite (benzoylecgonine, or BZE) was not found in preagricultural societies such as Chinchorro (3000–2000 B.C.) and Quiani (1500–1250 B.C.). However, they showed that coca was ubiquitous among the pre-Hispanic agropastoral societies of Arica (A.D. 700–1500). In later studies of agropastoral societies by

Cartmell et al. (1991) and Belmonte et al. (1998), samples from 158 inhumations, with hair available, were analyzed for two cemeteries, AZ-140 and AZ-71, from Arica. Individuals from these cemeteries date between A.D. 900 and 1400. If these individuals had consumed coca within a two-month period prior to death, the coca metabolite would be present in their hair, and the individuals would test positively. Coca metabolite was found in 89 of the 158 individuals tested, or 56 percent of the population with hair samples available.

This research found that among the Arica population, who were simple farmers and fisherfolk, all ages and both sexes of high and low status had access to and used coca.[5] This is in opposition to the ethnohistoric accounts for the Inka period, which give the impression that sumptuary rules meant elites had greater access to coca. From evidence gathered from individuals with positive coca tests and their associated grave goods, it can be shown that coca was probably used as a prehistoric labor enhancer for agricultural pursuits, for concentration in producing complicated weavings, as an aid in childbirth, and/or as a medicine to control symptoms of arthritis, tuberculosis, and other maladies. Through ethnographic analogy, coca was probably also used by climbers to provide extra strength for scaling the perilous coastal cliffs to gather guano for fertilizer as well as for preventing altitude sickness when ascending to the highlands at 3,000–4,500 meters or more above sea level (Allen 1988; Morales 1989; Spedding 1997:68–69).

In summary, recent archaeological studies demonstrate that coca use among agropastoral populations was likely common in the Andes prior to the Inkas. It also shows that its use was not restricted to a particular status or class of individuals, as some suggest for the Inkas (Hemming 1970:60 and many others). Coca's prehistoric use was likely more egalitarian in the lowlands and semitropical areas where it grows, which explains its availability and use in Arica. However, in areas where coca was an imported commodity, such as in the highlands, coca usage may have been restricted to those who had the resources to acquire high-quality coca leaves en masse or who could at least work for such people.

Coca's dual functions may account for why the early chroniclers sometimes seem contradictory: they mention that coca was a restricted substance controlled by the Inka nobility yet add that commoners constantly had coca-leaf quids in their mouths. In effect, coca in prehistory held dual characteristics: it was equally mundane and sacred.

Coca Postconquest:
The Spanish Conquerors' Perspective

Early in the sixteenth century, the Spanish conquerors who arrived at Cuzco believed they had found El Dorado, the Golden City. Francisco Pizarro and his successors were able easily to gain control of the empire and to maintain control with little effort due to the Inkas' well-developed governing system, a highly organized political hierarchy, including tax and tribute systems that involved corvée, or *mita,* labor. The Spanish ruling elite simply replaced the Inka elite but continued to transform the tribute system into a more intensified system with greater labor expectations. Because of the existing political system, the Spanish (unlike the English and French trappers in seventeenth-century North America; see Mancall, this volume) did not develop new ways to attract an indigenous workforce. By using the existing political system they were able to quickly redefine priorities.

The Spanish transformed Indian communities by moving and concentrating populations in centers, which were easier to control for mita and tax collecting (Morales 1989:3–4).[6] Tax and tribute increased, and forced labor replaced mita labor for some, especially with the growing emphasis on mining to extract precious metals to send back to Europe. Diseases the conquerors brought with them decimated indigenous populations by one half to two thirds, yet taxes and labor contributions from communities were not lowered accordingly (Allison and Gerzsten 1998:177; Godoy 1990:26; Klein 1996:24). This resulted in fewer individuals with greater burdens. Indigenous communities for the most part adjusted as best they could to the new hardships, which meant paying more and providing mita labor more often. The Inka mita system was based on an elaborate system of reciprocity; however, the Spanish elites transformed the system by reducing its reciprocity and extracting far more than it gave back. This was the initial step toward bringing the Andes into the global economy.

The development of Spanish enterprises—agriculture, herding, and mining—required a new labor force that was not readily available. The labor expectations would no longer be seasonal, as they had been under the mita system, but would now require year-round effort. The system placed new pressures on the local populations. The Spanish were quick to realize that a worker labored longer and more efficiently when given plenty of coca leaves to consume.

153

Therefore, coca played a vital role in the economy of the new mercantile capitalist system. The system concentrated initially on haciendas to grow coca and other agricultural products but was transformed in the 1540s by the great mining rush (Godoy 1990:24). The indigenous labor force was diverted, directly and indirectly, in support of the mining efforts. It was the transformation of an indigenous Inka labor system that enabled the Spanish elite to prosper.

The silver mines quickly became a major source of revenue for the local elite and the crown. Mining, however, required a large pool of laborers that needed constant replenishing. According to Klein (1996), tens of thousands of Indian laborers were brought to the mines, which were situated in the highlands at 4,000 meters or more above sea level in the area of what is now Potosí and Oruro, Bolivia. From 1540 to 1570 independent Indians ran the mines, but once the richest silver veins and ores ran out, the Spaniards took over and brought in new mercury amalgamation furnaces that required greater labor efforts. More workers were required to process the ore, and many suffered from health problems related to silica ingestion and mercury poisoning. The intensification of processing also resulted in greater fuel needs. Apparently, the highlands had already been on the way to becoming denuded during Inka times. There had been strict preconquest regulations about tree cutting and grass gathering, but these prohibitions were not followed in the postconquest era. Gathering fuel became harder, and workers had to travel greater distances to find grass and dung for the smelters (Godoy 1990: 28–30).[7]

Work in the mines was grueling. There were no airshafts, dust was a constant annoyance, and the life expectancy of a miner was six to twelve months (Allison and Gerzsten 1998). The miners, with the owners' approval and often assistance, consumed coca to sustain themselves, but coca was also needed as a sacrifice to the mineral huaca (Spedding 1997:49). Even today coca leaves are indispensable for miners, who chew them constantly as a connection with or protection from the "spirit owner of the minerals" and as "relief against the dust and foul air underground" (Spedding 1997:69). Nash (1993:198–200) describes the modern miners' coca consumption in more detail in her ethnographic account. She says that to *pijchar*, or chew, coca is the first thing a miner does upon entering a mine, and there are established morning and afternoon coca breaks. She quotes a tin miner who says that coca "gives us courage, it serves us as energy, and it serves us as food." In addition, many believe it prevents silicosis, and the leaves can help miners divine the future. Mine managers still supply good-quality coca leaves for their miners, knowing how essential it is to keep the workers on task. Miners also give sacrifices to the Tío, a male fertility god whose domain includes the underground and the minerals held there (Nash 1993:18).

Coca production had to be greatly increased to support early postconquest mining activities. The much greater production required more labor in the new coca fields, and laborers were imported from the highlands to the hot coca-producing valleys. In addition, porters were needed to transport packed baskets of leaves to the mines. This long, uphill journey required an additional supply of coca leaves for consumption by the porters along the way.[8]

Coca served as a cash crop for the Spanish hacienda owners. Coca can be planted in poor, rocky soils, it can be harvested three or four times per year, and the plants produce for thirty to forty years. Indigenous populations often had to be transplanted from the highlands to work the lowland fields. The development of Spanish mining and agriculture activities resulted in conflict among the Spanish elite for labor. The shortage of available laborers was a constant source of contention, and hacienda owners struggled to hold onto native laborers. Beginning in the 1550s the crown sought to mediate these conflicts by passing a series of protective ordinances. This legislation would protect the health of coca workers and porters by limiting the length of mita service, establish a minimum wage and an adequate food supply, limit expansion of existing plantations, and prevent the formation of new plantations for coca production at the expense of subsistence crops (Gagliano 1996). The latter two ordinances were meant to control the drain of indigenous labor to the coca fields from the mines and prevent a severe shortage of subsistence crops and supplies. The first two ordinances were meant to appease the reformists and some missionaries who were alarmed at the indigenous death rates and abuses on coca plantations (Gagliano 1994; Gagliano and Ronan 1997). The mita laborers and permanent field hands were to be paid in currency or coca leaves, and one of the ordinances forbade the workers to exchange their corn rations for coca leaves. Though protecting the workers, this legislation also was aimed at protecting existing hacienda owners by maintaining the value of coca by preventing a flooded coca market. Soon, however, with changes in administrators, the reformist coca legislation was ignored, and new coca plantations were licensed. Though the crown prohibited forced labor, it was evidently common, since King Philip II had to repeat the law and add protection of women and children in 1563. But the laws were not enforced, and complaints to the crown about the terrible conditions of Indian coca workers continued (Gagliano 1996:14).

Eight prohibitionist clergymen who attended the first and second conventions or councils of Lima in 1552 and 1567 urged the total eradication of coca plants. These outspoken missionaries felt that coca usage was the main obstacle for the conversion of Indians from idolatry to belief in Christianity. In effect, the clergy objected to coca's symbolic use. On the other hand, coca's importance as a stimulant for enhancing labor productivity was well understood by mercantile capitalists of the day. In 1569 Philip II sought a compromise: he decreed coca's protection and authorized its continued use by indigenous populations for anything but idolatry (Gagliano 1996:8–13). By this time, coca was entwined with Spanish efforts to intensify production. Whatever the personal philosophy of the local elites, the fact remained that time and again morality took a second place to production interests.

Labor shortages greatly affected agricultural pursuits. In an effort to expand the labor pool, the crown and colonial elites bought African slaves to work the lowland farms. It was thought that African slaves would be better suited to the subtropical subsistence agriculture and climate than the highland natives (Gagliano 1996:13). One of the main arguments the missionary reformers and others made against coca production was the inhumane condition of the native plantation workers. Some contemporary estimates gave a 40 percent mortality rate for coca workers each year from various causes, including disease. Unacclimatized workers who came from the high, cold, dry highlands to the steamy, hot lowland valleys suffered high death rates (Gagliano 1996:11). Lack of adequate food was also frequently blamed as a cause of death.

Eventually, a few coca plantations used African slaves as field laborers. In time, though, they were replaced by cheaper Indian labor when that population revived and had stabilized by the early eighteenth century (Klein 1996:30). African slave populations began to arrive in the Andes as early as 1529 (Thomas 1997:103) and, according to Raymond (1989:91), in 1650 made up approximately 6 percent of the population of Peru and approximately 4 percent of the Bolivian population. Indigenous populations made up 90 percent in each area. There are very few records of what types of work African slaves were given, but it appears that they were more highly valued than their indigenous counterparts, and they were given chiefly agriculture-related duties, as opposed to being sent to the highland mines.

In recent unpublished studies, Cassman and Cartmell discuss hair samples from four African slave mummies from Arica that tested positive for the coca metabolite. This new finding lends more evidence to the assertion that plantation owners encouraged the use of coca as a labor enhancer not only for indigenous laborers, who had used it from ancient times, but also for African slave laborers, who had no history of coca use and would have had limited resources to purchase or barter for it.

Conclusion

Prehistoric coca use among Andean agropastoral people was likely prevalent, especially in the lowlands, where coca grows wild or is cultivated. Therefore, perceptions about the highly restrictive nature of coca usage under the Inkas are not a reflection of Andean prehistory in general. The highest-quality coca leaves may have been under elite Inka control in the highlands surrounding the capital, but it would have been difficult for the Inkas to take control of general coca usage in all their conquered lands. Coca chewing was embedded in indigenous rituals, and its qualities as a mild stimulant were well understood. Much like the nineteenth-century BaTswana example of beer (see Suggs and Lewis, this volume), coca through the ages has been an indirect labor incentive that also promoted social exchanges between friends who say, "Come round for a chew of coca" (Spedding 1997:69). In contrast, postcontact Spanish elites used coca as a labor enhancer and discouraged its use in religious or ritual contexts. Spanish elites' economic interests easily outweighed their religious morals, and they were forced to redefine coca as a legitimate substance in order to tolerate and even encourage its use among indigenous populations. The intentionality of promoting coca as a labor enhancer by colonial elites is clearly demonstrated by the new evidence presented here that coca was even supplied to African slaves, who, we assume, would not have been able to purchase this substance on their own.

The Andean indigenous perspective has been and continues to be that coca is foremost a sacred substance needed for ritualistic sacrifice and is only indirectly or secondarily perceived as a labor enhancer. This cultural continuity may very well be a symbolic cultural construction of desire that is unconsciously based on a biological desire for coca as a stimulant (only after decades of consumption can coca become an addiction). Andean drug foods that include coca and chicha have survived to this day. As Jankowiak and Bradburd have suggested in this volume, the continuing use of a product within a culture is more likely to occur when the product also provides physical sustenance. In effect, symbols often have a material referent. This pattern is clearly evident in the

Andean cultural area, where folkways such as traditional dress and food are being abandoned in favor of nonindigenous consumption items, while coca and chicha remain vital substances.

10

Caffeine and Culture

E. N. Anderson

Extending the argument of Sidney Mintz (1984, 1998) that alcohol, sugar, caffeine, and other drug foods have been used to increase labor discipline and have helped to rationalize the global capitalist economy, this book suggests that drug foods were used to bring traditional people into the market or to create a dependency on the outside economy. Caffeine plants have spread along with clocks and work discipline, allowing workers to be on time and alert in a world where bodily rhythms are not necessarily synchronized with work hours. Thus, most contemporary workers have had at least occasional recourse to caffeine.

While there is ample evidence for the roles alcohol, sugar, tobacco, and opium played in habituating ever more people to modern work discipline, the roles of coffee, tea, and chocolate in this worldwide process have proved more elusive: their role in work discipline is real but not so brutally direct as rum's deliberate use to capture labor. I intend to show the complex reasons for consumption of these and similar plants.

Caffeine and other methylxanthine stimulants are commonly used for labor discipline. Isolated trading posts everywhere sell strong tea, colas, and coffee along with tobacco and alcohol. Large workplaces in rich nations and an increasing percentage of those in the Third World have methylxanthine sources available in vending machines, cafeterias, and offices. Coffee or tea is routinely provided at meetings, and cola drinks are usually available at outdoor worksites in hot weather.

However, the use of methylxanthines by individuals in what might be called self-motivation is still more important. Many people use methylxan-thine stimulus to wake up, get to work on time, stay alert on the job, and per-form over long hours. With short naps and caffeine people can perform at optimum levels over long periods (Bonnet and Arand 1994). They may then use alcohol after work hours to unwind and relax. Many academics, high-tech workers, and truck drivers use caffeine to work long hours at jobs that demand alertness and independent thinking. In extreme cases, this can become self-exploitation, suggested by stereotypes of professional writers abusing caffeine and countless cartoons of reporters surrounded by empty coffee cups.

Methylxanthine substances may be most important in creating a wider social context in which people can function better as human beings and live something like normal lives in spite of heavy work pressures. Workers and man-agers use these substances to help them socialize and lead a cheerful life dur-ing breaks and recreation times. They also use them as aids in organizing, resisting, and otherwise fighting back when the system becomes unbearable. Crosscultural comparisons show an association of caffeine venues like cafes, coffeehouses, and tea shops with radical, revolutionary, and grassroots politi-cal movements. Methylxanthines thus become not just a means of disciplining the workforce but also an important aid to organizing resistance to that disci-pline, helping people salvage some traces of humanity from the alienating machine.[1] Workers who are alienated from the products of their labor, individ-uals from society, and intellectual products from their creators characterize modern society and are a theme of this book.

Unlike alcohol, tobacco, and the hallucinogens, caffeine, the world's most widely used drug (Braun 1996; Gilbert 1984), has attracted little anthropologi-cal attention. Yet the cultural construction of caffeine consumption is one of the most interesting ethnobotanical stories.

Most cultural structuring of caffeine use occurs in regard to the great caf-feine drinks: coffee, tea, yerba maté, cola, and *guarana*. I will also consider with the caffeine drinks cacao and its products, which contain little caffeine but large quantities of theobromine, a closely related methylxanthine alkaloid that is the precursor of caffeine in its biological synthesis by coffee and tea plants. The stimulant effects of these methylxanthines are similar. The only other stimu-lant methylxanthine of any note is theophylline, which is abundant in tea. Pure caffeine, available in pill form, was often used by students and long-distance truck drivers and was given to U.S. pilots during the Gulf War (William Jankowiak, personal communication).

Coffee

Coffee is the second most important commodity, by value, in world trade; only petroleum outranks it (Bates 1997; Martin Diedrich, personal communication). Tea, chocolate, and the ever-present cola drinks are not far behind. In all, caffeine substances make up about 7.5 percent by value of world trade in plant commodities (Food and Agriculture Organization 1995).[2]

The stimulant effect of the methylxanthines is due primarily to their actions as antagonists of the brain's natural sleep inducer, adenosine (Braun 1996; Porkka-Heiskanen et al. 1997), "a behavioral, electrophysiological, and biochemical depressant. The methylxanthines inhibit binding of adenosine to its receptor sites" (Hirsh 1984:279). Effects on other depressant or relaxing neurotransmitters such as serotonin are possible. Thus, methylxanthines are not stimulants but instead counter actual depression of brain function (psychological depression is neurologically an agitated state, not a depressed one).

The effect of small doses of caffeine (tens or hundreds of milligrams) includes transient elevation of blood pressure, wakefulness, alertness, and often a feeling of cheerful well-being and activity. Larger doses over time may produce tremors, dizziness, insomnia, rapid heartbeat with perhaps some arrhythmia, ringing in the ears, and other symptoms (G. A. Spiller 1984). Frequent use causes the brain to produce more adenosine receptors, leading in turn to the need for more caffeine to produce the desired effect. Sudden withdrawal thus is often characterized by extreme lassitude and headaches as the body both relaxes and tries to deal with an excessive number of adenosine receptors. Caffeine consumption has been modeled using Gary Becker's mathematical model of addiction (Olekalns and Bardsley 1996), but methylxanthine alkaloids are relatively harmless substances that satisfy the world's passionate desire to stay awake.[3]

All significant sources of methylxanthines are tropical or subtropical plants, and coffee and tea, the most important, are virtually confined to tropical mountain environments.[4] Coffee is derived from the seeds of *Coffea arabica* and, to a lesser extent, *C. canephora (C. robusta)* and, very rarely, other species. Coffee accounts for some 54 percent of the caffeine consumed in the world (Gilbert 1984), but even this may be an underestimate. The average American five-ounce cup of coffee contains 83 milligrams of caffeine (Kirk 1985).

The worldwide spread of coffee is a very recent phenomenon (see Hattox 1985, from which the following history is taken; Sauer 1993:130–38; Ukers 1935; Wrigley 1988; Schapira, Schapira, and Schapira 1975). *Coffea arabica* is native to the mountains of southern Ethiopia, extending trivially into Kenya and Sudan (perhaps only as an ancient cultivar). Until medieval times it seems to have been known only in that area; beans were chewed or eaten. According to unconfirmed folklore, goatherds discovered the virtues of the plant after noticing that their goats were friskier after browsing on it. (Ukers 1935:6–11 provides a highly romanticized and fanciful but delightful account, correctly noting that there are no reliable accounts until the fifteenth century.) Coffee use apparently spread throughout Ethiopia but did not reach Yemen until the mid–fifteenth century. The origin area of coffee in Ethiopia is now the Kahve district; the word *kahve* (coffee) may have started as the name of a local ethnic group.

Coffee proved an instant success in Yemen. From Mocha, a major port whose name has been immortalized in coffee lore, coffee grown in the Yemen highlands reached Arabia and Turkey. Puritanical authorities were concerned that it might be intoxicating, but Muslim medical authorities correctly held that it was a valuable diuretic and stimulant rather than an intoxicant, and coffee was deemed allowable. More serious was the charge that coffeehouses were hotbeds of sedition (Hattox 1985; Ukers 1935). This charge led to frequent closings of coffeehouses in the Ottoman Empire.

In the last half of the seventeenth century, coffeehouses, often operated by Christians migrating from Ottoman lands, appeared in Paris and London. Vienna converted to coffee (and the associated pastries) during the long, rather benign, and unsuccessful Turkish siege of 1682–83 (Jacob 1935). From these nuclei, coffee spread worldwide. Its only serious competition arose in the early nineteenth century in the British Isles, where tea became cheaper (Smith 1996), partly because its trade was in British hands, while coffee was not. The replacement of coffee by tea in Ceylon (now Sri Lanka) due to the devastation of the coffee plants by leaf blight *(Hemileia vastatrix)* dealt the coup de grâce to British coffee drinking, and many British-influenced areas of the world still prefer tea.

Coffee's reputation for stimulating rebellion followed it to the West (Oldenburg 1989; Ukers 1935). By 1700 coffeehouses in France and England were seen as forums of political debate. Revolutions were planned in them. During the 1950s espresso houses in the United States were associated with beatniks, radicals, and other citizens viewed with fear and horror by the dominant majority. However, an odd dichotomy emerged. Coffee *shops* (and, on the whole, cafes) that served American staples like ham, egg, and pancake breakfasts, sandwich lunches, and thin steaks for dinner became identified with the stalwart, conservative, traditional Anglo-American world, while radical hangouts were known as coffee*houses*. Coffee shops still flourish everywhere in America. They are places for "regulars": workers who come every morning for the stimulation, both chemical and social, they need for their daily work. Long after they retire, many of these regulars still show up at the coffee shop every morning to have coffee with the younger generation that replaced them. Coffeehouses, in contrast, serve Italian pastries and other exotica. They are the haunt of students and young urban professionals. In both, politics is discussed but with very different outlooks: staunchly populist or conservative in the former, elitist or limousine-liberal in the latter (Roseberry 1996). A profound sociological gap has thus been encoded in the apparently trivial difference in names. Though recently, Starbucks and similar chains have greatly blurred the distinction, it still exists. Much intellectual activity and political debate occur in countless Latin American and European cafes and Malaysian and Indonesian *kedai kopi* (coffee shops). Coffee venues everywhere are centers of social activity, including the most intense forms: politics, debate, radical organizing.

In the United States coffee drinking peaked in 1962. Per capita use then dropped some 41 percent by the middle 1980s (Gilbert 1984; *Wall Street Journal,* 19 March 1986:1). Though consumption of standard coffees kept decreasing, the decline leveled off in the late 1980s as consumption of gourmet coffees rose. Home coffee consumption, which has fallen another 8 percent since 1985, is sharply age-linked: while 86 percent of those over sixty-five still drink coffee at home, only 64 percent of those age eighteen to twenty-four do (Dortch 1995:4).

The decline of coffee consumption primarily reflects its displacement by another caffeine drink: caffeinated soda, largely cola (Mintz 1998). Many people born after about 1960 prefer cold, sweet drinks such as cola and iced coffee for a number of reasons: buildings are kept warmer, cold drinks are more convenient in cars and trucks (they don't burn when spilled), there has been a demographic shift to the Sunbelt, and many younger consumers became habituated to soft drinks when they were children, when coffee was denied them. Residents of the colder northeastern United States and Canada continue to drink a lot of coffee (Gilbert 1984). Another possible reason for the decline in coffee consumption in the United States is that the amount of *C. robusta* in American coffee has increased from almost zero to about one quarter of typical coffee blends. *C. robusta* does not have *C. arabica*'s flavor but has twice its caffeine, so less coffee creates the same effect (M. A. Spiller 1984). This decline has, of course, greatly affected the political economy of coffee. Brazil continues to dominate the world market with its vast flood of medium-quality beans. However, countries that bank heavily on quality, such as Costa Rica, Jamaica, and Colombia, have done very well indeed, while countries that focus on mass production of bulk coffees, notably Mexico, have seen their coffee economy approach total ruin (Jan Rus, personal communication).[5]

However, the spectacular increase in the consumption of high-quality (virtually pure *C. arabica*) coffees is a dramatic countertrend too obvious to ignore. As in the early days of the coffee boom in the seventeenth and eighteenth centuries, modern gourmet coffees are typically consumed in specialized coffeehouses. Until the 1980s, gourmet coffee shops were confined to the upscale sections of America's most sophisticated cities. Now they are found on almost every corner in such cities and have spread even to small and remote towns. (In a tiny Oregon hamlet in 1996, I saw a sign advertising "Nite Crawlers/ Gourmet Espresso.") Often catering to precisely the generation that has switched from coffee to cola, they lure young people with fancy (often cold and heavily sugared) coffee drinks instead of the ordinary brew. Coffee connoisseurship extends to extremes like seeking out *kopi luwak* (beans taken from the dung of mammals of the genus *Paradoxurus,* which selectively eat the finest berries and excrete the beans), which brought $130 per pound in Los Angeles in 1993 (Perry 1993).

Modern coffeehouses often stage concerts, poetry readings, and various forms of political resistance. They often serve as a "feminist space," allowing the public discussion of feminist politics that once was privately talked out at Kaffeeklatsches (Kelly 1994). However, because these coffeehouses are domains of privilege, haunts of the rising leisured class (Roseberry 1996), they have not so far invited repression. Any revolution they unleash is apt to be a tame "reimagining" (Roseberry's term) rather than a conflict. Labor enhancement is, in a sense, combined with leisure. In modern coffeehouses, one finds people, alone or in groups, actually working—with laptop computers, cell phones, or documents.

The world over, coffee has been associated with specialized institutions (coffee shops, coffeehouses, cafes) that are often neighborhood meeting centers, the most important of the "third places" immortalized by Ray Oldenburg (1989). (The first two places are home and work.) Oldenburg notes that "third places have drawn their identity from the beverages they have served," and he cites coffeehouses' historic roles as "penny universities," houses of political agitation, fashionable meeting places, and middle-class venues for enjoyment (1989:183–99). Significantly, he does not find coffee used to addict and exploit. Coffee venues are largely places to go to wake up, thus differing from the next most common third place defined by alcohol (bars, saloons, pubs), which are places to relax and unwind. The same governmental authorities that feared coffeehouses in the 1950s in America sometimes rejoiced in alcohol venues, which tranquilized or addicted the working classes; however, industrial managers often preferred caffeine, since it helped rather than hindered work performance.

Coffee has also been associated with sacred and secular rituals. In Arabia and elsewhere in the Near East it was used by Sufi mystical movements to keep people awake during all-night rituals. There has long been a tension in Islam between organized, state-controlled religiosity and the spontaneous, individualistic, or community-based mysticism of the Sufi orders. This was yet another reason for the authorities to worry about coffee consumption (Hattox 1985).

In many cultures throughout the world, coffee drinking has become ritualized as the focal event in everyday sociability, ranging from minimally structured gatherings around office coffee machines to the extremely elaborate, highly ceremonialized coffee hours of eastern Europe such as the well-known Viennese *Jause* (Oldenburg 1989). In northern Europe, coffee is always available, and some Scandinavians drink up to fifty cups a day. Finland literally runs on coffee and is by far the world's leading consumer in per capita terms, brewing about 30 pounds per person per year. Other Scandinavian countries follow. (U.S. citizens brew a lowly 10 pounds; see *Los Angeles Times,* 7 March 1995, citing U.S. Department of Commerce figures.) Consumption is highly ritualized. In Finland, for instance, high-quality coffee is served with pastries, including *pulla,* a bread originally sacred for Easter and associated with fertility (Roberts 1989). Many firms and offices in the United States now offer complimentary coffee from the inevitable electric brewer. German and Scandinavian immigrants had much to do with introducing this concept of neighborliness and hospitality. Significantly, coffee—not tea, candy, cola, or even hamburgers—remains the universal solvent in all such settings.

E. N. Anderson

Tea

Tea is derived from the leaves of the tall bush *Camellia sinensis* (the closely related camellias of flower shops can actually produce inferior teas). About 43 percent of the world's caffeine consumption involves tea (Gilbert 1984:186). Tea is richer in caffeine than coffee; 3.5 percent of the weight of normal dry tea leaves is caffeine and theophylline, as opposed to 1.1 percent of the seed of *Coffea arabica* or 2.2 percent of the seed of *C. robusta* (Gilbert 1984:187). In 1995 world tea production was 2,627,000 metric tons (Food and Agriculture Organization 1995:174). India is the world's leading producer, followed by China; surprisingly, Kenya ranks third. Turkey and Georgia are also major producers.

Tea's origins are unclear (see Blofeld 1985; Eden 1976; Gardella 1994; Harler 1964; Yu 1974; Schafer 1967; Shalleck 1972). It was first documented in China, but it was exotic there. It originated in the region where modern China, India, and Burma come together, and people in this region had presumably been using it for many millennia. China probably received it from the poorly known but highly civilized local states that flourished in what is now Yunnan. One legend has tea originating when Bodhidharma, the Indian or central Asian missionary who brought Zen Buddhism to China, fell asleep during meditation; he was so infuriated that he cut off his eyelids and flung them to the ground, where they became tea bushes with eyelid-shaped leaves.

Though in mythology the ox-headed farm deity Shen Nung is said to have written about tea in 2737 B.C., it reached China's urban sphere sometime between fifteen hundred and two thousand years ago. Tea became widely popular during the T'ang Dynasty (A.D. 618–907), due in large measure to Lu Yu's book *The Classic of Tea,* written ca. A.D. 760. A poem by Lu T'ung well describes the lift of spirits brought by methylxanthines (Blofeld 1985:9–10). In the following Sung Dynasty, tea spread to the masses and was listed along with firewood and grain in a famous jingle about the necessities of life (Anderson 1988). The Chinese imperial government tried repeatedly to tax or monopolize the tea trade, with the usual mixed results (Gardella 1994; Smith 1991).

The Chinese name for tea, *ch'a,* spread around the world. The word *ch'a* may have originally referred to plant infusions in general, but it soon applied specifically to tea. The way it is pronounced reveals which part of China contributed tea to which country. From Japan to eastern Europe, the standard pronunciation is used. That Persia mediated the tea trade is revealed by a diagnostic marker: the Persian nominative ending –*i*. Thus, the Russian word *chai* proves that the Russians got tea via Persia and central Asia. Other parts of the world received tea from its most well known center of quality and abundance, Fujian Province (see Gardella 1994). In the Southern Min language, spoken widely in Fujian and Taiwan, *ch'a* became *t'e*, from which is taken all western European words for the drink. English "tea" was pronounced "tay" until the eighteenth century and is still so pronounced in Ireland and some other areas. The change to "tee" is confined to "standard" English dialects.

Today, of course, tea is identified with East Asian culture. Old men often become connoisseurs, and I have known people who held onto their I-Hsing teapots through emigration and refugee experiences when they had to abandon virtually all other possessions. (I-Hsing, or Ixing, China, is famous for its artistic teapots.) Vastly more widespread than tea ceremonies are the shops, meeting places, and hospitable homes where tea is served. Tea shops, stalls, and houses are the third places of East Asia, as coffee venues are in the West. Teahouses serve as meeting and discussion forums as well as the ordinary person's office. Local leaders too poor to rent a building regularly sit at a particular table in a particular teahouse at a particular time of day (Anderson 1970; Young 1974), where they can be found by anyone wishing to do business with them. In my fieldwork in East Asia, I spent countless hours seeking out men and women or talking to people who came to meet me at teahouses. Morning tea has now become a full-scale meal, especially in the Cantonese-speaking world. Vast "tea palaces" serve grades of tea from coarse to superb and sell a truly incredible variety of snacks, the famous dim sum. "Drinking tea" has thus become a major meal, usually a weekend brunch. Whole families or groups of friends inhabit their favorite teahouses for hours.

Teahouses in China have been attacked as coffeehouses have been in the Western world. A superb study by Qin Shao (2000) traces this harassment from Imperial times through the whole of the twentieth century. Teahouses were dens of iniquity—gambling, violence, lewdness, and low-class behavior in general. Still, Qin Shao's analysis clearly shows that the real problem is that teahouses are centers of local resistance, political or otherwise. Unpredictable and spontaneous behavior was anathema to bureaucrats, whether Imperial, Republican Chinese, or Communist.

Long before the Sung Dynasty, tea had become involved with Buddhism. Like coffee among the Sufis, it kept worshipers alert during all-night ceremonies. The Zen religion, along with the more secular connoisseurship of Lu Yu and his followers, led to the rise of tea ceremonies, now common in Chinese Taoist practice as well as some other communities. In China and neighboring areas, tea was soon integrated into sacrificial rites. Offering cups of tea, often in threes, is now perhaps the most basic and widespread of all offerings within East Asian religions. The cups are offered to sacred trees and rocks, to ancestors, and to high gods. In a minimal ceremony, only incense sticks and tea are offered; in elaborate sacrifice rituals, whole roast pigs and huge burning logs of sandalwood still do not displace tea from center stage.

Tea spread to Korea and thence to Japan, where connoisseurship and ritualization developed. In 1997 a special issue of the journal *Koreana* (vol. 11, no. 4) was devoted to Korean tea usage. In Japan, ritualization of methylxanthines reached its apogee in the highly refined tea ceremony, the *cha-no-yu,* and the way of life associated with it (Castile 1971; Fujioka 1973; Kondo 1985; Kramer and Kondo 1986; Okakura 1964, a classic account; and Sen 1979). Dorinne Kondo's now-classic account of the tea ceremony (Kondo 1985; Kramer and Kondo 1986) reveals many symbolic shadings and uncovers layers of cultural significance to which no brief summary can do justice; she discusses the ceremony in a context of class, tradition (and its creation), cultural reaffirmation, management of self and emotion, and much more.

Tea was soon traded to England. The British Empire sought new production areas, expanding into Ceylon, India, and later East Africa. In the nineteenth century, fast tea clippers and packets rushed the leaf to rapidly expanding populations of drinkers at home (Forrest 1973; Ukers 1936:113–38).[6]

Tea, like coffee and chocolate, was a luxury before the early to mid-1800s. The real price of tea had fallen rapidly (Forrest 1973), but only when duties were reduced in 1833 did tea become readily available to English consumers (Burnett 1969:212). Tea's affordability after 1833 helps explain its universal use as the comfort and stimulant of all levels of British society. In other parts of Europe, it was coffee that became cheaper; differences in pricing in the nineteenth century probably explain the crazy-quilt pattern of preferences evident in modern Europe.

Ireland, England, New Zealand, and Australia remain the world centers of tea drinking. However, Iran, Saudi Arabia, and neighboring countries are also great tea-drinking zones. Their attachment dates from earlier times when the Silk Road brought tea from China. Tea consumption remains low in the United States but is expanding rapidly. The spread of tea to India and the harsh life of workers on tea plantations there have often been described (Misra 1986; Piya

Chatterjee, personal communication). India is now the major exporter of the leaf, but many Chinese and Japanese connoisseurs sneer at the quality of India's product.

Tea quality ranges from the lowly leaves that go into "instant" tea to the exclusive Taiwan and Southeast China mountain products that cost up to hundreds of dollars per pound. Like coffee, tea appeals to all classes and can be a daily necessity or a rare luxury.

Chocolate

Chocolate is the product of the cacao tree *(Theobroma cacao)* and is apparently native to South America and perhaps Central America, but it has been domesticated in Mexico (Coe and Coe 1996; Young 1994). Cacao is difficult to raise and difficult to prepare; the beans require a carefully controlled fermentation process to bring out the flavor (Dand 1997; Presilla 2001). The fruit was no doubt initially gathered for its sweet pulp; only later did people discover that the seeds, if carefully cleaned, roasted, and ground, developed a heavenly flavor (Coe and Coe 1996; Presilla 2001; Young 1994). After learning to use the fruit and grow the tree, local people probably used the fresh seeds to make a beverage and later discovered fermentation.

The Olmec people, creators of Mesoamerica's first great civilization, may well have been the domesticators or at least the popularizers of this plant. Cacao was the caffeine drink of the great pre-Columbian civilizations of Mesoamerica. The Nahuatl word for the chocolate drink was *chocolatl* or *chocolate,* soon borrowed into Spanish and then into English. There are many origin theories for the word *chocolatl;* it may be the Mayan word *choko* (hot) added to the Nahuatl word *atl* (water) (Shively and Tarka 1984:151).

Like methylxanthine drinks in other countries, in Native America chocolate was intensely ritualized. It was the drink of royalty and of ritual (Coe and Coe 1996). It was sometimes flavored with vanilla, another Mesoamerican cultigen. It was also flavored with honey and with various flowers. Usually, however, it was prepared by beating up ground seeds with toasted cornmeal and a dash of powdered chile pepper, producing a thick, foaming, richly flavored drink.[7] Cacao beans also became the standard currency, recognized throughout the region.

Because it is difficult to produce and, inevitably, expensive, high-quality chocolate remains a luxury, not a source of daily caffeine, which makes it relatively unimportant as a device for labor discipline, either imposed or self-

169

imposed. However, cheap chocolate bars do alternate with cups of coffee for many workers, providing sugar for immediate nutrient energy and fat for longer-term energetic drive, along with methylxanthines. Thus, not only workers but mountaineers and other travelers carry chocolate bars as a combined stimulant and source of nutrition.

There are widespread folk beliefs that chocolate is an aphrodisiac and that the phenylalanine in chocolate is mood elevating (see, e.g., McGee 1984:408 for a serious discussion and Boynton 1982 for a humorous but revealing one). Chocolate sweets combine sugar and theobromine, which would seem to account adequately for these claims. Much more obvious is the role of chocolate in courting, as a traditional gift from men to women. Chocolate is associated with indulgence and thus with pleasure and sin. Perhaps these associations have influenced beliefs about the effects of chocolate; in any case, America is clearly in the grip of yet another fad focused on a methylxanthine plant.

Other Caffeine Drinks

Cola is the name of a pair of West African trees *(Cola nitida* and C. *acuminata)* whose nuts contains 2.4–2.6 percent caffeine (Uphof 1968:143) as well as a flavor that Americans and many others find pleasurable. As with other caffeine sources, the nuts were used in West Africa as ceremonial and ritual items in both sacred and secular rites. They were prized by elites and were important in hospitality at all social levels. They were so important in trade that, like cacao, they came to be used as currency. They were and are important in local legend, song, story, ideology, religion, and belief.

Their worldwide consumption stems from the development in the 1880s of Coca-Cola, whose flavor and caffeine originally came from cola nuts. Today, cola drinks are essentially sugar-water with artificial flavoring. Their caffeine is a by-product of decaffeinating coffee. Cola and coca leaves (the latter now decocainated) are now only used in trace amounts for flavoring.

The spectacular success of cola drinks needs no elaboration here (see Mintz 1998). They are now the drink of choice among young people throughout the world and have replaced coffee and tea as the caffeine drink of the rising generation. The current Mexican idiom for "totally isolated" is "donde no va el truc de Coca" [where even the Coca-Cola truck doesn't go]. True epicurism seems never to have developed around cola drinks, but young people discuss the merits of various colas, and it is widely held that Mexican Coca-Cola is more tasty than the U.S. product, allegedly because it is stronger and contains cane sugar rather than high-fructose corn syrup (the company remains notoriously secretive about its formulations). Mintz (1998) has found that Coca-Cola was originally used to stimulate the workforce in the American South. Combining those two great drugs, sugar and caffeine, in a manner available to all, it subsequently has spread worldwide. In spite of the incredible spread of Coca-Cola from regional drink to universal American cultural marker ("Coca-Colonization"), there seems to be little scholarly literature on the drink's social implications.

Yerba maté *(Ilex paraguayensis)*, a holly native to south-central South America (Reed 1995, 1996), occupies the same cultural position in that region that caffeine drinks do elsewhere: it is the common ground of hospitality and friendship, and a ritual of consumption has developed around it, complete with the songs and poetry so beloved by the Latin American public sphere (Barretto 1991 quotes many of these songs). Yerba maté remains the caffeine drink of choice in rural Paraguay, Uruguay, Argentina, and extreme southern Brazil but is losing ground to the international drinks. In Argentina, where it is universal and considered a social experience, people are expected to drink from the same *maté* gourd. Coffee has come to Argentina as an after-dinner or occasional breakfast drink, and English settlers and businessmen introduced tea and made tea time a national institution, but maté remains the preeminent caffeine drink (Rodolfo Otero, personal communication). Strangely, in spite of its excellent taste, caffeine content (similar to tea), and alleged but unproved health values, yerba maté has never spread significantly outside South America, though it is widely available in herb stores and South American markets.

Another caffeine holly is yaupon *(I. vomitoria)*, source of the "black drink" ritually consumed by Native American peoples in the southeastern United States as part of a purifying rite. Vast quantities of warm yaupon tea were consumed until vomiting occurred (see Hudson 1979). The resulting strong caffeine stimulation was interpreted as a gift bestowed by the supernatural beings on the purified drinkers. The ritual took place during war expeditions, council meetings, and other situations requiring long-continued alertness. Black drink was quickly adopted by white and black settlers and remains a folk medicine in the American South.

Other South American caffeine drinks include species of *Paullinia,* including *guarana (Paullinia cupana)* (Erickson et al. 1984; Perez Arbelaez 1956: 684–85). The seeds of *guarana,* which contain about 3.5 percent caffeine, are

171

prepared as a paste, kneaded into a loaf, then powdered and added to water to prepare a drink. The powder may be up to 4 percent caffeine (Erickson et al. 1984:281–82). *Guarana,* the traditional caffeine drink of much of Brazil, is very popular, especially along the Amazon, and has become somewhat popular in the United States due to Brazilian immigrant influence. It is made into a canned soft drink that competes with cola drinks and is associated with good times and sociability.

Conclusion

Humans have responded in strikingly similar ways to methylxanthine sources. Clearly, biology and chemical pharmacology as well as human neurophysiology make certain cultural responses likely. This has implications for cultural ecology and anthropology. We are not speaking here of biological determinism. No "instincts" or biological "laws" or innate "fixed action patterns" determine methylxanthine use. However, culture does not happen in a detached mental space. Culture is, rather, learned actions that are embodied (cf. Bourdieu 1977), and the body that practices them comes with a brain prone to drowsiness that sometimes will not arouse itself on demand. The brain also has its own ways of reasoning about the plant, wakefulness, and emotional involvement. Sociability and ceremony, in particular, are stimulated when the brain is alert. Unlike many symbolic foods, caffeine drinks are important because of their actual and unique physiological effect, not because of symbolic associations alone.

Several common themes emerge in the long history of human interaction with methylxanthine-rich plants. All these plants and the drinks made from them have become enormously important in hospitality, friendship, and interpersonal interaction. They have been incorporated into social rituals, usually secular but sometimes sacred. Often the drink is the explicit focus of a ceremony. Each drink has its own connoisseurs. There are specialized journals (*Coffee Journal* for coffee and tea, *Chocolatier* for chocolate), utensils (Japanese tea ceremony wares, Paraguayan maté gourds, and Mexican coffee services—see the 1978 issue of the leading Mexican art journal *Artes de México,* issue 192). The plants' role in world trade has become truly spectacular. To the historic importance of coffee, tea, and chocolate we must now add the phenomenon widely known as Coca-Colonization.

The drinks all started among small-scale indigenous societies. They have gained worldwide importance due to the explosive growth in trade that began in the fifteenth century. Unlike other agricultural commodities, they did not start slowly and spread steadily. With the exception of tea, which had spread throughout East Asia by A.D. 1000 but remained localized in that part of the world until the seventeenth century, chocolate, cola, and coffee remained rare, obscure, or local until modern times. Nothing shows the explosive nature of the spread of these drinks better than their names. They all spread so quickly that their names did not change, being borrowed into all languages: *ch'a, t'e, café, cacao, chocolate, cola, maté.*

The plants appeal to all classes: the highest-quality forms are luxuries for the rich, while the lower grades have become small but important indulgences for the workers. Methylxanthine beverages have very often been associated with activities that authorities have held to be subversive and dangerous (though cola drinks seem to be associated with more conforming youths and so avoid any stigma). The appeal of these drinks does not lie in their flavor or their health value. All these plants produce bitter brews with little nutritional or medicinal value. They are usually an acquired taste, disliked by novice drinkers and made tolerable only by intense sweetening or long habituation.

The late but explosive spread of these plant substances correlates perfectly with the spread of clocks and work discipline. Robert Bates, summarizing extensive unpublished literature, says, "[P]eople...take [coffee] not solely for pleasure but also as a stimulus to harder work, less sleep, and greater achievement" (1997:xiii). The same is, of course, true for other caffeine drinks. In China, the rapid spread of tea throughout the empire and its shift from luxury to necessity coincided precisely with the very early development during the T'ang and Sung Dynasties of a highly rationalized court bureaucracy regulated by water-clocks and early mechanical clocks (Anderson 1988). In early modern Europe, the spread of clocks and mechanical timekeeping, the development of large-scale work enterprises, and Weberian "rationality" (Weber 1946) were part of a single process; it is impossible to imagine one without the others.

Mintz (1998) has shown that the coffee break was deliberately engineered by factory owners, often in tandem with religious leaders who wished to get the working class weaned from alcohol. Quakers' early promotion of cocoa as an alternative to beer lies behind their dominance of the English chocolate industry (Coe and Coe 1996:242–45). Other religious interests later promoted tea as an alternative to alcohol, possibly giving us the word "teetotaler" (Forrest 1973:88). Coca-Cola, for a long time a medicinal drink and an alternative to alcohol, was also manufactured and promoted by religious men in search of temperance. Of course, caffeine drinks have their own religious opponents; they are banned by most branches of the Mormon Church and discouraged by the Seventh-Day Adventists and some other religious affiliations.

Mintz also notes the close link between caffeine and sugar, which provide a dynamite combination, guaranteed to energize the most exhausted factory worker. During the nineteenth century, exploding demand for factory products, driven by the expansion of work discipline and long work hours in the factories, promoted the development of more and more sophisticated transport, production, processing, and entrepreneurship. The prices of caffeine drinks crashed, dropping to the point at which coffee and tea were within the reach of the poorest workers. Mintz (1998) believes they spread from factory to home. I find little evidence for this. Except perhaps in England and America, the popularity of drinks like tea and chocolate long predated factories. Burnett (1966, 1969), in his research on employment in England, considers tea in detail in his studies of the horrors of industrial life; however, he gives no indication that tea consumption was other than voluntary. As with coffee in the United States, people choose to drink it to discipline their own labor.

During the 1950s, some employers complained that coffee breaks, which were becoming increasingly common, were pure loss—they took workers away from their jobs for several minutes at a time. Others argued that coffee breaks increased productivity and more than offset any loss in work time. This proved to be the case, and coffee breaks quickly became accepted.

Over the last few centuries, there has been a progressive shift in socially accepted drugs from depressants (especially alcohol but also tobacco and opiates) to stimulants. Tobacco continues to spread in the Third World but is on the decline, especially among the young, in the First World as well as in Mexico (Michael Kearney, personal communication). Caffeine drinks have surged far ahead of alcoholic ones, and strong stimulant drugs such as cocaine and methamphetamines have become dangerous drugs of abuse, while opiate use has declined or leveled off. This change has accompanied a progressive cultural shift in much of the world toward longer work hours, longer commutes, more intellectually demanding jobs, and, above all, more of the discipline of the clock.

There are cases in which tea, coffee, and cola have been used to extract more labor. Bradburd and Jankowiak (this volume) point out the enormous importance of alcohol and tobacco in binding Native American peoples to the trading posts and motivating them to bring in more furs. Tea was used in Canada in situations in which the use of alcohol was discouraged. The Hudson's Bay Company, in particular, tried to avoid using liquor as a labor motivator and fell back on tea as a substitute (Bryce 1968). Even today, strong tea is sold in Canadian trading posts and remote stores, and some Native American people drink enough to endanger their health. Strong tea is also sold (in leaf) or supplied (brewed) in most of East Asia today and is often marketed aggressively to minorities; its effect on labor power is not irrelevant. Very often in China, tea is supplied by the management to stimulate workers to perform at a higher level. In India, tea is as universal in offices as coffee is in America, and the whole tea trade is importantly linked with issues of power and class (Piya Chatterjee, personal communication).

Today, throughout the world, outdoor work in the heat now seems to require the support of cola drinks. As with tea and coffee, employers are quick to make these cold drinks available to their workers, both to seem benevolent and to stimulate them to work more.

Less appreciated is the role of caffeine drinks in actual business transactions. China (and overseas Chinese communities) may provide an extreme case, with its tea shops that serve as offices for the less affluent and sites of business discussion even among the more affluent. China is not, however, an isolated case. Cafes in Latin America and the Mediterranean region serve the same function and are almost as important in local business. Daniel Bradburd has suggested that the development of social spaces in the interstices of alienation may serve as a very subtle kind of labor enhancer (personal communication). Indeed it does. In fact, this development is not always subtle. Cafes and teahouses are as necessary to business in much of the world as pens and paper. Their status as offices-away-from-the-office depends on the mental alteration produced by their chief product. In the traditional Chinese world, for instance, business deals were always concluded over tea and/or alcoholic drinks (Anderson 1988). Apparently, the slight alteration of mental state was necessary to the deal.

The role of methylxanthines in culture truly problematizes the materialist versus idealist debate in the social sciences. Material substances are these alkaloids that directly affect mental functioning, and they dramatically show the uselessness and perniciousness of the mind-body distinction for serious social science research.

Caffeine use, however, is not just a product of the alienation of time and labor, it provides a solution (in more ways than one) for the problem. In the modern world, caffeine drinks are important both as a work stimulus and as a stimulus for sociability and human interaction. They adapt us to the machine, and they also help to save us from the machine. The coffeehouse, cafe, tea shop, cola stop, and maté group allow human community in a chaotic world. They also continue to be the meeting places of friendly neighbors, political activists, folksingers, scholars, aspiring poets, organizers of worthy causes, and all the others among us who wish to make life worth living. Perhaps they are our last, best hope (Oldenburg 1989).

11

Drugs in Work and Trade

New Directions for the Study of Drug Use

Daniel Bradburd and William Jankowiak

Our introduction described a patterned trajectory for drug trade and use in European economic expansion. Drugs were first traded in early contact situations to gain access to labor or to increase quantities of locally available goods; then, in later colonial periods, when enhanced control over local peoples assured access to labor, people were supplied with or used drugs to increase the duration or intensity of their labor; finally, with industrialization, coffee, tea, and other mild stimulants became the favored labor-enhancing drugs, replacing alcohol and other depressants. The individual essays in the volume confirm this broad vision. Hays, Brady and Long, Ambler, and Mancall describe drugs being used to secure access to labor or goods. Angrosino; Gordon; Cassman, Cartmell, and Belmonte; and Suggs and Lewis explore linkages between drug consumption and the duration and intensity of labor. Anderson's essay on caffeine documents the explosive growth of its use in an industrializing world.

Brady and Long and Hays provide close and detailed accounts of tobacco's "introduction" to Australia and Melanesia, showing how both preexisting patterns of use and the nature of contact shaped later consumption. Ambler and Mancall provide more macrolevel views of the role of alcohol in the West African slave trade and in the North American fur and skin trade.

Brady and Long argue that peoples in Australia consumed native (wild) tobacco and other nicotine-containing plants, notably, *pituri*. Thus the introduction of cultivated tobacco by European settlers did not bring a new and unknown product to Australia; rather, cultivated tobacco replaced indigenous tobacco in long-established trade networks. Possession of (relatively) large quantities of a commodity similar to an already highly valued indigenous good helped Europeans establish "friendly" relations with Aborigines. In time, addiction to tobacco transformed these relations into something quite like bond service, a situation with strong parallels to the "tot" system in southern Africa. Brady and Long develop this theme, pointing out that it was not merely unscrupulous ranchers who drew natives in through the exchange of tobacco; anthropologists used tobacco as a gift to informants and as a trade good to build collections of native art, and missionaries used it as an inducement for conversion.[1] Brady and Long's work also shows that once tobacco was introduced and in demand, the directional arrow of exploitation becomes more difficult to discern, to the point of suggesting a relationship of mutual exploitation.

There are remarkable parallels between Hays's essay and Brady and Long's work (see also Shineberg 1967). Hays describes the development of a tremendous desire for tobacco among the peoples of New Guinea that Europeans recognized and exploited, both to gain access to labor and to increase the intensity and duration of native labor. As did Mancall in his discussion of alcohol in North America, Hays describes considerable local variation in European tobacco's acceptance by New Guinea's peoples. However, in New Guinea, rejections of trade tobacco seem less rejections of tobacco than expressions of a continued preference for locally produced and processed forms of tobacco, which, it appears, were far stronger than trade tobacco. In short, Hays concludes that matters of taste help determine the drug of choice.

Both Ambler and Mancall show that alcohol was a vital component of trade. Their essays also show that questions of intent and agency were complex, that national political and economic interests could drive the trade, that national and local interests often conflicted, and that native demands and desires played a vital role in shaping exchanges. Like Hays, Ambler also demonstrates that demand was shaped by local tastes, for example, privileging rum over brandy. He further notes that, like tobacco in Australia, in West Africa rum was incorporated into traditional patterns, replacing earlier indigenous drinks and probably intensifying the drinking experience. The significance of a link between trade with natives and the development of alcohol industries in the Caribbean (for rum) and in Europe (at first for brandy and later for grain alcohols) is shown in both accounts. Indeed, Mancall argues that for all the controversy over trade in liquor and all the pros and cons cited by traders and missionaries, ultimately the brute economic logic of the trade that carried the day was only partly that drugs promoted trade or were a means of giving cheap goods for dear—although these were clearly present. He suggests that trade was primarily driven by the need to dispose of rum produced in the West Indies. While Ambler is not quite as emphatic about this as Mancall, his text also suggests that the needs of metropolitan alcohol producers were significant in shaping the West African trade. (Gordon suggests this was also important in Southwest Africa.) Angrosino's discussion of Trinidadian planters pushing their workers to consume rum rather than ganja seems a local example of this economic logic at play.

In their considerations of how drug use was linked to the duration and intensity of labor, Angrosino, Suggs and Lewis, Gordon, and Cassman, Cartmell, and Belmonte all show that consumption was often driven by demand, that determination of who used what drug was often contested within as well as across groups, and that the combinations of political, economic, and cultural leverage marshaled by different groups shaped the outcomes of these contests.

Angrosino details the historical struggle over whether alcohol or ganja would be the drug of "choice" for indentured East Indian laborers in Trinidad. In so doing, he provides insights into the motivations of both workers and their employers. In Trinidad, planters' control over the labor of indentured East Indian laborers was a given, and workers used drugs to overcome the drudgery of their labor and of their existence and to keep themselves working. It was, however, the intertwining of economic and cultural factors that determined whether ganja (traditionally consumed by the workers as a medicine and a labor enhancer) or alcohol (favored by the planters) would emerge as the drug of choice. Angrosino demonstrates that planters preferred their laborers consuming rum rather than ganja, even though there was evidence that drunkenness promoted far more violence and discord than did a marijuana "high" largely because rum was a substance that the planters (and even temperance advocates) knew and because its consumption provided planters with an additional economic return ganja could not match.

While it is not his central intent to do so, Angrosino also shows that both rum and ganja increased the labor output of Indian indentured workers by providing a social context for and a means of tuning out the drudgery of the laborers' otherwise intolerable daily existence. Through the creation of a "consuming community," drugs made life sustainable, and in doing so they made labor sustainable. Anderson, Suggs and Lewis, and Gordon also provide evidence of this.

Suggs and Lewis explore alcohol's changing role in promoting group labor as the BaTswana shifted from a mixed, to a colonial, and then to a postcolonial economy. Traditionally, among the BaTswana the provision of alcohol promoted group solidarity in ways far different from those described by Angrosino or Anderson and was thus indirectly linked to increasing labor. Specifically, as a "key symbol," alcohol represented *the group*. Although alcohol was consumed by the chiefs and elders (all male) while the labor was done by the women and younger men, Suggs and Lewis argue that this system worked because consumption not only promoted group solidarity, it revealed the group for which the labor was being performed and, in so doing, helped legitimate the demands of labor made in the name of the group. The desire to participate in the consumption and distribution of alcohol led men to press their women to work harder or longer, promoting intensification of production. Where distributing alcohol permitted a household to mobilize labor to increase grain production by more than the amount consumed as alcohol, manipulation of access to drink did increase wealth and intensify production.

In the colonial period and later, chiefs and elders resisted encroachments on their traditional, legitimate rights to demand labor from those to whom they provided drink. The transfer of these rights to Europeans, whose supplying of alcohol was seen to legitimate their control of the labor of single, young men, and still later instances of young men asserting their status by using cash wages to buy themselves beer show the close symbolic link of beer to the control of labor.

Gordon argues that beer was a key symbol for German settlers in colonial Southwest Africa that was later reworked to become a national symbol in newly independent Namibia. His study of alcohol in Namibia's political and economic development reveals several interesting variations on themes noted above and also provides a particularly good example of the subtle play of power manifest in the "enclaving" of a drug. Gordon persuasively demonstrates that while alcohol may be supplied as a means either of gaining access to labor or of increasing its intensity, in colonial Namibia the withholding of alcohol from natives through a rigidly enforced policy of prohibition helped distinguish the

European colonizers from the native population. The consumption of a tall, cold beer became a kind of defining characteristic of what it meant to be a colonist. He strongly suggests that this affected the colonists' willingness to remain engaged in a colonial project that was otherwise difficult and not very rewarding. Beer consumption, he suggests, became a marker of and reward for European status, which helped colonists build their sense of superior identity. Like the rum and ganja consumed by Indians in Trinidad, vast amounts of cold beer made the colonial existence livable in the otherwise hostile environment of Southwest Africa. Thus, after Southwest Africa became a South African (trust) territory, South African attempts to control the colonists' alcohol consumption generated tremendous settler resistance.

Cassman, Cartmell, and Belmonte's essay on the history and prehistory of coca in the Andes shows that coca use was not severely limited or restricted by the Inkas in pre-Columbian times. They also show that even though powerful elements of the Spanish community attempted to prohibit coca's use on moral or religious grounds, it was such an effective labor enhancer that (like alcohol in North America) scruples were consistently overcome by practical considerations. Their work lends support to the view that drugs and drug foods are used to gain access to labor predominantly in contact situations in which other means of control are unavailable. In areas like the Andes, where there were preexistent states and preexistent means of controlling labor, drugs were instead used as a means of increasing the intensity and duration of labor.

Anderson's essay reveals the remarkable range of caffeine-containing beverages consumed by indigenous peoples the world over. Anderson also points out that for all their broad geographic distribution, until modern times indigenous caffeine drinks were locally consumed by relatively small numbers of people. As a whole, caffeinated beverages—coffee, tea, colas—account for 7.5 percent of world trade; the only commodity whose annual trade value exceeds that of coffee is petroleum. Anderson links this tremendous transformation to the rise of clocks and work discipline, arguing that increased consumption of methylxanthines—the active ingredients in caffeinated beverages—was part of a shift from consumption of depressants like alcohol to the consumption of stimulants. Anderson further argues that this consumption is largely self-motivated, as people seek to work harder and more efficiently. While Anderson stresses the complexities of caffeine consumption, noting, for instance, the ways in which consumption is commonly ritualized and how those rituals create social solidarity, he also strongly emphasizes the existence of a biological substrate.

The linkage of methylxanthines with work is not, Anderson argues, accidental. Methylxanthines are adenosine inhibitors and literally work as physical not psychological antidepressants. People thus consume caffeine because it enables them to work longer, harder, and better. It is a labor enhancer whose value has been recognized both by those who consume it and, as Anderson tellingly points out, by modern employers who freely supply coffee to their employees. Anderson's piece thus demonstrates the use of caffeine as a labor enhancer and supports our contention that the industrial revolution brought about a shift in the kinds of drug foods consumed to increase the intensity and duration of labor.

The essays we have just described enrich our understanding of the intertwined relationship of drugs to labor and European expansion. They show that individual cases were extraordinarily complex, and they also show that the web of ties linking people, drugs, and labor was never simple or mechanical. Nonetheless, some characteristics of drug trade and drug use appear repeatedly in the essays, and taking note of them helps us better understand the processes that are the focus of this book and also provides insights into some more general aspects of drug trade and drug use.

While drug trade was generally exploitative, probably often so in its intent, and drugs were used to create "incommensurable exchanges" that made them a very useful means of pushing trade, local peoples repeatedly expressed specific desires for kinds of tobacco, for varieties of liquor, or for marijuana rather than rum; they played competing traders against each other; and they manipulated their control of labor and of goods to gain for themselves the greatest possible quantities of the most desired drugs. Exchange value was contested, and, in early contact situations, local agency often helped shape the balance of trade. While the breadth and scope of drug trade suggests that it was both profitable and effective, it still did not provide a simple mechanical way for suppliers of drugs to gain robotic control over workers. At a minimum, taste, fashion, and style thus played a role in the trade in drugs, and the degree to which their role is similar to or differs from the role they play in the trade of other commodities is an area that needs further consideration.

That said, many of the authors suggest that drugs' psychoactive properties make them nearly unique commodities: they alter consciousness, provide energy, relieve pain, palliate hunger and thirst, increase (at least people's perceptions of their) mental acuity, and promote sociability, often simultaneously. Combined, these properties made drugs strikingly attractive in both pre- and postcontact situations. Brady and Long's and Hays's descriptions of the diffusion and trade of tobacco and tobacco-like products provide dramatic evidence for how highly valued indigenous drugs were in Australia and Melanesia. This evidence, coupled with, for example, the Coes' description of how valued cacao was in pre-Columbian Central America (Coe and Coe 1996), highlights that demand for drugs—a craving more than a simple desire—makes trade for them demand driven in a way matched by few other commodities.

That drug trade is demand driven not only helps explain why drugs were such a potent force for European economic expansion, it also illuminates (even as it is illuminated by) aspects of the "war on drugs" waged by the United States. Specifically, if the drug trade is driven by demand, if the quest for drugs is such that indigenous peoples have sustained continent-wide trade networks to have access to them, then it seems very unlikely that any drug policy that does not deal effectively with demand (not supply) can succeed. Equally, the inability of the most powerful nation on earth to halt its citizens' drug use—in the face of billions of dollars spent, vast quantities of manpower and material mobilized, and the incarceration of large numbers of its citizen—speaks to drugs' incredible potency as a trade good. When we consider that European expansion inverted this situation, as agents of (what were then) the most powerful and wealthy nations introduced drugs in trade to peoples living in far smaller, weaker polities, it is easier to understand why few if any of those advances were successfully resisted. As many illicit drugs currently consumed in the United States and Europe are produced in remote areas of Colombia, Myanmar, and Afghanistan at the margins of the modern world system, the current flow of drugs from periphery to center ironically reverses those of the historical processes this work describes. That we wage a "war" on drugs with so little apparent understanding of their role in our economy seems another of the great ironies and conundrums of our current attitudes and policies to their use and trade.

With the essays sensitizing us to the link between drugs and labor, we can better appreciate the importance of that link in our own lives, where drugs are deeply embedded into labor processes that are constantly tweaked to increase productivity, itself obsessively measured. That whole industries seem to run on caffeine will surprise no one.[2] Perhaps no one will be surprised at evidence of alcohol's continuing role in workers' adaptations to heavy labor, where its solitary consumption remains an anodyne to alienation, drudgery, and discontent, while drinking socially is central to perceptions of the self and to deflecting

183

the stresses of modern work. Anderson's suggestion that modern workers clustered around the coffee urn may simultaneously be self-medicating to enhance their labor efficiency, creating solidarity by complaining about work and, ironically, by countering the alienation arising from that very labor, increasing their ability to keep working effectively all at the same time is further evidence of the complex relationship of drugs to labor. In this context, it seems difficult to disassociate the mass consumption of antidepressants from work and the pressures of work performance or to see drugs like Ritalin as other than aids to work performance or, in our terms, labor enhancers.

Precisely because drugs are seen as powerful, potent, and unusual commodities, access to them is often restricted in both indigenous and postcontact conditions. While drugs may be "enclaved" for many reasons, ranging from fear of (real or imagined) social disorder to reserving them as marks of distinction, Gordon, Suggs and Lewis, Hays, Brady and Long, and Cassman, Cartmell, and Belmonte show that people can use both having rights to and being prohibited from drug consumption as sources of solidarity and identity. And, everywhere, there are complexities within complexities. If collectively consuming a prohibited drug promotes solidarity, the right to consume a good proscribed for others may be a source of group identity that also confers and marks distinction. In Southwest Africa/Namibia both occurred simultaneously as white settlers' legal consumption of cold lager marked their "national" identity versus white South Africans and their elevated status versus native Africans, while the latter's illegal consumption of drink was an act of resistance that fostered an oppositional identity and political consciousness. That forbidden fruit becomes attractive is a commonplace; Gordon's postindependence consumption figures demonstrate it. His discussion and Suggs and Lewis's description of why young BaTswana men see modern beer consumption as a status-affirming act help explain why that is so. Associated with this is the strong suggestion that drug consumption is often seen as a reward. This was the case for German settlers, BaTswana males (young and old alike), Australian Aborigines submitting to work discipline, and contemporary Americans who indulge themselves with chocolate as a comfort, a reward, and a motivation for slogging through work or life.

Another very important characteristic that the essays highlight is the ability of drugs to foster conviviality and to create communities centered about their consumption. Moreover, sharing drugs and the drug experience creates powerful social bonds that play out in other arenas. Suggs and Lewis show

that access to drugs can be central to the successful mobilization of work parties and cooperative labor; Angrosino documents drug consumption playing a
vital role in creating and maintaining "support groups" that help workers survive degrading or punishing work conditions; Gordon, Angrosino, and Anderson describe communities of consumption that are sites of resistance, sometimes
simply by existing in the face of controls and prohibitions, sometimes because
the drugs' properties, the people's circumstances, and the existence of a group
engenders more obviously political behavior.

In the United States, a number of examples show drugs playing a central
role in sociability, conviviality, and communities of consumption. Included
among these are the wonderfully named happy hour end of the work day, students' binge drinking, and the mass consumption of the drug Ecstasy at "raves."
Both happy hour and binge drinking are often associated with a "work hard,
drink hard" attitude tying together work, sociability, identity, and reward. While
the happy hour (and the parallel heavy drinking of Japanese "salary men") is
accepted if not sanctioned, binge drinking and raves are considered problematic. As we suggested earlier, in traditional societies the ritualization of drug use
and of drugs' enclaving, described here by Suggs and Lewis and Hays and
alluded to by others, seems related to the tremendous complexities of creating
and enforcing an effective message for control. Certainly, the comparative
data in this volume, showing that the enclaving of drugs is rarely straightforward, that consuming them often conveys status, that their consumption can be
legitimated as an act of resistance, and that their shared consumption can be the
basis for group identity, suggest that prohibiting any group (e.g., those under
twenty-one) from consuming a generally available drug or setting any single
drug or category of drugs outside the boundaries of appropriate consumption
while others are freely available will, at the least, put those actions into symbolic play in ways that make simple prohibition far from simple.

Finally, the essays provide a platform for considering trade and consumption of drugs not covered in this volume. While we have made only brief mention of opium and of opiates, it is apparent that Great Britain's (and Japan's less
well known) opium trade with China was an attempt to create incommensurable
trade, in this instance, on a grand scale,[3] while examination of opium consumption itself shows that, like coca, alcohol, and tobacco, people frequently
used it as a stimulant or an analgesic to help them work longer or harder (Rush
1990; Westermeyer 1982; Gangulay, Sharma, and Krishnamachari 1995). There
is even scattered evidence for opium-centered communities of consumption that

differ little from those described above.[4] We suspect that a more detailed examination of both indigenous, postcontact, and contemporary consumption of numerous other drugs would provide additional examples of similar regimes of drug use.

Overall, then, the essays in this volume demonstrate that trade in and use of drugs were intimately linked to attempts to gain access to control over labor. They reveal variation in the ways drugs were used as inducers and enhancers, and they illustrate the ways in which precontact patterns of indigenous use shaped the postcontact experience and the ways in which the needs of merchants, traders, and the metropolitan and colonial producers shaped their role in trade. They show that drug foods were welcomed and resisted and that preferences for particular drug foods were shaped both by external forces and by the actively expressed desires of contacted populations. They show as well that once introduced, the desire for drugs often created demand-driven trade relations in which the wishes of the contacted peoples played as powerful a role as the desires of the European traders. Over and over, the essays show that drugs, like other important goods, are embedded in systems of meaning and of power and take on multiple and contested meanings such that relationships centered about the use of drugs were complex and variable. They also show that because of their pharmacological properties (their ability to, among other things, relieve pain, assuage hunger and thirst, and promote convivial relations), drugs are *not* just like other commodities, and their link with labor and trade is different from those of most other commodities. It has been the aim of this volume to call attention to these aspects of drugs, their trade, and their use with the aim of increasing our understanding of the nature of drugs and their use and of the nature of European economic expansion. We have also tried to suggest some of the implications that flow from this study with the hope that the current volume will provide a base for future work in this area.

Notes

1. Drugs, Desire, and European Economic Expansion

1. For tobacco, see Goodman (1993) and von Gernet (1995); for tea and coffee, see Smith (1995), Pendergrast (1999), Weinberg and Bealer (2001), Braun (1996), and Mathee (1995); for chocolate, see Coe and Coe (1996). Anderson (this volume) provides a comprehensive view of caffeine drinks; for distilled spirits, see Mathee (1995), Braun (1996), Burnett (1999), and Courtwright (2001).

2. A partial listing of works includes Trocki (1999) on Britain's opium trade with China and Spence (1975, 1990) on the use of introduced opium by Chinese coolies. Burnett (1999), Courtwright (2001), Gutman (1977), Schivelbusch (1992), and Thompson (1967) examine alcohol consumption by laborers in Europe and North America. For coffee, tea, and sugar consumption in Europe and their association with patterns of labor and home life, see Schivelbusch (1992), Smith (1995), Mathee (1995), and Mintz (1985). For descriptions of indigenous use of alcohol, tobacco, and coca in precontact periods, see Goodman (1993), von Gernet (1995), and Hugh-Jones (1995). Accounts of alcohol and tobacco in trade and contact in the Americas, Africa, and the insular Pacific include White (1983), Mancall (1995a), Eber (1995), Shineberg (1967), and Gordon (1996). Nash (1979; see also Hugh-Jones 1995) describes coca use associated with mining and other labor in Spain's American colonies; Lovejoy (1995) describes the use of kola nuts as hunger suppressants and aids to labor. The role of stimulants like coffee, tea, and caffeinated soft drinks in contemporary American and European society has been described by Pendergrast (1993, 1999), Courtwright (2001), Burnett (1999), and Anderson (this volume). The contested use of alcohol as a means of attracting, keeping, and compensating labor in southern Africa has been explored by Gordon (1996), Crush and Ambler (1992), van Onselen (1976), and Scully (1992). Marshall (1976, 1979, 1990), Marshall and Marshall (1979), Eber (1995), and MacAndrew and Edgerton (1969) explore the impact of (primarily) alcohol on native populations in the Americas and the island Pacific.

3. Our model of drug trade in contact situations is not chronological; we posit stages of drug use contingent on the nature and circumstances of the contact situation, particularly, the degree of control that the contacting European populations were able to exert over the contacted peoples and, later, the nature of the labor

being undertaken by contacted or colonized populations. Like all models, ours simplifies reality.

4. Drugs are pharmacological agents that alter cortical stimulation and modify mental activity. Drugs can be stimulants or depressants; they can be analgesics; they can suppress hunger and thirst; they can provide an enhanced ability to work or to focus on work; and they can alter consciousness in subtle or marked ways. Drugs like amphetamines, morphine, cocaine, and, importantly for our purposes, nicotine, alcohol, and, quite likely, caffeine boost the brain's production of dopamine, which apparently "facilitates a learning of association between the pleasurable effects of a drug and other stimuli.... [B]ecause this stimulus is so strong," drug cravings make users feel as if they are "always hungry or thirsty [for drugs]" (DiChiara in Raloff 1996:38). See Iversen (1996:206–7) for a discussion of nicotine and Ponteieri et al. (1996:255) for a discussion of nicotine and an outline of the role of dopamine in drug abuse.

5. This dislocation played a role in Native American opposition to the introduction of alcohol and to its use in trade (Mancall 1995a; Phillips 1961; White 1983) as well as its association with current (and historical) European and American attempts to restrict the use of drugs.

6. The perception that drugs promote sociability is broadly reported in two literatures: writings on the pharmacological properties of drugs, which note that they induce feelings of euphoria; and the ethnographic literature on consumption, which recounts many people's perceptions that drugs promote social intercourse. See Hugh-Jones (1995:51ff.) for an interesting discussion of coca use among the Barasana. In this volume, Anderson, Angrosino, and Gordon all specifically discuss socialability, drug use, and labor.

7. Goodman writes of early drug use in Europe that "[t]ea, coffee, chocolate and tobacco entered Europe...at myriad seaports and inland ports....Undoubtedly the fact that tea, coffee, chocolate and tobacco were relatively non-perishable and come to the consumer in a processed and fairly standardized form, contributed to [their] widespread availability" (1995:131).

8. Sugar is not, of course, a drug in the sense of tobacco or the opiates. Mintz, however, has appropriately noted similarities between the patterns of consumption and trade of sugar and other goods, for which he has coined the term "drug food" (1979, 1985). Tobacco appears to have been the vehicle for opium's introduction into China; adding sugar to coffee, tea, and, particularly, chocolate seems central to their mass consumption in Europe. The Portuguese also adulterated tobacco with sugar for their African trade. Sugar not only can be mixed with alcohol, it is an important component in its manufacture.

9. Mintz quotes Jan DeVries that "two features of economic life—often attributed to so-called precapitalist economies—had to be radically modified to enlarge demand. First, more families...had to become involved with the market both as pro-

ducers for sale and as buyers of consumption goods. Second, the disposition to satisfy only pre-existing levels of consumption and to work no more than these required...had to change" (1985:163). Drugs helped solve both these problems.

10. There was, of course, resistance to drug use, but until recently resistance was often a stage in the process of introduction, which was overcome by public demand. States recognized the enormous revenue opportunities found in taxing drugs or establishing government monopolies in them, which influenced their desire to prohibit the import or sale of drugs.

11. Mathee (1995) traces the movement of coffee, tea, and distilled alcohol throughout the world from the sixteenth through the eighteenth centuries. Courtwright (2001) provides a fuller and more elaborate description of material in Mathee, and he extends the historical horizon into the late twentieth century. Within a larger work, Wolf (1982:332ff.) provides an excellent overview of patterns of production, exchange, and (largely metropolitan) consumption of sugar, tea, coffee, cocoa, and opium. Mintz's (1985) study of sugar established the linkage between the rise of Britain's colonial empire, the rise of British industrialization, and increased British consumption of sugar and tea. Goodman (1993; see also Price 1995; Schivelbusch 1992; Mathee 1995) provides an excellent account of the growth of tobacco use. Schivelbusch (1992) has discussed the introduction of various stimulants, including coffee, tea, and tobacco, into the European diet, and the Coes (1996) have similarly provided an account of trade in chocolate. Pendergrast's recent work (1999) focuses on trade in coffee, as do works by Weinberg and Bealer (2001) and Braun (1996), which provide accounts of coffee's use from its discovery to Starbucks.

12. Recognition of addiction and an absence of moral judgment characterize Thomas De Quincey's *Confessions of an English Opium Eater,* published in 1821 to wide notoriety (De Quincey 1986).

13. Given that views of these goods and their appropriate use "at home" and in trade were both openly contested and far from monolithic, a uniform view of the appropriate role of drugs in contact situations was unlikely.

14. White's (1991) work, among many others, describes the incredible complexity of these frontier zones, illustrating the ways in which mutual dependencies were created and how the balance ultimately shifted toward European hegemony. Drugs were but one element of this long, contested process.

15. The figures are drawn from Murdock and White (1969), whose coded levels of political complexity we use.

16. The classic case of drug trade to open markets is, of course, opium trade and China. Fay (1975), Spence (1975), Waley (1958), and Trocki (1999), among others, discuss various aspects of this trade. Because it involves the opening of trade between two highly developed state systems, we have chosen not to focus on it in this chapter.

17. Contacted people were anything but passive recipients of goods. Shineberg (1967:154) notes that captains failed at trade because the goods they were carrying were inferior, not desirable, or had fallen out of fashion, including tastes in tobacco. We return to this point below.

18. There was great conflict about the liquor trade within the French colonial system. Prohibitions were raised and dropped several times as different parties were able to temporarily push their views. Similar conflicting views over the legitimacy of the trade existed in other countries' colonies and later in the newly independent United States. Many conflicts pitted groups such as missionaries against traders, but the record suggests that individuals were equally conflicted about the trade. Mancall (1995a) and Phillips (1961) provide details.

19. Early coureurs de bois kept few records, and our knowledge of their ways comes primarily from the records of Jesuits, with whom they were locked in competition (Phillips 1961:109).

20. McLeod (1965) rarely describes himself deliberately providing liquor or tobacco to induce trade; he mentions alcohol (and, slightly less frequently, tobacco) in nearly every entry, suggesting its distribution was a central issue in his life.

21. Burke notes this dialectic of need and pressure in European expansion into Zimbabwe: "As the European community's need for food obtained from local cultivators increased and Lobengula's control over ivory become less exclusive, the desire for an access to the prestige, novelty, and intrigue of manufactured commodities accelerated. Many visitors in the 1870s and 1880s described the experience of being besieged by crowds hoping for 'presents,' and those who traveled beyond Bulawayo into Mashona land and the Zambezi valley met with increasingly larger and more assertive demands from local elites for a variety of goods as the price for their safe passage" (1996:56). In addition to beads, clothing, guns, and shot, traders carried "Boer brandy…jam…coffee…tea…chocolate…sugar…chicory…and snuff boxes or tobacco products, though there was also a thriving regional trade in tobacco grown to the north of Bulawayo" (Burke 1996:64).

22. Alcohol was generally not as popular in the Pacific as it was in North America. Trade in the Pacific reflected this, and captains offered tobacco rather than alcohol as a means to further trade.

23. Drugs were not the first items offered but were introduced later. Several factors seem to be involved. First, as the preceding discussion shows, European attitudes toward the use of drugs like alcohol in trade were mixed, and opposition to drugs could, at times, limit their use in trade. Second, in the earliest periods of contact, prior to the period of what might be called the routinization of exchange, there was little need to introduce particularly exotic goods, and, moreover, access to those goods was limited. Widespread access to distilled spirits is a relatively recent phenomenon, contingent upon both the availability of sugar as an ingredient in the fermentation process and the spread of the technology of distilling itself. Tobac-

co was not available for trade until it was being produced in some quantity by European colonies in the New World. Additionally, in the earliest stages of contact, neither an accumulation of durable goods that might reduce their value nor, perhaps, the kind of intense competition that later promoted intensification of drug trade was present.

24. The famous English opium trade with China (Trocki 1999; Spence 1975) may represent a special case. Here the question was not gaining access to a good (the trade for tea had already been established), and, strictly speaking, the British were not concerned with controlling labor, since that had been taken care of at the Chinese end. The British were concerned with meeting the cost of importing their own drug—tea—without damaging their balance of trade. From the perspective of the nation-state, the introduction of opium into the tea trade increased the profitability—the balance of payments—for the British at China's expense. It was a means of using drugs to increase the profitability of a venture, though not by creating trade or by stimulating workers to work longer or harder.

25. Firth (1973:13) claims that the Germans established smoking schools in the Bismarck Archipelago to teach the natives how to appreciate the finer benefits of smoking. This "trade" was associated with the expansion of plantations and mines and a need for labor on them. Local populations quickly proved unwilling to sustain the long hours required for efficient production, and laborers had to be sought from elsewhere (Oliver 1989:64). Many plantations adopted a strategy of supplying drugs to attract and hold onto a viable, if not reliable, labor pool. Lemert noted that on the Cook Islands and Samoa "liquor is an indispensable means of recruiting labor for certain kinds of work.... [Workers] are usually rounded up by [the] foreman with the promise [after work] of alcohol" (1979:199). In areas of what had been New Spain, the institution of debt peonage *(changa)* emerged out of the practice of advancing provisions, frequently an alcoholic drink called *chicha,* which then had to be paid for with labor (de Barrios 1980). Navarette-Pellicer's (1988) account of the Tzeltzal in Chiapas notes that alcohol was used as an instrument of "domination and control," and it details the ways in which alcohol—in this case, *aguardiente* (raw brandy)—was used to transform self-sufficient farmers into peons whose labor was necessary to support the hacienda and, indirectly, the Mexican capitalist economy. This was accomplished first by using the general desire for aguardiente to drive people to market their labor. Navarette-Pellicer also describes a more specific kind of entrapment in which agents for *hacenderos* gave Indians aguardiente, getting them drunk, then demanded their labor to pay for the cost of the liquor consumed, provided more alcohol, and then trucked the intoxicated Indians to the hacienda, where they were forced to work.

26. The essays in Crush and Ambler (1992) provide an exhaustive discussion of the contested role of alcohol in labor and race relations in southern Africa.

27. To some degree, this is the reapplication of European understandings to

new markets. Thus from early on one finds products like tea being promoted to Europeans under the same guise. "Reading through the promotional medical literature [of the sixteenth to eighteenth centuries] on tea, coffee, chocolate and tobacco, one is struck by the repetitive theme that outdistancing their many virtues was their uncanny ability to assuage and satisfy hunger and thirst" (Goodman 1995:134).

28. Courtwright (2001:137ff) provides excellent examples of drugs used as labor enhancers in Europe and elsewhere.

29. For reasons partly derived from Galen's system of humors, coffee consumption was believed to have a decidedly negative impact on male sexual performance.

30. There are but a few examples of concerted later efforts to control use of caffeine, most notably, those of Harvey Wiley, head of what became the U.S. Food and Drug Administration. He attempted to restrict its use in the early twentieth century. Otherwise, caffeine is generally seen as a work aid. For example, Balzac's immense productivity is often linked to his enormous coffee consumption, and I have heard colleagues in the math department describe a mathematician as "a device for converting caffeine into equations." With the exception of some areas of the arts, where consumption of alcohol (or other depressant drugs) is associated with disinhibition and the release of creativity, in the West, alcohol, unlike caffeine, generally loses its association with productivity. Even as regards creativity, alcohol consumption (and, all the more so, hard drug use) is usually described in cautionary tales of seduction and then ruin (see, for example, descriptions of the lives of F. Scott Fitzgerald, Ernest Hemingway, and Jackson Pollack). The efficacy of methylxanthines in enhancing mental acuity is not uncontested (see Braun 1996; Weinberg and Bealer 2001); there is also some evidence that they can enhance physical performance (Braun 1996:143).

31. As suggested above, nonstimulants can also be labor enhancers. Florida house painters are reported to consume marijuana to overcome tedium.

32. Additional discussions of the link between industrialization and prohibition can be found in Mintz (1985), Roberts (1981), Rorabaugh (1979:219), Rumbarger (1989), Courtwright (2001), and Schivelbusch (1992).

33. The continuing—and, for opiates, cocaine, and marijuana, increasing—consumption of drugs in the face of countervailing prohibitions again highlights the powerful attraction of drugs, the degree to which drug use and the drug trade are demand driven, and the multiplicity of meanings and understandings that can be applied to drugs and their use.

34. Kondo's (1990) discussion of the modern Japanese workplace illustrates some complexities of alcohol use and what its consumption means and does in workers' lives. Though she makes no reference to alcohol or alcoholic beverages in her index, Kondo describes numerous links between drink, work, and masculine identity, including male artisans seeing the ability to consume large amounts of

alcohol as a significant marker of their masculinity, a construction of self closely associated with their willingness to work enormously long hours for no overtime pay. Employers provide kegs of draft beer at company socials as part of their ongoing attempts to generate a sense of good feeling and family union among their workers. To the degree that their perception of themselves as vital and powerful is central to their ability and desire to work long hours and to the degree that alcohol plays a part in their construction of self, its use is, in our terms, labor enhancing. The same may well be true of the group feeling arising from the employers' provision of alcohol at ritualized social occasions within the work year. Kondo's work is centrally concerned with exploring the ambiguities, complexities, and contradictions of workers' lives, and she makes it clear that she does not see structures like these embodying pure hegemony, false consciousness, or class consciousness. Not surprisingly, drug use plays complex and contradictory roles both in Kondo's account and elsewhere.

35. George Orwell's *Down and Out in Paris and London* (1933) provides another classic account of workers using alcohol to overcome the drudgery of labor and, in a sense, to keep going. He describes *plongeurs* (dish washers) drinking two liters of wine a day, noting that "one seemed to work faster when partially drunk," and later concludes a discussion of weekend drinking in his working-class quarter by noting, "For many men in the quarter, unmarried and with no future to think of, the weekly drinking bout was the one thing that made life worth living" (Orwell 1961:65, 96).

2. Mutual Exploitation?

1. In fact, there are two indigenous populations in Australia: Aborigines and the Torres Strait Islanders. The Torres Strait lies on the border between Australia and Papua New Guinea to the north, and its population is of Melanesian origin.

2. The term *squatter* originally meant a trespasser on the land; the meaning changed in the 1830s to refer to a substantial stock holder.

3. While bush tobacco was usually chewed, a Kimberley man, Jack Sullivan, reported that Aborigines smoked bush tobacco in the 1930s: "It was strong and made you a little giddy, no different from that Sunlight plug tobacco or Havelock tobacco which is a little stronger, and which everyone prefer [sic], you might as well say....They reckoned it was dinkum [real] tobacco, and never ate anything else. It was their tobacco the same as the white tobacco made in America" (1983:33).

4. Similarly, Wilbert (1987) notes that tobacco relieves thirst and hunger and is considered a food among South American Indians. Wilbert remarks on the potency of tobacco and its ability to make people "drunk." See Thomson (1939) for similar comments from Australia.

5. The photograph was probably taken by Rev. J. R. Love, date unknown, but certainly early twentieth century.

Notes

6. Creed (1878:267) reported that Cape York people smoked an herb that grew there in bamboo pipes. A Yanyuwa man told Baker (1999) that he had cultivated a tobacco garden for himself in the Borroloola region, Northern Territory, in the 1930s.

7. Roth (1984:100) observes that the Kalkadoon would often prepare their tobacco in a manner similar to pituri; Watson (1983:51) discusses the change from pituri with ash to tobacco with ash and suggests the ash would "free-base" the nicotine similarly. Duncan-Kemp (1964) provides accounts of people smoking pituri and of smoking pituri and wild tobacco in turn. She includes photographs of people smoking using extremely large pipes made of hollow reeds and wooden tubes. Thomson suggested that the smoking of pituri "must be a recent innovation after the introduction of tobacco" (1939:82).

8. Horne and Aiston (1924:65) observed that the tin matchbox was also a common receptacle for both pituri and the chewed quids.

9. It seems that harvesting expeditions could comprise up to eighty men; each one would return home carrying up to seventy pounds of the dried and packaged drug (Watson 1983). Special half-moon-shaped woven bags were made to carry pituri.

10. "Kangaroo" was a Guugu Yimidhir word for a particular macropod; Capt. James Cook introduced it as the term for all similar macropods (Peterson 1979).

11. The ceremonial uses of tobaccos and pituri in Australia do not appear to be as ubiquitous as in the Americas, where the ritual use of tobacco forms a unique aspect of aboriginal religion (Paper 1988; Wilbert 1987) and where, of course, indigenous people were the ones to introduce Europeans to the substance.

12. Indeed, Aboriginal people frequently liken introduced tobacco to bush tobacco. Showing one of us a *Nicotiana* plant near Amanbidji, Northern Territory, a Ngarinman woman said, "Two-fella same; Log Cabin and this one." Log Cabin is a popular brand of loose tobacco.

13. The navigator Matthew Flinders met a fleet of six praus in 1803, and in 1856 on one of his expeditions Alfred Russell Wallace took a Macassarese servant who had been to Australia several times (Macknight 1976:18).

14. Aborigines were employed by European trepang fishermen, however. In one account, a Borroloola man described working on a lugger between 1910 and 1920 and being paid in tobacco and rations (Read and Read 1991:81).

15. Macknight examined the supplies listed in the boats' contracts and found, for example, that in 1885–86 sixteen praus carrying 457 men imported an average of 2.5 pounds of tobacco per man. This could have been smoked entirely by the crew, but it would seem that "a considerable amount was given to Aborigines" (Macknight 1976:30).

16. Apart from the drawings and paintings by early British artists such as Augustus Earle that depicted Aborigines smoking pipes, Aboriginal artists them-

selves painted the clay pipe in rock art. See Edwards (1979:32–33) for a rock art painting in the Alligator Rivers Region, Northern Territory.

17. Many clay pipe fragments have turned up in archaeological excavations, for example, at the first Government House site in Sydney (Wilson and Kelly 1987). Pipes were also made of unusual objects such as an emu leg (see illustration in Rudgley 1993:136), shells, and crab claws, which are still used today in northern Australia (Thomson 1939). In 1885 only 1.4 percent of tobacco was consumed as cigarettes in the colony, but by 1904 11 percent of tobacco was smoked in cigarettes (Wilson and Kelly 1987). In 1884 the newly invented mechanized Bonsack machine was able to make 120,000 cigarettes a day (Walker 1980:276; Burnham 1993). Rolling one's own cigarettes became a fad in the late nineteenth century.

18. Tobacco was grown in Australia as early as 1818, when crops were planted at Emu Plains and in the Hunter Valley in New South Wales, and later in Victoria and Queensland. However, imported leaf was preferred by colonists (Muir 1969–71).

19. This is interesting in view of the fact that at least one damages case is in process against the Australian government for supplying cigarettes to Australian troops during the Vietnam war (*Australian,* 14 February 1998). During World War II cigarettes were given out free and included in survival rations for soldiers (Burnham 1993:101).

20. Church Missionary Society missionaries attribute the lifting of the ban to the Berndts' criticisms (Cole 1980:67). Aborigines were not averse to having missions as sources of tobacco. For example, an Aboriginal elder at Croker Island, Northern Territory, told one of us (M.B.) in 1984 that his father had invited missionaries to establish themselves there in order to expedite the Aborigines' supply of tobacco.

21. An earlier ethnographer, Carl Lumholtz, working in Queensland, similarly asked people to collect "all things creeping on the ground or flying in the air" in exchange for tobacco (Lumholtz 1980:115).

22. "We pursued our usual policy of issuing Aborigines who helped us in our research with a small daily quantity of tobacco, this being done with the knowledge and consent of the Mission…inevitably the demand exceeded the supply" (Berndt and Berndt 1951–52:24).

23. Some of Poignant's photographs of people smoking Macassan pipes are in McCarthy (1957).

24. The Berndts' 1944–46 survey of Aboriginal labor on Northern Territory cattle stations notes that the tobacco supplied to Aborigines varied from two to four plugs per week and that "walkabout rations" for the off-season included twelve sticks, together with sugar, flour, tea, and baking powder. The tobacco was in some cases of very poor quality and badly deteriorated with worm holes (Berndt and Berndt 1987:70). This low-grade black twist tobacco, distributed as wages, was

known across a wide area as *nicki nicki,* which is possibly derived from an Aboriginal pronunciation of the New Guinea word for twist, "niggerhead" (Arthur 1996).

25. A history of the relationship between pastoralists and their Aboriginal laborers in the Channel Country of southwestern Queensland described the work: "Forty people worked on the construction of the house. Others prepared the ground for the acres of fruit and vegetable gardens, spread the manure, carried the water for the gardens and weeded and tended them. Aboriginal women worked in the homestead, sweeping, washing, dusting and pulling the punkah fans at night to waft cool air over the Duncans as they relaxed in their living room. They dug and cleaned wells; they fought bushfires; in droughts they pulled living beasts out of quagmires and separated the calves from dying cows; they took the yarded cattle out for their daily food and water; they branded cattle, one year doing over a thousand; they searched for lost stockmen; and they helped build the stockyards so well that Duncan-Kemp called them 'a monument for generations to come.' For this, Duncan-Kemp notes, they received no monetary recompense. Their pay was tea, tobacco, clothing and food: two bullocks were killed every month for the camp of 200 Aborigines" (Watson 1998:34–35).

26. In 1884, as a result of a huge rise in the death rate of laborers, particularly those from New Guinea, a royal commission was set up to inquire into recruiting practices. Some workers were repatriated, and in 1885 New Guinea workers were given tobacco as compensation to pass on to the friends of those who had died in Australia (Corris 1973:101).

27. Tobacco smoking appears to have been unknown in most of Papua New Guinea before the arrival of Europeans. Wild tobacco found there today is said to be of New World origin (Lepowsky 1982).

28. Rolls (1993:405) asserts that the Macassan trepang fishers often paid in opium, although he does not say where this occurred or whether the payment was for work or in return for the use of coastal resources.

29. As a result, there are examples of occasions when Aborigines recognized whites' unwillingness to share on demand. The anthropologist Fred Myers once reacted angrily to a demand for cigarettes and was surprised to be sympathized with by the asker, who said that Myers gave things away too easily. The Aboriginal man then instructed the anthropologist to hide cigarettes in his socks so that he could tell people he had none (Peterson 1997:179).

30. This reticence could be interpreted as being disrespectful, which in turn is associated with the concept of shame, a complex notion encompassing guilt, embarrassment, respect, and coyness (Peile 1997).

31. Even today, it is common for Aboriginal people, at no notice, "to join a vehicle travelling hundreds of kilometres away, taking with them no money and few provisions, and will have no idea when or how they will return" (Hamilton 1987:49).

32. Enterprising individuals in one Western Desert community collect the

most favoured ash and sell it (ten dollars for a powdered-milk tin of ash) to those living away from the source.

5. Alcohol and the Fur Trade

1. There are documented cases of alcohol use within particular Native American families, though such pathologies are not necessarily determined by genetics; for an exploration of one family's history of alcohol use, see Kunitz and Levy (1994:139–67). It should be noted that many American Indians do believe that their physiological responses to alcohol differ from non-Indians; see May and Smith (1988:324–34).

2. The most thorough assessment of the goals of the English and the French missionaries as well as Native American responses can be found in Axtell (1985).

3. Throughout his history of Plymouth, Bradford (1952) mentions the importance of the beaver trade, recognizing the value of the commerce for Puritans eager to maintain trade relations with London merchants.

4. See Shurtleff (1853–54, 1:106, 323, 2:84–85, 258, 3:425, 4, pt. 2:297, 1857:242–43, 247–48); *Acts and Laws* (1761:220); Bachellor (1904, 1: 117, 739–40); Bartlett (1856–65, 1:279, 307–8, 413–14, 2:487, 500–501); Trumbull and Hoadly (1850–90, 1:254–55, 263, 338, 2:119, 3:94, 5:5, 6:31–32, 7:472–73, 1894–96, 1:657–58, 685–86, 740–41, 751, 755, 3:1096–98, 4:93); Mitchell and Flanders (1896–1908, 2:168–70, 3:250, [310–13], 5:320–30, 6:283–93); Browne et al. (1883–1972, 5:260, 557, 8:327–28, 15:260, 17:178, 22:511, 26:348, 38:15–16, 147–48); Hening (1810–23, 3:468, 5:273, 7:117, 8:116); Cooper and McCord (1836–41, 2:67, 309); Chandler (1904–16, 18:223–24); Mancall (1995a:103–10).

5. See Saunders (1885–90, 1:231, 4:507, 5:583, 902, 1141–42, 6:616–17, 23:2).

6. Rum and Ganja

1. Sucrose is an energy source, sweetener, preservative, flavor enhancer, bulking agent, and stabilizer. The multipurpose nature of a sugar crop has "supported the evolution of cane...from a luxury to a regular part of the diet in one country after another" (Hagelberg 1985:88). The British had a particular craving for sugar. By 1800 the average per capita consumption of sugar in Britain was eighteen pounds per year, and that figure had doubled by 1840, when the British government removed import taxes on sugar (Rogozinski 1992:107).

2. Carter (1996:231) acknowledges that the virtual equation of slavery with indenture is the prevailing theme in the literature, although she counts herself a dissenter, mainly because the ties between the indentured Indians and their homeland were never severed, as they had been for the African slaves.

3. Mahabir has chosen to transcribe his informants' comments in poetic form. My translation into standard English is as follows: "Ganja sold for three cents, and so none of us got drunk; rum was selling for forty cents, and nobody wanted it.

They smoked ganja, and they were singing and eating [because it made them happy]. It cost sixty dollars to buy a license to sell ganja at a shop, but it was usually sold [without license] out of people's houses [thereby keeping the price low]."

4. This practice bears some superficial resemblance to the South African tot system discussed by Scully (1992). In South Africa, however, it was the poor small-scale farmers who used payments of alcohol to recruit and retain a labor force, since they were unable to compete with the cash wages paid by the larger growers. Larger-scale South African planters, in fact, seemed to have argued against the tot system because they could afford to look more "progressive." There was no significant small-scale farmer class in Trinidad to compete with the large plantations, and if indeed the estates used payments in alcohol it was not because they were competing for scarce labor (the labor of the Indians having already been bonded to them in indenture) but because they profited from the transaction and were willing to overlook the sociomedical costs. The proliferation of alcohol as a labor enhancer was also marked in the northern Rhodesian mining industry (Ambler 1992), but in that case, the purveyors of alcohol were private entrepreneurs, not the managers-owners of the industry itself. The owners tried to regulate the distribution and consumption of alcohol, recognizing that while its easy availability was a strong inducement to migrating labor, its effects could easily get out of hand and create an unruly workforce. Again, the situation, while superficially similar to that of Trinidad, really reflects very different economic and social realities.

5. My translation: "When you smoke ganja you no longer feel sick. In the old days, they would smoke, and they wouldn't get fevers or coughs, nor would they end up in jail [for fighting—a typical outcome with rum]."

6. My translation: "In those days there was good rum, boy, good rum. And we drank it on Saturdays, but on Sundays we didn't want any so that on Monday when we turned out to work we wouldn't be drunk."

7. Inside the Windhoek Lager

1. Sumptuary laws—those laws that attempt to regulate habits or consumption on moral or religious grounds—were an important part of the ideological toolbox of colonialism yet have received little attention. This is, to say the least, surprising, because as Hunt (1996) has pointed out, sumptuary laws are strongest on the borders of modernity. As such, it could be argued, sumptuary legislation made a significant contribution to state formation insofar as it provided the basis for more extensive and regularized patterns of law enforcement.

2. Habitus is defined by Bourdieu as "a system of lasting, transposable dispositions, which, integrating past experiences, functions at every moment as a matrix of perceptions, appreciations and actions and makes possible the achievement of infinitely diversified tasks, thanks to analogical transformations of schemes permitting the solution of similarly shaped problems" (1977:83).

3. In this context it is also important to note the absence of commercially marketed sorghum or millet beer, despite administration attempts to market it in township or location beer halls from the late thirties to the sixties, when European alcohol consumption was legalized.

4. In recent politics, Nujoma has consistently sided with the periphery, mostly led by Zimbabwe, against South Africa on issues like the war in the Congo.

5. The 1921 census, for example, reported a total European population of 19,432, of whom 10,775 were adults (6,909 males, 3,866 females, and 8,657 children) (Southwest Africa 1923).

6. Needless to say, opinions differed as to whether all alcoholic beverages should be prohibited or only to natives or whether only dangerously intoxicating spirits should be banned. A summary of the St. Germain Convention is found in Buell (1928:942–53). It was a development linked to the Act of Brussels of 1890, in which the major powers declared their concern at the misuse of liquor abuse by natives. Later the Church Missionary Society and the Native Races and Liquor Trade United Committee in England also proved to be articulate campaigners, pointing out, for instance, that between 1901 and 1910 the duties levied on spirit imports in southern Nigeria furnished between 53 and 61 percent of the colony's revenue. A sense of context is also necessary here. Prohibition came into force in the United States in January 1920.

7. This was later increased to 3 percent (Siiskonen 1994:78).

8. The diffusion of *khali* to Namibia is, however, problematic, because the official on the Rand charged with suppressing it, Major Pritchard, became the first native commissioner in the territory, and thus it is unclear whether it was a diffusion from the Rand mines or whether this was simply the name of the beverage he imposed upon local alcoholic beverages, given their similar contents (see Moodie 1992:164–66).

9. Thus, more than twenty years later, in 1949 the administration claimed that "in order to secure the advancement of the native, and to prevent as far as possible his lapsing into crime, it is forbidden to place in the care of, or to give, sell or deliver to, any coloured person, any intoxicating liquor except for medicinal purposes, on the production of a prescription from a qualified medical practitioner. It is further unlawful for a master to give his servant 'tots' of liquor; it is also unlawful to brew kaffir beer without permission" (South Africa 1949:1171).

10. For delightful vignettes of small-town life in southern Namibia that stress the role of special drinking customs, see Con Weinberg's (1975) memoir about being a country doctor during the interwar years.

11. See "The Proud Boast and Toast of South West Africa Is Its Glorious Beer," *South West Africa Annual* (1953): 81–87.

12. In part this was shaped by the military situation pertaining at the time, which offered few alternative sources of income generation, but the situation per-

sisted after demilitarization. This raises many interesting and important questions: given the lack of cash-earning opportunities in this area (they are largely restricted to government and service sector jobs), where do people get money to spend on liquor? Part of it is derived from migrant worker remittances from the south. The other source is aggressive trading of goats, sheep, and cattle for liquor in the more isolated peripheral areas like the Kaokoveld. Unregulated truckers from Owambo and even Otjiwarongo would easily trade a bottle of sparkling wine valued at N$7 for a goat worth between N$270 and N$400. Three cartons of such wine would fetch an ox valued at N$1,500 in the region and N$3,500 on the national commercial market. One resident described the practice thus: "'This business is a dirty trick because the Ovahimba are cheated day and night. Whenever traders arrive in the villages they give residents some wine bottles known as *orupara* to get people into the mood,' Tjavara said. After orupara more liquor flows and this also means more animals exchanging hands. On many occasions residents only realize how many bottles they took the previous days when nursing their hang-overs. 'Just imagine how many of the Ovahimba have already given away their goats, sheep, and cattle to traders for nothing. Many end up abandoning their kraals after all their livestock is lost,' Tjavara continued" (*New Nation,* 12–14 August 1998).

13. A recent example culled from the *Mail and Guardian* (2 August 1999) is entitled "There's More to Namibia than Deserts and Good Beer" and deals with economic opportunities. It concludes with a note: "The brightest star at the moment is Namibian Breweries, makers of Windhoek Light and Lager, strongly favoured by the health conscious and yuppie market in South Africa. Namibian Breweries has consistently come through with earnings growth between 25 percent to 30 percent, accounts conservatively and has a strong capital base."

8. Alcohol as a Direct and Indirect Labor Enhancer

1. The introductory paragraphs to this section draw heavily from Suggs (1996:596–97).

2. Peters (1994) and Good (1992) offer alternative and more hegemonic views of the chieftaincy and the *kgotla* system.

3. Lobengula was then chief of the Matabele, a group that left South Africa during Shaka's Mfecane and moved through BaTswana territories before settling in what is today southern Zimbabwe. At the time, tensions between Khama and Lobengula over territorial boundaries were of concern to the colonial authorities as well as to the two groups' peoples. An assegai is a short stabbing spear utilized by the Matabele in combat.

4. See Adler (1991) for a similar argument surrounding the change from artisanal drinking patterns in Britain to pub-based consumption in the emergent industrial economy.

5. Akyeampong's (1996) amazing analysis of power, drink, and cultural

change in the social history of Ghana demonstrates comparatively Akan elders' recognition of similar threats to authority and control.

6. This is similar to Adler's conceptualization of artisan drinking communities, where, she notes, drinking opportunities "occupied a significant symbolic place in the affirmation and reproduction of the social relations that formed the basis of preindustrial English society" (1991:382).

7. Of course, the payment in tots that cut across separating lines of descent and ethnicity must also have helped to construct a class identity in the place of kin-based identities emphasizing common labor status of individuals rather than cooperative corporate control. The work of Akyeampong (1996), Ambler (1992), Suggs (1996), and others has clearly begun to demonstrate the ways that the symbolic character of alcohol and its consumption forged class identities (and/or reflected their foundation) in cash contexts. That is, tradition is malleable, and if it was the recognition of pattern that made the exploitative payments in kind acceptable (the initial lens through which such behavior would be interpreted), the traditions could also be brought to bear as a means of linking new "others" to "self" in identity. Our perspective goes a long way toward explaining why, as Moodie says, "black miners tenaciously clung to alcohol as a necessary accompaniment of informal sociability" and why "whatever the regulations, consumption of alcohol was seen as a right for adult men" (1992:162).

9. Coca as Symbol and Labor Enhancer

1. Traditional coca production requires handling and processing different from modern cocaine; therefore, there is little or no crossover with cultivation, harvesting, and marketing for illegal cocaine. For traditional uses, coca leaves must be treated delicately to avoid bruising, discoloration, and embitterment by drying too slowly or picking too soon or too late. The color and taste of an individual coca leaf are very important to its overall quality. No such special care is needed for the production of coca-product exports such as cocaine; any leaf in any state will do. Traditional coca consumption is usually practiced by adults, especially men, who place several leaves in their mouths with a bit of vegetable ash paste after saying a prayer; they suck the wad of leaves to extract the juices. In this form coca is a mild stimulant (Spedding 1997). Ironically, in the last three to four decades, coca cultivation in South America has increased a thousandfold to supply cocaine and crack consumption in the United States and Western Europe. These derivatives of coca leaves require approximately a hundred kilos of leaves to produce one gram of basic paste, the illegal substance (Mac Gregor 1993:113).

U.S.–led coca plant eradication threats are generally unacceptable to the traditional coca users and employers, just as they were in the sixteenth century, when religious prohibitionists fought against coca use. There is an enormous unofficial contribution to the gross national or domestic product of nations such as Peru and

Bolivia that cannot be overlooked and mirrors the early Spaniards' main concern and reason for protecting its continued production (Leóns and Sanabria 1997:19–20; Mac Gregor 1993:8–13). During the sixteenth century consumption was for internal use and had a long history and wide acceptance among the populace. Now the cocaine paste exports are for use by a minority of foreigners for purposes that go against mainstream societal mores and in the long term have no beneficial side effects. Coca is still used today by indigenous Andean populations in ritualistic and labor-enhancing contexts, while cocaine, which is returned to the European and American markets, is used not to enhance labor performance but rather to escape from labor itself, an irony that would not have been lost on the pre-contact populations as it has been lost on postcolonial societies.

2. Most people who know Quechua as well as followers of Murra and other ethnohistorians prefer Inka spelled with a *k,* though Inca with a *c* is still very common (George Urioste, personal communication, 2000).

3. It is said that the quality of coca leaves is highly variable, with altitude, age of the plant, time of harvest, drying method, and transport all substantially affecting the final product. Possibly, Inka nobles had control of the best coca from the best fields, while poorer-quality coca was generally available to commoners. At this stage this hypothesis needs testing, although Spedding (1997:49) suggested with similar reasoning that the Inka monopoly was on distribution, not production.

4. In the coastal oasis of the modern city of Arica, northern Chile, and generally in the south-central Andes, preservation of organic materials is remarkable. There are hundreds of prehistoric and historic mummified human remains and associated grave goods housed at the Museo Arqueológico de San Miguel, Universidad de Tarapacá, Arica, Chile.

5. Looking more specifically at the individuals who tested positively, we see that all ages and both genders consumed coca. The positive coca consumers included fifty adults age fifteen to sixty, twelve subadults age three to eleven, nineteen infants age four to twenty-four months, and eight newborns. Obviously, the newborns, infants, and younger subadults tested positive due to their mothers' ingestion and transfer of the metabolite from the placenta or breast milk (Cartmell et al. 1991). The fewest number of individuals consuming coca were youths from age six to puberty. Status was measured by the quantity and quality of textiles, the most common grave good accompanying an individual (Cassman 1997).

6. In many cases, especially in Peru, the social and economic systems known as *ayllu* were dissolved. Ayllus were groups of extended families that controlled a defined territory collectively and practiced endogamy. Ayllus survived in the Bolivian highlands, since there were fewer Spanish settlements and contacts (Godoy 1990:26–27).

7. There is no mention of the effect of denuding the highlands on the camelid population, but that must have greatly affected their numbers and may explain the

lack of mention of camelids as pack animals and the Spanish emphasis on human porters.

8. In Bolivia, where coca lands had not initially been taken as Spanish landed estates as in the Cuzco area, indigenous communities retained ownership of land and worked their own fields. However, these traditional communities were taxed on their production. The coca harvest tax was assigned to individual Spaniards who held the communities in *encomiendas* (Klein 1996:23–24). Some indigenous members of the nobility with their own coca fields provided some coca to the miners (Spedding 1997:49), but Spanish coca traders had a monopoly on the enormous new market created for laborers in the mines.

10. Caffeine and Culture

1. For many years I researched these substances, and I have carried out fieldwork on the uses of tea in China and Canada, the production of coffee in Mexico, coffee ceremonialization among Finnish Americans, chocolate folklore in the United States, and other relevant phenomena. Otherwise unattributed statements refer to my own work.

2. As of 1997, coffee was worth an average of $3,424 per ton; cacao beans brought $1,691; tea leaves, $2,080 (Food and Agriculture Organization 1997:25). By contrast, wheat, the world's most important plant commodity, brought only $148, and soybeans, $278 (Food and Agriculture Organization 1997:25). World consumption in 1993 (the latest year for which I can find figures) was 98,428,000 bags of coffee; 2,508,900 metric tons of tea; and 2,287,400 metric tons of cocoa (UNCTAD 1993). Coffee exports in 1995 earned $14,936,790,000 for some of the world's poorest nations; tea, $2,085,588,000; cocoa, $4,962,139,000 (UNCTAD 1995).

3. Many medical conditions, notably cancer, have been blamed on methylxanthines. However, there seem to be no negative health consequences from caffeine consumption by adults (Ernster 1984; World Health Organization 1991) beyond the withdrawal syndrome described in the text and a possible heightened cholesterol level among those who habitually drink coffee brewed by boiling it. This latter procedure, virtually confined to Scandinavia, releases saturated fats from the beans. Coffee and tea contain substances that bind iron and make it less available in digestion and can thus cause anemia in extreme cases, but this is rare (see Muñoz et al. 1988). Caffeine may endanger fetuses and infants (Braun 1996).

4. Caffeine plants are now vital to the economies of many nations. Most of these are tropical montane countries that otherwise offer little of interest to the world and have few chances for development. Many of these nations depend largely on coffee or tea for their foreign export earnings; some small West African nations depend largely on cacao. Critics of the world trade in drug plants have often attacked export-oriented cash cropping (e.g., Lappé and Collins 1977), including coffee and tea production. However, it is difficult to envision any other profitable

uses for tropical rainforest and montane environments that are not ecologically devastating. Cacao and coffee, in particular, are not only erosion-controlling dense evergreen woody plants but are traditionally grown under the shade of tall trees, producing both superior cacao and coffee as well as a forestlike environment that is almost as good for birds and other wildlife as a natural forest (personal observation during extensive travel and research in producing areas of China, Taiwan, Malaysia, Indonesia, Mexico, and several other countries; see also Hernández Castillo and Nigh 1998; Pennybacker 1997; and Sherry 2000 for coffee; Dand 1997; Young 1994 for cacao). Moreover, the shade trees are often valuable food or timber trees in their own right. In today's world, where quality is important, shade growing makes sense. Therefore, conservationists have been promoting shade-grown coffee, especially when local cooperatives produce it (Pennybacker 1997; Sherry 2000); open-grown coffee produces more beans but less quality and less wildlife. By far the most important coffee producer is Brazil, with up to one third of world production in productive years (Food and Agriculture Organization 1995:171; *Los Angeles Times,* 7 March 1995). Production freezes in Brazil cause spectacular fluctuations in supply (Lucier 1988). In 1993 Brazil produced 1,279,000 metric tons of coffee; in 1995, after a sharp freeze, only 930,000, barely ahead of Colombia's 810,000. Colombia produces about one seventh of the world supply; Mexico and Indonesia are also important. Coffee is grown in virtually every country whose territory includes tropical mountains; even the United States grows high-quality coffee on the Hawaiian volcanoes. World production of cacao was 2,529,000 metric tons in 1995 (Food and Agriculture Organization 1995:173). The Ivory Coast was by far the world leader, with 860,000 tons. Ghana weighed in second with 325,000. Brazil is a significant producer in the Western Hemisphere.

5. Tropical commodity prices are notoriously unstable, leading to budgetary problems for many nations (Bates 1997; de Graaff 1986; Jacob 1935; Lucier 1988; Paige 1997; Renard 1993; Uribe 1954; and many others—the literature on caffeine-plant political economy is large). Producer countries have often tried to form cartels, but these invariably collapse due to the problem of getting many disparate and often economically desperate countries to make binding agreements. Consumer countries have tried to keep prices low, but they are equally powerless in the face of Brazilian freezes and the difficulties of quality production everywhere (Bates 1997; Lucier 1988). World methylxanthine trade is a case of not so extreme exploitation by the rich of the poor, though there are those who would disagree, holding the coffee trade to be intensely exploitative (Roseberry, Gudmundson, and Kutschbach 1995). Similar problems plague the trade in tea and other methylxanthine plants. Where local small-scale producers can aggressively control marketing, as in Colombia at certain times in the past (Bates 1997) or as in recent Mexican cooperative enterprises (Hernandez Castillo and Nigh 1998), rural smallholders can make a decent living—if prices hold.

6. Technology reached a peak in the tea clippers that sailed from Canton to England and America. In many ways the all-time pinnacle of marine technology, tea clippers optimized across three disparate dimensions, being designed for maximum speed, maximum load, and maximum safety. Rarely has so much skill gone into so complex an optimizing task—and all this just to get the tea to market before the competition could do it.

7. Chocolate may or may not have been used in *molli* (sauce or stew), now *mole;* the great chocolate *moles* of modern Mexican cuisine are colonial creations, fusions of Arab-Andalucian with Nahuatl cooking (Coe and Coe 1996). Aztecs said that "an ordinary amount...gladdens one, refreshes one, consoles one, invigorates one" (Sahagún 1963:119). In southern Mexico, chocolate used as a savory spice with chile is still common, and drinks made of chocolate, chile, and toasted cornmeal are widely found. For the history of world chocolate use from the Spanish in Mexico through modern industrial production, see Coe and Coe 1996; McGee 1984:397–409; Shively and Tarka 1984; and Dand 1997. The chocolate fad was preceded by a period when imitation chocolate briefly swept the U.S. market, following the rising cacao prices of the early 1970s (Dand 1997). The imitation lacked chocolate flavor as well as stimulant value and resembled chocolate only in color and texture. For a brief period, genuine chocolate products were virtually impossible to find in American supermarkets. Consumer acceptance, however, was very low; sales of "chocolate" products plummeted. Chocolate consumption bottomed out in 1981. The food industry reversed itself, and chocolate consumption had recovered by 1985 (*USA Today,* 13 February 1986). Young correctly notes that "attempts to manufacture an acceptable synthetic chocolate...have failed" (1994:79).

11. Drugs in Work and Trade

1. Once one is aware of these exchanges they become apparent everywhere. See, for example, Shostak's (1983) description of people's demands for and her provision of tobacco early in her fieldwork.

2. Agar (1986), for example, describes long-distance truckers keeping themselves awake with coffee and other stimulants, including vast amounts of sweet food.

3. Just as both Ambler and Mancall argue that one leg of the economic logic of liquor trade was the need to provide income for Caribbean producers, part of the logic of the British opium trade was a (hidden) desire to defray the costs of their India colony.

4. While there is an enormous literature on opium and its use, there is little systematic information on why people actually consumed it. We base our view on material quoted in Westermeyer (1982), Rush (1990), Gangulay, Sharma, and Krishnamachari (1995), Berridge (1999), and Kerimi (2000).

Bibliography

Acker, C.

1995 From All Purpose Anodyne to Marker of Deviance: Physicians' Attitudes towards Opiates in the US from 1890 to 1940. In *Drugs and Narcotics in History*. Edited by R. Porter and M. Teich. 114–32. Cambridge: Cambridge University Press.

Acts and Laws

1761 *Acts and Laws of His Majesty's Province in New Hampshire, in New England*. Portsmouth, N.H.: D. Fowler.

Adamson, A. H.

1972 *Sugar without Slaves: The Political Economy of British Guiana 1838–1904*. New Haven, Conn.: Yale University Press.

Adler, M.

1991 From Symbolic Exchange to Commodity Consumption: Anthropological Notes on Drinking as a Symbolic Practice. In *Drinking: Behavior and Belief in Modern History*. Edited by S. Barrows and R. Room. 376–98. Berkeley: University of California Press.

Agar, M.

1986 *Independents Declared: The Dilemmas of Independent Trucking*. Washington, D.C.: Smithsonian Institution Press.

Akerman, K.

1980 Material Culture and Trade in the Kimberleys Today. In *Aborigines of the West*. Edited by R. M. and C. H. Berndt. 243–57. Perth: University of Western Australia Press.

Akyeampong, E.

1996 *Drink, Power, and Cultural Change: A Social History of Alcohol in Ghana, c. 1800 to Recent Times*. Portsmouth, N.H.: Heinemann Press.

Albertis, L. M. d'

1881 *New Guinea: What I Did and What I Saw*. London: Sampson, Low, Marston, Searle and Rivington.

Allen, C.

1988 *The Hold Life Has: Coca and Cultural Identity in an Andean Community*. Washington, D.C.: Smithsonian Institution Press.

Allison, M., and E. Gerzsten

1982 *Paleopathology in South American Mummies*. Richmond: Medical College of Virginia.

1998 *A History of the American Holocaust*. Chapel Hill, N.C.: Professional Press.

Ambler, C.

1987 *Alcohol and Disorder in Precolonial Africa*. Working Papers no. 126, African Studies Center, Boston University.

1992 Alcohol and the Control of Labor on the Copperbelt. In *Liquor and Labor in Southern Africa*. Edited by J. Crush and C. Ambler. 1–55. Athens: Ohio University Press.

Ambler, C., and J. Crush

1992 Alcohol in Southern African Labor History. In *Liquor and Labor in Southern Africa*. Edited by J. Crush and C. Ambler. 1–55. Athens: Ohio University Press.

Anderson, B.

1991 *Imagined Communities*. New York: Verso.

Anderson, C.

1995 The Economics of Sacred Art: The Uses of a Secret Collection in the South Australian Museum. In *Politics of the Secret*. Edited by C. Anderson. 97–107. Sydney: University of Sydney Press.

Anderson, E. N.

1970 *The Floating World of Castle Peak Bay*. Washington, D.C.: American Anthropological Association.

1988 *The Food of China*. New Haven, Conn.: Yale University Press.

Angelo, A. C.

1948 Kimberleys and North-West Goldfields: Early Days. *Western Australian Historical Society* (December):38–46.

Angrosino, M. V.

1974 *Outside Is Death: Alcoholism, Ideology, and Community Organization among the East Indians of Trinidad*. Winston-Salem, N.C.: Overseas Research Center.

Appadurai, A., ed.

1986 Introduction: Commodities and the Politics of Value. In *The Social Life of Things*. Edited by A. Appadurai. 3–63. Cambridge: Cambridge University Press.

Arriaza, B., W. Salo, A. Aufderheide, and T. Holcomb

1995 Pre-Columbian Tuberculosis in Northern Chile: Molecular and Skeletal Evidence. *Journal of the American Association of Physical Anthropology* 98:37–45.

Arthur, J. M.

1996 *Aboriginal English*. Melbourne: Oxford University Press.

Atkinson, A., and M. Aveling, eds.

1987 *Australians: A Historical Library. Australians 1838*. New South Wales: Fairfax, Syme and Weldon Associates.

Bibliography

Austen, L.

1945 Cultural Changes in Kiriwina. *Oceania* 16:15–60.

Austin, G.

1995 Between Abolition and *Jihad*: The Asante Response to the Ending of the Atlantic Slave Trade, 1807–1896. In *From Slave Trade to "Legitimate" Commerce: The Commercial Transition in Nineteenth-Century West Africa*. Edited by R. Law. 93–118. Cambridge: Cambridge University Press.

Axtell, J.

1985 *The Invasion Within: The Contest of Cultures in Colonial North America*. New York: Oxford University Press.

1988 At the Water's Edge: Trading in the Sixteenth Century. In *After Columbus: Essays in the Ethnohistory of Colonial North America*. Edited by J. Axtell. 154–60. New York: Oxford University Press.

Bachellor, A. S., ed.

1904 *Laws of New Hampshire*. Manchester, N.H.

Backhouse, J.

1843 *A Narrative of a Visit to the Australian Colonies*. London: Hamilton, Adams and Company.

Baker, R.

1999 *Land Is Life: From Bush to Town: The Story of the Yanyuwa People*. Sydney: George Allen and Unwin.

Barnes, J., and G. Winter

2001 Stressed Out? Bad Knee? Relief Promised in a Juice. *New York Times*, 27 May:A1.

Barretto, M.

1991 *El maté, su historia y cultura*. Buenos Aires: Ediciones del Sol.

Bartlett, J. R., ed.

1856–65 *Records of the Colony of Rhode Island and Providence Plantations in New England*. 10 vols. Reprint, New York: AMS Press, 1968.

Basedow, H.

1929 *The Australian Aboriginal*. Adelaide: F. W. Preece and Sons.

Bates, R.

1997 *Open Economy Politics: The Political Economy of the World Coffee Trade*. Princeton, N.J.: Princeton University Press.

Belmonte, E., J. C. Romero, M. Ortega, V. Cassman, and P. Arévalo

1998 Research Paper Summaries for Fondecyt Grant Uso de Coca en Ritual Funerario: Análisis Interdisciplinario. Universidad de Tarapacá, Arica, Chile.

Bennion, L., and T.-K. Li

1976 Alcohol Metabolism in American Indians and Whites: Lack of Racial Differences in Metabolic Rate and Liver Alcohol Dehydrogenase. *New England Journal of Medicine* 294:9–13.

Berlin, I.

1998 *Many Thousands Gone: The First Two Centuries of Slavery in North America.* Cambridge, Mass.: Harvard University Press.

Berndt, C. H., and R. M. Berndt

1951–52 An Oenpelli Monologue: Culture-Contact. *Oceania* 22:24–34.

Berndt, R. M., and C. H. Berndt

1942 Preliminary Report of Fieldwork in the Ooldea Region. *Oceania* 12.4:321.

1987 *End of an Era: Aboriginal Labour in the Northern Territory.* Canberra: Australian Institute of Aboriginal Studies Press.

Berridge, V.

1999 *Opium and the People: Opiate Use and Drug Control Policy in Nineteenth and Early Twentieth Century England.* London: Free Association Books.

Bevan, T. F.

1890 *Toil, Travel, and Discovery in British New Guinea.* London: Kegan Paul, Trench, Trubner and Company.

Bhana, S., and A. Bhana

1991 An Exploration of the Psycho-Historical Circumstances Surrounding Suicide among Indentured Indians, 1875–1911. In *Essays on Indentured Indians in Natal.* Edited by S. Bhana. 137–88. Leeds, England: Peepal Tree Press.

Bishop, C.

1974 *The Northern Ojibwa and the Fur Trade: An Historical and Ecological Study.* Toronto: Holt, Rinehart and Winston.

Blake, J.

1977 *West Africa: Quest for God and Gold, 1454–1578.* 1937. Reprint, London: Curzon Press.

Blofeld, J.

1985 *The Chinese Art of Tea.* London: George Allen and Unwin.

Bolam, A. M.

1978 *The Trans-Australian Wonderland.* 1923. Facsimile ed., Perth: University of Western Australia Press.

Bonnet, M. H., and D. L. Arand

1994 The Use of Prophylactic Naps and Caffeine to Maintain Performance during a Continuous Operation. *Ergonomics* 37:1009–20.

Booth, M.

1998 *Opium: A History.* New York: St. Martin's Press.

Bosman, W.

1967 *A New and Accurate Description of the Coast of Guinea Divided into the Gold, the Slave, and the Ivory Coasts.* Edited by J. R. Willis. 1705. Facsimile ed., New York: Barnes and Noble.

Bourdieu, P.

1977 *Outline of a Theory of Practice*. New York: Cambridge University Press.

1984 *Distinction*. Cambridge, Mass.: Harvard University Press.

Boynton, S.

1982 *Chocolate: The Consuming Passion*. New York: Workman Publishers.

Bradburd, D., and W. Jankowiak

N.d. Getting Hooked by the World Market: Drug Foods, Desire, and Capitalist Expansion. Ms.

Bradford, W.

1952 *Of Plymouth Plantation*. Edited by S. E. Morison. New York: Barnes and Noble.

Brady, M.

1987 Leaving the Spinifex: The Effect of Rations, Missions and the Atomic Tests on the Southern Pitjantjatjara. *Records of the South Australian Museum* 20:35–45.

1992 *Heavy Metal: The Social Meaning of Petrol Sniffing in Australia*. Canberra: Australian Institute of Aboriginal Studies Press.

Braun, S.

1996 *Buzz: The Science and Lore of Caffeine and Alcohol*. London: Penguin.

Brereton, B.

1974 The Experience of Indentureship: 1845–1917. In *Calcutta to Caroni: The East Indians of Trinidad*. Edited by J. La Guerre. 25–38. London: Longmans.

1981 *A History of Modern Trinidad 1783–1962*. Kingston, Jamaica: Heinemann.

Brewer, J., and R. Porter, eds.

1993 *Consumption and the World of Goods*. London: Routledge.

Breytenbach, C.

1989 *Namibia: Birth of a Nation*. Monague, South Africa: Luga.

British Parliamentary Papers: The Slave Trade

1968 Vol. 9: *Correspondence with Foreign Powers and with British Commissioners Relating to the Slave Trade*; vol. 10: *Correspondence with the British Commissioners at Sierra Leone Relating to the Slave Trade, 1824–1825*; vol. 13: *Correspondence with the British Commissioners at Sierra Leone Relating to the Slave Trade, 1831*. Shannon: Irish University Press.

Brockmann, C.

1912 *Briefe eines deutschen Mädchens aus Südwest*. Berlin: E. S. Mitler.

Brooks, G. E.

1970 *Yankee Traders, Old Coasters and African Middlemen: A History of American Legitimate Trade with West Africa in the Nineteenth Century*. Brookline, Mass.: Boston University Press.

1993 *Landlords and Strangers: Ecology, Society, and Trade in Western Africa, 1000–1630*. Boulder, Colo.: Westview Press.

Browne, W. H., et al., eds.

1883–1972 *Archives of Maryland.* 72 vols. Baltimore: Maryland Historical Society.

Bryce, G.

1968 *The Remarkable History of the Hudson's Bay Company.* 1904. Reprint, New York: Burt Franklin.

Buell, R.

1928 *The Native Problem in Africa.* New York: Macmillan.

Burke, T.

1996 *Lifebuoy Men, Lux Women.* Durham, N.C.: Duke University Press.

Burnett, J.

1966 *Plenty and Want.* Harmondsworth: Penguin.

1969 *A History of the Cost of Living.* Harmondsworth: Penguin.

1999 *Liquid Pleasures: A Social History of Drinks in Modern Britain.* London: Routledge.

Burnham, J. C.

1993 *Bad Habits: Drinking, Smoking, Taking Drugs, Gambling, Sexual Misbehaviour and Swearing in American History.* New York: New York University Press.

Carr, D. J., and S. G. M. Carr, eds.

1981 *People and Plants in Australia.* Sydney: Academic Press.

Carstairs, G. M.

1954 Daru and Bhang: Cultural Factors in the Choice of Intoxicant. *Quarterly Journal of Studies on Alcohol* 15:220–37.

1966 Bhang and Alcohol: Cultural Factors in the Choice of Intoxicants. In *The Marijuana Papers.* Edited by D. Solomon. 103–29. New York: New American Library.

Carter, M.

1996 *Voices from Indenture: Experiences of Indian Migrants in the British Empire.* New York: Leicester University Press.

Cartmell, L., A. Aufderheide, A. Springfield, C. Weems, and B. Arriaza

1991 The Frequency and Antiquity of Prehistoric Coca-Leaf-Chewing Practices in Northern Chile: Radioimmunoassay of a Cocaine Metabolite in Human-Mummy Hair. *Latin American Antiquity* 2.3:260–68.

Cassinelli, L. V.

1986 Qat: Changes in the Production and Consumption of a Quasilegal Commodity. In *The Social Life of Things.* Edited by A. Appadurai. 236–60. Cambridge: Cambridge University Press.

Cassman, V.

1997 A Reconsideration of Prehistoric Ethnicity and Status in Northern Chile: The Textile Evidence. Ph.D. diss., Department of Anthropology, Arizona State University, Tempe.

Castile, R.

1971   *The Way of Tea.* New York: Weatherhill.

Chan, A. W. K.

1986   Racial Differences in Alcohol Sensitivity. *Alcohol and Alcoholism* 21:93–104.

Chandler, A. D., ed.

1904–16   *Colonial Records of the State of Georgia.* 26 vols. Athens: Franklin Printing and Publishing Company.

Cheesman, E.

1935   *The Two Roads of Papua.* London: Jarrolds.

Chen, S. H., et al.

1992   Gene Frequencies of Alcohol Dehydrogenase$_2$ and Aldehyde Dehydrogenase$_2$ in Northwest Coast Amerindians. *Human Genetics* 89:351–52.

Chignell, A. K.

1915   *An Outpost in Papua.* 2nd ed. London: Smith, Elder and Company.

Chikamatsu, S.

1982   *Stories from a Tearoom Window.* Rutland, Vt., and Tokyo: Charles Tuttle.

Choquette, L.

1991   Recruitment of French Emigrants to Canada, 1600–1760. In *To Make America: European Emigration in the Early Modern Period.* Edited by I. Altman and J. Horn. 131–71. Berkeley: University of California Press.

Cieza de León, P.

1959   *The Incas.* Translated by H. de Onis. Norman: University of Oklahoma Press.

Clarke, C. G.

1986   *East Indians in a West Indian Town.* London: George Allen and Unwin.

Cleland, J. B., and T. H. Johnston

1937–38   Notes on Native Names and Uses of Plants in the Musgrave Ranges Region. *Oceania* 8:208–15.

Coe, S., and M. D. Coe

1996   *The True History of Chocolate.* London: Thames and Hudson.

Cole, K.

1980   *Dick Harris: Missionary to the Aborigines. A Biography of the Reverend Canon George Richmond Harris MBE, Pioneer Missionary to the Aborigines of Arnhem Land.* Victoria: Keith Cole Publications.

Colson, E., and T. Scudder

1988   *For Prayer and Profit: The Ritual, Economic and Social Importance of Beer in Gwembe District, Zambia, 1950–1982.* Stanford, Calif.: Stanford University Press.

Comaroff, J.

1975   Talking Politics: Oratory and Authority in a Tswana Chiefdom. In *Political Language and Oratory in Traditional Societies.* Edited by M. Bloch. 141–60. London: Academic Press.

Comaroff, J., and J. Comaroff

1997 Postcolonial Politics and Discourses of Democracy in Southern Africa: An Anthropological Reflection on African Political Modernities. *Journal of Anthropological Research* 53.2:123–46.

Cooper T., and D. J. McCord, eds.

1836–41 *Statutes at Large of South Carolina.* 10 vols. Columbia, S.C.: A. S. Johnson.

Cornell, F.

1986 *The Glamour of Prospecting.* Cape Town: D. Philip.

Coronel, R. F.

1991 El Valle sangriento: De los indígenas de la coca y el algodón a la Hacienda Cañera Jesuita. Colección Tesis Historia. Quito, Ecuador: Abya-Yala Publicaciones.

Corris, P.

1970 Pacific Island Labour Migrants in Queensland. *Journal of Pacific History* 5:45–64.

1973 "Blackbirding" in New Guinea Waters, 1883–84. *Journal of Pacific History* 3:85–105.

Coughtry, J.

1981 *The Notorious Triangle: Rhode Island and the African Slave Trade, 1700–1807.* Philadelphia: Temple University Press.

Courtwright, D.

1995 The Rise and Fall and Rise of Cocaine in the United States. In *Consuming Habits: Drugs in History and Anthropology.* Edited by J. Goodman, P. Lovejoy, and A. Sherratt. 206–28. London: Routledge.

2001 *Forces of Habit: Drugs and the Making of the Modern World.* Cambridge, Mass.: Harvard University Press.

Crais, C.

1992 *White Supremacy and Black Resistance in Pre-Industrial South Africa.* Cambridge: Cambridge University Press.

Creed, Dr.

1878 Notes from Dr. Creed, M.L.A. on the Aborigines of the North Coast. *Journal of the Royal Anthropological Institute* 7:266–68.

Cronon, W.

1983 *Changes in the Land: Indians, Colonists, and the Ecology of New England.* New York: Hill and Wang.

Crosby, A. W.

1986 *Ecological Imperialism: The Biological Expansion of Europe, 900–1900.* New York: Cambridge University Press.

Crush, J., and C. Ambler, eds.

1992 *Liquor and Labor in Southern Africa.* Athens: Ohio University Press.

Curr, E. M.

1883 *Recollections of Squatting in Victoria Then Called Port Phillip District (from 1841 to 1857)*. Melbourne: George Robertson.

Curtin, P.

1990 *The Rise and Fall of the Plantation Complex*. Cambridge: Cambridge University Press.

Curto, J. C.

1989 Alcohol and Slaves: The Luso-Brazilian Alcohol Commerce at Mpinda, Luanda, and Benguela during the Atlantic Slave Trade, c. 1480–1830 and Its Impact on the Societies of West Central Africa. Ph.D. diss., University of California, Los Angeles.

Dakin, K., and S. Wichmann

2000 Cacao and Chocolate: A Uto-Aztecan Perspective. *Ancient Mesoamerica* 11:55–75.

Dand, R.

1997 *The International Cocoa Trade*. New York: John Wiley and Sons.

de Barrios, V.

1980 *Guide to Tequila, Mescal and Pulque*. Mexico City: Editorial Minutiae Mexicana.

de Graaff, J.

1986 *The Economics of Coffee*. Wageningen: Pudoc.

De Quincey, T.

1986 *Confessions of an English Opium Eater*. 1821. Reprint, London: Penguin.

Dietler, M.

1990 Driven by Drink: The Role of Drinking in the Political Economy and the Case of Early Iron Age France. *Journal of Anthropological Archaeology* 9:352–406.

Dingle, A. E.

1980 "The Truly Magnificent Thirst": An Historical Survey of Australian Drinking Habits. *Historical Studies* 19.75:227–49.

Dobkin de Rios, M.

1984 *Hallucinogens: Cross-Cultural Perspectives*. Albuquerque: University of New Mexico Press.

Donnan, E., ed.

1930 *Documents Illustrative of the History of the Slave Trade to America*. Vol. 2, *The Eighteenth Century*. Washington, D.C.: Carnegie Institution of Washington.

Dortch, S.

1995 Coffee at Home. *American Demographics* (August):4–6.

Dove, M.

1988 The Ecology of Intoxication among the Kantu' of West Kalimantan. In *The Real and Imagined Role of Culture in Development: Case Studies from Indonesia*. Edited by M. R. Dove. 139–82. Honolulu: University of Hawaii Press.

Drysdale, I.

1974 *The End of Dreaming.* Adelaide: Rigby.

Duelke, B.

1998 *"Same but Different . . .": Tradition und Geschichte im Alltag einer nordaustralischen Aborigines-kommune.* Studien zur Kulturkunde no. 108. Cologne: Rudinger Koppe Verlag.

Dumett, R.

1974 The Social Impact of the European Liquor Trade on the Akan of Ghana (Gold Coast and Asante), 1875–1910. *Journal of Interdisciplinary History* 5 (summer):69–101.

Duncan-Kemp, A. M.

1933 *Our Sandhill Country: Nature and Man in South-Western Queensland.* Sydney: Angus and Robertson.

1964 *Where Strange Paths Go Down.* Brisbane: W. R. Smith and Paterson.

Dunn, R.

1972 *Sugar and Slaves: The Rise of the Planter Class in the English West Indies, 1624–1713.* Chapel Hill: University of North Carolina Press.

Dupeyrat, A.

1955 *Festive Papua.* London: Staples Press Limited.

Dyck, L. E.

1993 Absence of the Atypical Mitochondrial Aldehyde Dehydrogenase ($ALDH_2$) Isozyme in Saskatchewan Cree Indians. *Human Heredity* 43:116–20.

Eber, C.

1995 *Women and Alcohol in a Highland Maya Town.* Austin: University of Texas Press.

Eden, T.

1976 *Tea.* 3rd ed. London: Longmans.

Edwards, R.

1979 *Australian Aboriginal Art: The Art of the Alligator Rivers Region, Northern Territory.* Canberra: Australian Institute of Aboriginal Studies Press.

Elder, J. D.

1970 Drug Addiction and Society. In *West Indian Social Problems.* Edited by M. Cross. 63–81. Port-of-Spain, Trinidad: Columbus Publications.

Elkin, A. P.

1951 Reaction and Interaction: A Food Gathering People and European Settlement in Australia. *American Anthropologist* 53.22:64–186.

Eltis, D.

1991 Precolonial Western Africa and the Atlantic Economy. In *Slavery and the Rise of the Atlantic System.* Edited by B. Solow. 97–119. Cambridge: Cambridge University Press.

2000 *The Rise of African Slavery in the Americas.* New York: Cambridge University Press.

Erickson, H. T., M. Pinheiro, F. Correa, and J. R. Escobar

1984 Guarana *(Paullinia cupana)* as a Commercial Crop in Brazilian Amazonia. *Economic Botany* 38:273–86.

Ernster, V.

1984 Epidemiological Studies of Caffeine and Human Health. In *The Methylxanthine Beverages and Foods.* Edited by G. A. Spiller. 377–400. New York: Alan R. Liss.

Evans, R., K. Saunders, and K. Cronin

1975 *Exclusion, Exploitation and Extermination: Race Relations in Colonial Queensland.* Sydney: ANZ Book Company.

Fabri, F.

1884 *Bedarf Deutschland der Kolonien?* Gotha: F. A. Perhes Verlag.

Fairweather, I.

2002 "Without Culture There Is No Future": The Performance of Heritage in Post-Apartheid Northern Namibia. In *Challenges for Anthropology in the "African Renaissance."* Edited by D. Lebeau and R. J. Gordon. 32–43. Windhoek: Gamsberg-Macmillan.

Fay, P.

1975 *The Opium War 1840–1842.* Chapel Hill: University of North Carolina Press.

Fernandez, H.

1998 *Heroin.* Center City, Minn.: Hazelden.

Ferre, S.

1997 Adenosine-Dopamine Interactions in the Ventral Striatum: Implications for the Treatment of Schizophrenia. *Psychopharmacology* 133.2:107–20.

Finsch, O.

1887 Über Naturprodukte der westlichen Südsee, besonders der deutschen Schutzgebiete. *Deutsche Kolonialzeitung* 4:519–30, 543–51, 593–96.

Firth, S.

1973 German Firms in the Western Pacific Islands, 1857–1914. *Journal of Pacific History* 8:10–28.

Food and Agriculture Organization of the United Nations (FAO)

1995 *Production Yearbook.* Rome: FAO.

1997 *The State of Food and Agriculture 1997.* Rome: FAO.

Foreign Office (British)

1969 *Peace Handbooks: German African Possessions.* 1919. Reprint, New York: Greenwood.

Forrest, D.

1973 *Tea for the British: The Social and Economic History of a Famous Trade.* London: Chatto and Windus.

Foster, R.

1991 Making National Cultures in the Global Ecumene. *Annual Review of Anthropology* 20:235–78.

———, ed.

1996 *Nation-Making: Emergent Identities in Postcolonial Melanesia.* Ann Arbor: University of Michigan Press.

Fujioka, R.

1973 *Tea Ceremony Utensils.* New York: Weatherhill.

Gagliano, J. A.

1994 *Coca Prohibition in Peru: The Historical Debates.* Tucson: University of Arizona Press.

1996 The Coca Debate in Colonial Peru. In *Drugs in the Western Hemisphere: An Odyssey of Cultures in Conflict.* Edited by W. O. Walker III. 8–22. Jaguar Books on Latin America no. 12. Wilmington: Scholarly Resources.

Gagliano, J. A., and C. Ronan, eds.

1997 *Jesuit Encounters in the New World: Jesuit Chroniclers, Geographers, Educators and Missionaries in the Americas 1549–1767.* Rome: Institutum Historicum SI.

Gálvez, B. de

1951 *Instructions for Governing the Interior Provinces of New Spain, 1786.* Translated and edited by D. Worcester. Berkeley: Quivira Society.

Ganguly, K. K., H. K. Sharma, and K. A. V. R. Krishnamachari

1995 An Ethnographic Account of Opium Consumers of Rajasthan (India): Socio-Medical Perspective. *Addiction* 90:9–21.

Gardella, R.

1994 *Harvesting Mountains: Fujian and the China Tea Trade, 1757–1937.* Berkeley: University of California Press.

Garland, E., and R. J. Gordon

1999 The Authentic (In)authentic: Bushman Anthro-Tourism. *Visual Anthropology* 12.2–3:267–88.

Garrett, B. E., and R. R. Griffiths

1997 The Role of Dopamine in the Behavioral Effects of Caffeine in Animals and Humans. *Pharmacology, Biochemistry and Behavior* 57.3:533–41.

Garry, N. E.

1930 Papers Relating to Her Stay in the Northern Territory 1930–32. Items 1 and 2, Ms. 3977. Mitchell Library, Sydney.

Gates, C. M., ed.

1965 *Five Fur Traders of the Northwest.* 1933. St. Paul: Minnesota Historical Society.

Gilbert, R. M.

1984 Caffeine Consumption. In *The Methylxanthine Beverages and Foods*. Edited by G. A. Spiller. 185–214. New York: Alan R. Liss.

Gill, K., et al.

1999 An Examination of ALDH₂ Genotypes, Alcohol Metabolism and the Flushing Response in Native Americans. *Journal of Studies on Alcohol* 60:149–58.

Goddard, C., and A. Kalotas

1995 *Punu: Yankunytjatjara Plant Use.* Alice Springs: Institute of Aboriginal Development Press.

Godoy, R.

1990 *Mining and Agriculture in Highland Bolivia: Ecology, History, and Commerce among the Jukumanis.* Tucson: University of Arizona Press.

Goldman, D., et al.

1993 DRD₂ Dopamine Receptor Genotype, Linkage Disequilibrium, and Alcoholism in American Indians and Other Populations. *Alcoholism: Clinical and Experimental Research* 17:199–204.

Good, K.

1992 Interpreting the Exceptionality of Botswana. *Journal of Modern African Studies* 30.1:69–95.

Goodall, H.

1996 *Invasion to Embassy: Land in Aboriginal Politics in New South Wales, 1770–1972.* St. Leonards, New South Wales: George Allen and Unwin.

Goode, E.

1969 *Marijuana.* New York: Aldine.

Goodman, J.

1993 *Tobacco in History: The Cultures of Dependence.* London: Routledge.

1995 Excitantia: Or, How Enlightenment Europe Took to Soft Drugs. In *Consuming Habits: Drugs in History and Anthropology*. Edited by J. Goodman, P. Lovejoy, and A. Sherratt. 126–47. London: Routledge.

Goodman, J., P. Lovejoy, and A. Sherratt, eds.

1995 *Consuming Habits: Drugs in History and Anthropology.* London: Routledge.

Gordon, D.

1996 From Rituals of Rapture to Dependence: The Political Economy of Khoikoi Narcotic Consumption, c. 1487–1870. *South African Historical Journal* 35:62–88.

Gordon, R. J.

1998 Vagrancy, Law and "Shadow Knowledge." In *Namibia under South African Rule*. Edited by P. Hays, J. Silvester, M. Wallace, and W. Hartmann. 51–77. Athens: Ohio University Press.

Graburn, N., and B. Strong

1973 *Circumpolar Peoples.* Pacific Palisades, Calif.: Goodyear Publishing Company.

Graham, H. N.

1984 Tea: The Plant and Its Manufacture; Chemistry and Consumption of the Beverage. In *The Methylxanthine Beverages and Foods*. Edited by G. A. Spiller. 29–74. New York: Alan R. Liss.

Gundermann, H., and H. Gonzalez

1989 *La cultura Aymara*. Santiago: Museo Chileno de Arte Precolombino and the Ministry of Education.

Gunson, N., ed.

1974 *Australian Reminiscences and Papers of L. E. Threlkeld: Missionary to the Aborigines 1824–1859*. Vols. 1 and 2. Australian Aboriginal Studies no. 40. Canberra: Australian Institute of Aboriginal Studies Press.

Gutman, H.

1977 Work, Culture and Society in Industrializing America, 1815–1919. In *Work, Culture and Society in Industrializing America*. Edited by H. Gutman. 1–26. New York: Random House.

Guy, K. M.

2002 Rituals of Pleasure in the Land of Treasures: Wine Consumption and the Making of French Identity in the Late Nineteenth Century. In *Food Nations*. Edited by W. Belasco and P. Scranton. 34–47. New York: Routledge.

Haagen, C.

1994 *Bush Toys: Aboriginal Children at Play*. Canberra: Australian Institute of Aboriginal Studies Press.

Haddon, A. C.

1901 *Head Hunters Black, White, and Brown*. London: Methuen.

1946 Smoking and Tobacco Pipes in New Guinea. Philosophical Transactions, Series B, 232. London: Royal Society of London.

Hagelberg, G. B.

1985 Sugar in the Caribbean: Turning Sunshine into Money. In *Caribbean Contours*. Edited by S. W. Mintz and S. Price. 85–126. Baltimore, Md.: Johns Hopkins University Press.

Haggblade, S.

1983 *Sorghum Beer: The Impact of Factory Brews on a Cottage Industry*. Gaborone, Botswana: Ministry of Commerce.

1984 The Shebeen Queen or Sorghum Beer in Botswana. Ph.D. diss., Department of Economics, Michigan State University, East Lansing.

Hair, P. E. H., and R. Law

1998 The English in Western Africa to 1700. In *The Oxford History of the British Empire*. Vol. 1, *The Origins of Empire: British Overseas Enterprise to the Close of the Seventeenth Century*. Edited by W. R. Louis. 241–63. Oxford: Oxford University Press.

Hallet, R., ed.

1965 *The Niger Journals of Richard and John Lander.* 1832. Reprint, New York: N.p.

Hamilton, A.

1972 Blacks and Whites: The Relationships of Change. *Arena* 30:34–48.

1987 Coming and Going: Aboriginal Mobility in North-West South Australia 1970–71. *Records of the South Australian Museum* 20:47–57.

Hamper, B.

1992 *Rivethead: Tales from the Assembly Line.* New York: Warner Books.

Harler, C. R.

1964 *The Culture and Marketing of Tea.* London: Oxford University Press.

Harms, R.

2002 *The Diligent: A Voyage through the Worlds of the Slave Trade.* New York: Basic Books.

Hatley, T.

1993 *The Dividing Paths: Cherokees and South Carolinians through the Era of Revolution.* New York: Oxford University Press.

Hattox, R. S.

1985 *Coffee and Coffeehouses.* Seattle: University of Washington Press.

Hays, T. E.

1991 "No Tobacco, No Hallelujah": Missions and the Early History of Tobacco in Eastern Papua. *Pacific Studies* 14.4:91–112.

Haythornthwaite, F.

1956 *All the Way to Abenab.* London: Faber and Faber.

Heath, D. B.

1974 *Contemporary Cultures and Societies of Latin America.* 2nd ed. New York: Random House.

Hemming, J.

1970 *The Conquest of the Incas.* Miami: Harcourt Brace.

Hening, W., ed.

1810–23 *The Statutes at Large: Being a Collection of All the Laws of Virginia.* 13 vols. New York, Richmond, and Philadelphia: Printed by and for Samuel Pleasants Jr., Printer to the Commonwealth.

Hernandez Castillo, R. A., and R. Nigh

1998 Global Processes and Local Identity among Mayan Coffee Growers in Chiapas, Mexico. *American Anthropologist* 100:136–47.

Hernsheim, E.

1983 *South Sea Merchant.* Translated by P. Sack and D. Clark. Boroko: Institute of Papua New Guinea Studies.

Hirsch, E.

1995 Efficacy and Concentration: Analogies in Betel Use among the Fuyuge (Papua

New Guinea). In *Consuming Habits: Drugs in History and Anthropology*. Edited by J. Goodman, P. Lovejoy, and A. Sherratt. 88–102. London: Routledge.

Hirsh, K.

1984 Central Nervous System Pharmacology of the Dietary Methylxanthines. In *The Methylxanthine Beverages and Foods*. Edited by G. A. Spiller. 235–302. New York: Alan R. Liss.

Hobsbawm, E., and T. Ranger, eds.

1986 *The Invention of Tradition*. New York: Cambridge University Press.

Hopkins, A. G.

1973 *An Economic History of West Africa*. London: Longmans.

Horne, G. A., and G. Aiston

1924 *Savage Life in Central Australia*. London: Macmillan.

HRA (Historical Records of Australia)

1925 Series 1 (26 vols., 1788–1848): vol. 25 (1846) and vol. 26 (1847). Sydney: Commonwealth Parliament.

Hudson, C. M., ed.

1979 *Black Drink*. Athens: University of Georgia Press.

Hughes, H. I.

1978 Good Money and Bad: Inflation and Devaluation in the Colonial Process. *Mankind* 11:308–18.

Hugh-Jones, S.

1995 Coca, Beer, Cigars and *Yagé*: Meals and Anti-Meals in an Amerindian Community. In *Consuming Habits: Drugs in History and Anthropology*. Edited by J. Goodman, P. Lovejoy, and A. Sherratt. 47–66. London: Routledge.

Hunt, A.

1996 *Governance of the Consuming Passions*. New York: St. Martin's Press.

Hutchinson, H. W.

1957 *Village and Plantation Life in Northeastern Brazil*. Seattle: University of Washington Press.

Indian Hemp Drugs Commission of Great Britain

1969 *Marijuana Report, 1893–1894*. Silver Springs, Md.: Thomas Jefferson Press.

Iversen, L.

1996 Smoking…Harmful to the Brain. *Nature* 382:206–7.

Jacob, H.

1935 *Coffee: The Epic of a Commodity*. New York: Viking.

Jankowiak, W.

1993 *Sex, Death, and Hierarchy in a Chinese City*. New York: Columbia University Press.

Jankowiak, W., and D. Bradburd

1996 Using Drug Foods to Capture and Enhance Labor Performance: A Cross-Cultural Perspective. *Current Anthropology* 37.4:717–20.

N.d.   Chemical Stimulants, Conquest, and the Management of Labor: A Cross-Cultural Perspective. Ms.

Jayawardena, C.

1963   *Conflict and Solidarity in a Guianese Plantation.* London: Athlone Press.

Jenness, D., and A. Ballantyne

1920   *The Northern D'Entrecasteaux.* Oxford: Clarendon Press.

Jensen, M., ed.

1955   *English Historical Documents IX.* London: Eyre and Spottiswoode.

Jessop, J., ed.

1985   *Flora of Central Australia.* Australian Systematic Botany Society. Sydney: Reed Books.

Johnson, J.

1878   Abeokuta Past and Present. *Church Missionary Society Intelligencer* 3 (February):543.

Johnston, T. H., and J. B. Cleland

1933–34 The History of the Aboriginal Narcotic *Pituri. Oceania* 4:201–68.

Karp, I.

1980   Beer Drinking and Social Experience in an African Society: An Essay in Formal Sociology. In *Explorations in African Systems of Thought.* Edited by I. Karp and C. S. Bird. 83–119. Bloomington: Indiana University Press.

Kawabata, Y.

1959   *Thousand Cranes.* Translated by E. Seidensticker. New York: Alfred A. Knopf.

Kea, R.

1995   Plantations and Labour in the South-East Gold Coast from the Late Eighteenth to the Mid Nineteenth Century. In *From Slave Trade to "Legitimate" Commerce: The Commercial Transition in Nineteenth-Century West Africa.* Edited by R. Law. 119–43. Cambridge: Cambridge University Press.

Kelly, E.

1994   Grounds for Criticism: Coffee, Passion, and the Politics of Discourse in Feminist Space. Paper delivered at the Food and Culture Conference, Portsmouth, N.H.

Kendall, A.

1973   *Everyday Life of the Incas.* London: B. T. Batsford.

Kerimi, N.

2000   Opium Use in Turkmenistan: A Historical Perspective. *Addiction* 95.9:1391–1433.

Khama, S.

1888   Letter to Sir Sidney Shippard, Concerning Relations with the Matabele. Enclosure 2 in Despatch no. 70 G. 30.3.88. Document HC 123. Botswana National Archives.

Kidd, R.

1997 *The Way We Civilize: Aboriginal Affairs—The Untold Story.* St. Lucia: University of Queensland Press.

Kinnock, G.

1989 *Namibia: Birth of a Nation.* London: Quartet.

Kirk, J.

1985 The Debatable Effects of Caffeine. Ms.

Klass, M.

1961 *East Indians in Trinidad.* Prospect Heights, Ill.: Waveland.

1991 *Singing with Sai Baba: The Politics of Revitalization in Trinidad.* Boulder, Colo.: Westview.

Klein, H.

1996 Coca Production in the Bolivian Yungas. In *Drugs in the Western Hemisphere: An Odyssey of Cultures in Conflict.* Edited by W. O. Walker III. 22–34. Jaguar Books on Latin America no. 12. Wilmington: Scholarly Resources.

Knauft, B.

1987 Managing Sex and Anger: Tobacco and Kava Use among the Gebusi of Papua New Guinea. In *Drugs in Western Pacific Societies: Relations of Substance.* Edited by L. Lindstrom. 73–98. ASAO Monograph no. 11. Lanham, Md.: University Press of America.

Kondo, D.

1985 The Way of Tea: A Symbolic Analysis. *Man,* n.s. 20:287–306.

1990 *Crafting Selves: Power, Gender, and Discourses of Identity in a Japanese Workplace.* Chicago: University of Chicago Press.

Kramer, R., and D. Kondo

1986 Correspondence: The Way of Tea. *Man,* n.s. 21:538–41.

Krech, S., III, ed.

1981 *Indians, Animals, and the Fur Trade: A Critique of Keepers of the Game.* Athens: University of Georgia Press.

Kube, S.

1985 Salve Gambrinus! Der Kampf wider den Durst und den tierischen Ernst. In *Vom Schutzgebiet bis Namibia, 1884–1984.* Edited by R. J. Gordon. 343–46. Windhoek: Interessen-Gemeinschaft.

Kunitz, S. J., and J. E. Levy

1994 *Drinking Careers: A Twenty-Five-Year Study of Three Navajo Populations.* New Haven, Conn.: Yale University Press.

Langton, M.

1993 Rum, Seduction and Death: Aboriginality and Alcohol. *Oceania* 63:195–206.

Lanning, E. P.

1967 *Peru before the Incas.* Englewood Cliffs, N.J.: Prentice-Hall.

Lappé, F. M., and J. Collins
1977 *Food First.* Boston: Houghton Mifflin.

Latham, A. J. H.
1973 *Old Calabar, 1600–1891: The Impact of the International Economy upon a Traditional Society.* Oxford: Clarendon Press.

Laurence, K. O.
1994 *A Question of Labour: Indentured Immigration into Trinidad and British Guiana, 1875–1917.* New York: St. Martin's Press.

Law, R.
1990 *The Slave Coast of West Africa 1550–1750: The Impact of the Atlantic Slave Trade on an African Society.* Oxford: Clarendon Press.

Lawson, J.
1967 *A New Voyage to Carolina.* Ed. Hugh T. Lefler. Chapel Hill: University of North Carolina Press.

Leahy, M.
1936 The Central Highlands of New Guinea. *Geographical Journal* 7:229–62.

Lemert, E.
1979 Forms and Pathology of Drinking in Three Polynesian Societies. In *Beliefs, Behavior, and Alcoholic Beverages: A Cross Cultural Survey.* Edited by M. Marshall. 192–207. Ann Arbor: University of Michigan Press.

Leóns, M. B., and H. Sanabria
1997 Coca and Cocaine in Bolivia: Reality and Policy Illusion. In *Coca, Cocaine and the Bolivian Reality.* Edited by M. B. Leóns and H. Sanabria. 1–46. Albany: State University of New York Press.

Lepowsky, M.
1982 A Comparison of Alcohol and Betel Nut Use on Varnatinai (Sudest Island). In *Through a Glass Darkly: Beer and Modernization in Papua New Guinea.* Edited by M. Marshall. 325–42. Boroko, Papua New Guinea: Institute of Applied Social and Economic Anthropology.

Lindstrom, L.
1982 *Grog Blong Yumi:* Alcohol and Kavaon Tanna, Vanuatu. In *Through a Glass Darkly: Beer and Modernization in Papua New Guinea.* Edited by M. Marshall. 421–32. Boroko, Papua New Guinea: Institute of Applied Social and Economic Anthropology.

Long, J.
1922 *John Long's Voyages and Travels in the Years 1768–1788.* Ed. M. M. Quaife. Chicago: R. R. Donnelly and Sons.

Long, J. P. M.
1992 *The Go-Betweens: Patrol Officers in Aboriginal Affairs Administration in the Northern Territory 1936–74.* Darwin: North Australia Research Unit.

Look Lai, W.

1993 *Indentured Labor, Caribbean Sugar: Chinese and Indian Migrants to the British West Indies, 1838–1918.* Baltimore, Md.: Johns Hopkins University Press.

Love, J. R. B.

1915 *The Aborigines: Their Present Condition as Seen in Northern South Australia, the Northern Territory, North-West Australia and Western Queensland.* Melbourne: Arbuckle, Waddell and Fawckner.

Lovejoy, P.

1995 Kola Nuts: The "Coffee" of the Central Sudan. In *Consuming Habits: Drugs in History and Anthropology.* Edited by J. Goodman, P. Lovejoy, and A. Sherratt. 103–25. London: Routledge.

Low, T.

1990 *Bush Medicine: A Pharmacopoeia of Natural Remedies.* Melbourne: Angus and Robertson.

Lucier, R.

1988 *The International Political Economy of Coffee: From Juan Valdez to Yank's Diner.* New York: Praeger.

Lumholtz, C.

1980 *Among Cannibals, an Account of Four Years' Travels in Australia and of Camp Life with the Aborigines of Queensland.* 1889. Reprint, London and Canberra: John Murray and Australian National University Press.

Lyon, P., and M. Parsons

1989 *We Are Staying: The Alyawarre Struggle for Land at Lake Nash.* Alice Springs: Institute of Aboriginal Development Press.

Lyons, A. P.

1916 Daru Patrol Reports for 1916–17. Report of Patrol and Traverse of the Aramira [sic] River W.D. Ts. [Torres Straits]. Australian Archives, Canberra, Australia.

MacAndrew, C., and R. Edgerton

1969 *Drunken Comportment: A Social Explanation.* Chicago: Aldine.

MacDougall, W.

1956 *Report on Patrol of Central Reserves April–July 1956.* South Australia: Long Range Weapons Establishment.

Mac Gregor, F., ed.

1993 *Coca and Cocaine: An Andean Perspective.* Translated by J. Cavanagh and R. Underhay. Westport, Conn.: Greenwood Press.

MacGregor, W.

1892 *Despatch Reporting Administrative Visits to Tagula and Murua, &c. British New Guinea: Annual Report from 1st July, 1890, to 30th June, 1891.* App. 1:31–32. Brisbane: Government Printer.

1893 *Despatch Reporting Visits to the D'Entrecasteaux and Trobriand Groups: Annual Report on British New Guinea from 1st July, 1891, to 30th June, 1892.* App. A:1–7. Brisbane: Government Printer.

1894 *Despatch Reporting Visit to Various Islands at the Eastern End of the Possession: Annual Report on British New Guinea from 1st July, 1892, to 30th June, 1893.* App. B:3–7. Brisbane: Government Printer.

Macknight, C. C.

1976 *The Voyage to Maregé: Macassan Trepangers in Northern Australia.* Melbourne: Melbourne University Press.

MacPherson, J.

1921 The Use of Narcotics and Intoxicants by the Native Tribes of Australia, New Guinea, and the Pacific. *Sydney University Medical Journal* (May):108–22.

Macquarie, L.

1821 Macquarie's Diary. Ms. A772. State Library, New South Wales.

Mahabir, N. K.

1985 *The Still Cry: Personal Accounts of East Indians in Trinidad and Tobago during Indentureship (1845–1917).* Tacarigua, Trinidad: Calaloux Publications.

1994 Marijuana in the Caribbean. *Caribbean Affairs* 7.4:28–40.

Maharaj, O.

N.d. *The Indentures.* Port-of-Spain, Trinidad: National Freedom Organisation.

Mamozai, M.

1989 *Schwarze Frau, weisse Herrn.* Hamburg: Rowolt.

Mancall, P.

1991 *Valley of Opportunity: Economic Culture along the Upper Susquehanna, 1700–1800.* Ithaca, N.Y.: Cornell University Press.

1995a *Deadly Medicine: Indians and Alcohol in Early America.* Ithaca, N.Y.: Cornell University Press.

1995b *Envisioning America: English Plans for the Colonization of North America, 1580–1640.* Boston and New York: St. Martin's Press.

Marett, R.

1969 *Peru.* New York: Praeger.

Margry, P., ed.

1876–86 *Découvertes et établissements des français dans l'ouest et dans le sud de l'Amérique Septentrionale (1614–1754).* 6 vols. Paris: Impr. D. Jouaust.

Marshall, M.

1976 A Review and Appraisal of Alcohol and *Kava* Studies in Oceania. In *Cross-Cultural Approaches to the Study of Alcohol.* Edited by M. Everett, J. Waddell, and D. Heath. 103–18. Paris: Mouton.

1979 *Weekend Warriors.* Palo Alto, Calif.: Mayfield.

1981 Tobacco. In *Historical Dictionary of Oceania.* Edited by R. D. Craig and F. P. King. 288–89. Westport, Conn.: Greenwood Press.

1990 *Silent Voices Speak.* Belmont: Wadsworth Publishing Company.

1991 The Second Fatal Impact: Cigarette Smoking, Chronic Disease, and the Epidemiological Transition in Oceania. *Social Science and Medicine* 33:1327–42.

Marshall, M., and L. Marshall

1979 Holy and Unholy Spirits: The Effects of Missionization on Alcohol Use in Eastern Micronesia. In *Beliefs, Behavior, and Alcoholic Beverages: A Cross Cultural Survey.* Edited by M. Marshall. 205–36. Ann Arbor: University of Michigan Press.

Martell, A.

1975 The Canadian Presbyterian Mission to Trinidad's East Indian Population 1868–1912. M.A. thesis, Department of History, Dalhousie University, Halifax, Nova Scotia.

Martin, C.

1978 *Keepers of the Game: Indians, Animals, and the Fur Trade.* Berkeley: University of California Press.

Martin, L.

1997 *Commerce and Economic Change in West Africa: The Palm Oil Trade in the Nineteenth Century.* Cambridge: Cambridge University Press.

Mathee, R.

1995 Exotic Substances: The Introduction and Global Spread of Tobacco, Coffee, Cocoa, Tea and Distilled Liquor, Sixteenth to Eighteenth Centuries. In *Drugs and Narcotics in History.* Edited by R. Porter and M. Teich. 24–51. Cambridge: Cambridge University Press.

May, P. A., and M. B. Smith

1988 Some Navajo Indian Opinions about Alcohol Abuse and Prohibition: A Survey and Recommendations for Policy. *Journal of Studies on Alcohol* 49:324–34.

McCarthy, F. D.

1957 *Australia's Aborigines: Their Life and Culture.* Melbourne: Colorgravure Publications, Herald and Weekly Times Ltd.

McElroy, A., and P. Townsend

1985 *Medical Anthropology in Ecological Perspective.* Boulder, Colo.: Westview Press.

McGee, H.

1984 *On Food and Cooking.* New York: Scribner's.

McGrath, A. M.

1987 *Born in the Cattle: Aborigines in the Cattle Country.* Sydney: George Allen and Unwin.

McLaren, J.

1973 *My Crowded Solitude.* South Melbourne: Sun Books.

McLeod, A.

1965 Diary of Archibald McLeod. In *Five Fur Traders of the Northwest*. Edited by C. M. Gates. St. Paul: Minnesota Historical Society.

McNeill, W. H.

1976 *Plagues and Peoples*. New York: Doubleday.

Merrell, J. H.

1989 *The Indians' New World: Catawbas and Their Neighbors from European Contact through the Era of Removal*. Chapel Hill: University of North Carolina Press.

Metcalf, G.

1987 A Microcosm of Why Africans Sold Slaves: Akan Consumption Patterns in the 1770s. *Journal of African History* 28:377–94.

Miller, J.

1985 *Koori: A Will to Win*. Sydney: Angus and Robertson.

Miller, J. C.

1988 *Way of Death: Merchant Capitalism and the Angolan Slave Trade 1730–1830*. Madison: University of Wisconsin Press.

Mintz, S.

1979 Time, Sugar and Sweetness. *Marxist Perspectives* 2:56–73.

1985 *Sweetness and Power: The Place of Sugar in Modern History*. New York: Viking.

1987 Author's Rejoinder. *Food and Foodways* 2:171–97.

1993 The Changing Roles of Food in the Study of Consumption. In *Consumption and the World of Goods*. Edited by J. Brewer and R. Porter. 261–73. London: Routledge.

1996 *Tasting Food, Tasting Freedom: Excursions into Eating, Culture, and the Past*. Boston: Beacon Press.

1998 Quenching Homologous Thirsts: The Curious History of Tea and Coca-Cola. Lecture delivered at the University of California, Riverside, 22 April.

Misra, S. R.

1986 *Tea Industry in India*. New Delhi: Ashish Publishing House.

Mitchell, J. T., and H. Flanders, eds.

1896–1908 *Statutes at Large of Pennsylvania from 1682 to 1801*. Harrisburg: Clarence M. Busch, State Printer of Pennsylvania.

Molamu, L.

1989 Alcohol Use in Botswana: An Historical Overview. *Contemporary Drug Problems: An Interdisciplinary Quarterly* 16.1:3–42.

Moodie, D.

1992 Alcohol and Resistance on the South African Gold Mines, 1903–1962. In *Liquor and Labor in Southern Africa*. Edited by J. Crush and C. Ambler. 162–86. Athens: Ohio University Press.

Moogk, P.

1994 Manon's Fellow Exiles: Emigration from France to North America before 1763. In *Europeans on the Move: Studies on European Migration, 1500–1800.* Edited by N. Canny. 236–60. Oxford: Oxford University Press.

Moore, D. R.

1979 *Islanders and Aborigines at Cape York: An Ethnographic Reconstruction Based on the 1848–1850 "Rattlesnake" Journals of O. W. Brierly and Information He Obtained from Barbara Thompson.* Canberra: Australian Institute of Aboriginal Studies Press.

Morales, E.

1989 *Cocaine: White Gold Rush in Peru.* Tucson: University of Arizona Press.

Morgan, E. S.

1975 *American Slavery, American Freedom: The Ordeal of Colonial Virginia.* New York: Norton.

Mortimer, W. G.

1996 The History of Coca. In *Drugs in the Western Hemisphere: An Odyssey of Cultures in Conflict.* Edited by W. O. Walker III. 2–8. Jaguar Books on Latin America no. 12. Wilmington: Scholarly Resources.

Muir, T.

1969–71 Tobacco in Early Australia. *Australian Tobacco Growers' Bulletin* 6:15–19. Sydney: Grolier Society of Australia.

Muñoz, L. M., B. Lonnerdal, C. L. Keen, and K. G. Dewey

1988 Coffee Consumption as a Factor in Iron Deficiency Anemia among Pregnant Women and Their Infants in Costa Rica. *American Journal of Clinical Nutrition* 48:645–51.

Munro, G. B.

1921 The Brandy Parliament of 1678. *Canadian Historical Review* 2:174–79.

Murdock, G. P., and D. White

1969 Standard Cross Cultural Sample. *Ethnology* 8:329–69.

Murra, J.

1986 Notes on Pre-Columbian Cultivation of Coca Leaf. In *Coca and Cocaine: Effects on People and Policy in Latin America.* Edited by D. Pacini and C. Franquemont. 49–52. Cultural Survival Report no. 23. Cambridge: Cultural Survival.

Nash, J.

1993 *We Eat the Mines and the Mines Eat Us: Dependency and Exploitation in Bolivian Tin Mines.* New York: Columbia University Press.

National Archives of Namibia

1915 GN 51/1915. South West Africa Administration 2/14/2.

1919 Native Affairs. Memoranda and Reports. South West Africa Administration 2/134/2.

Bibliography

1925 Magistrate to NAC, 14 August. A466/25.

1950 Commission of Enquiry into the Sale of Liquor and Desecration of Sundays. South West Africa Administration 283/2.

National Institute on Alcohol Abuse

1996 *Alcohol Alert* no. 33.

1998 *Alcohol Alert* no. 39.

National Institute on Drug Abuse

1998 National Institute on Drug Abuse Research Report Series: Nicotine Addiction. www.nida.nih.gov/research.

Navarette-Pellicer, S.

1988 *La flor del aguardiente.* Mexico City: Instituto Nacional de Antropología Historia.

Neehall, R. G.

1958 Presbyterianism in Trinidad. S.T.M. thesis, Department of Ministry, Union Theological Seminary.

Newman, P.

1964 *British Guiana: Problems of Cohesion in an Immigrant Society.* London: Oxford University Press.

Niehoff, A., and J. Niehoff

1960 *East Indians in the West Indies.* Milwaukee: Milwaukee Public Museum.

North-Coombes, M. D.

1991 Indentured Labour in the Sugar Industries of Natal and Mauritius. In *Essays on Indentured Indians in Natal.* Edited by S. Bhana. 12–88. Leeds, England: Peepal Tree Press.

Norton, T.

1974 *The Fur Trade in Colonial New York, 1686–1776.* Madison: University of Wisconsin Press.

O'Callaghan, E. B., and B. Fernow, eds.

1856–87 *Documents Relating to the Colonial History of the State of New York.* 15 vols. Albany: Weed, Parsons and Company, Printers.

Okakura, K.

1964 *The Book of Tea.* New York: Dover.

Oldenburg, R.

1989 *The Great Good Place.* New York: Paragon House.

Oldevig, M.

1948 *The Sunny Land.* Cape Town: Howard Timmins.

Olekalns, N., and P. Bardsley

1996 National Addiction to Caffeine: An Analysis of Coffee Consumption. *Journal of Political Economy* 104:1100–1104.

Oliver, D.

1989 *The Pacific Islands.* 3rd ed. Honolulu: University of Hawaii Press.

Orwell, G.

1961 *Down and Out in Paris and London.* 1933. Reprint, San Diego: Harcourt Brace.

Padden, R. C.

1967 *The Hummingbird and the Hawk: Conquest and Sovereignty in the Valley of Mexico, 1503–1541.* Columbus: Ohio State University Press.

Paige, J. M.

1997 *Coffee and Power: Revolution and the Rise of Democracy in Central America.* Cambridge, Mass.: Harvard University Press.

Pan, L.

1975 *Alcohol in Colonial Africa.* Helsinki: Finnish Foundation for Alcohol Studies.

Paper, J.

1988 *Offering Smoke: The Sacred Pipe and Native American Religion.* Edmonton: University of Alberta Press.

Peile, A. R.

1997 *Body and Soul: An Aboriginal View.* Edited by P. Bindon. Western Australia: Hesperian Press.

Pendergrast, M.

1993 *For God, Country and Coca Cola.* New York: Touchstone.

1999 *Uncommon Grounds: The History of Coffee and How It Transformed Our World.* New York: Basic Books.

Penfold, S.

2002 "Eddie Shack Was No Tim Horton": Donuts and the Folklore of Mass Culture in Canada. In *Food Nations.* Edited by W. Belasco and P. Scranton. 48–66. New York: Routledge.

Pennybacker, M.

1997 Habitat-Saving Habit. *Sierra* (March–April):18–19.

Perez Arbelaez, E.

1956 *Plantas útiles de Colombia.* Madrid: Rivadeneyra; Bogotá: Camacho Roldan.

Perry, C.

1993 Recycled Coffee. *Los Angeles Times,* 14 October:food sec., 2.

Peters, P.

1994 *Dividing the Commons: Politics, Policy and Culture in Botswana.* Charlottesville: University Press of Virginia.

Peterson, N.

1979 Aboriginal Uses of Australian Solanaceae. In *The Biology and Taxonomy of the Solanaceae.* Edited by J. G. Hawkes, R. N. Lester, and A. D. Skelding. 171–88. Linnaean Society Symposium Series no. 7. London: Academic Press.

1993 Demand Sharing: Reciprocity and the Pressure for Generosity among Foragers. *American Anthropologist* 95.4:860–74.

1997 Demand Sharing: Sociobiology and the Pressure for Generosity among For-
agers. In *Scholar and Sceptic: Australian Aboriginal Studies in Honour of L.
R. Hiatt*. Edited by F. Merlan, J. Morton, and A. Rumsey. 171–90. Canberra:
Australian Institute of Aboriginal Studies Press.

1998 Welfare Colonialism and Citizenship: Politics, Economics and Agency. In
*Citizenship and Indigenous Australians: Changing Conceptions and Possibil-
ities*. Edited by N. Peterson and W. Saunders. 101–17. Melbourne: University
of Cambridge Press.

Phillips, P.

1961 *The Fur Trade*. Norman: University of Oklahoma Press.

Plomley, N. J. B., ed.

1966 *Friendly Mission: The Tasmanian Journals and Papers of George Augustus
Robinson 1829–1834*. Hobart: Tasmanian Historical Research Association.

Plowman, T.

1984 The Origin, Evolution and Diffusion of Coca, *Erythroxylum* Spp., in South and
Central America. In *Pre-Columbian Plant Migration*. Edited by D. Stone.
146–56. Papers of the Peabody Museum of Archaeology and Ethnology vol.
76. Cambridge, Mass.: Harvard University Press.

1986 Coca Chewing and the Botanical Origins of Coca (*Erythroxylum* Spp.) in South
America. In *Coca and Cocaine: Effects on People and Policy in Latin America*. Edited by D. Pacini and C. Franquemont. 5–34. Cultural Survival Report
no. 23. Cambridge: Cultural Survival.

Poignant, R.

1996 *Encounter at Nagalarramba*. Canberra: National Library of Australia.

Ponteieri, F., G. Tanda, F. Orzi, and G. Di Chiara

1996 Effects of Nicotine on the Nucleus Accumbens and Similarity to Those of
Addictive Drugs. *Nature* 382:255–57.

Pool, G.

1991 *Samuel Maherero*. Windhoek: Gamsberg-Macmillan.

**Porkka-Heiskanen, T., R. E. Strecker, M. Thakkar, A. A. Bjorkum,
R. W. Greene, and R. W. McCarley**

1997 Adenosine: A Mediator of the Sleep-Inducing Effects of Prolonged Wakefulness. *Science* 276:1265–68.

Poster, M., ed.

1988 *Jean Baudrillard, Selected Writings*. Stanford, Calif.: Stanford University
Press.

Postma, J.

1990 *The Dutch in the Atlantic Slave Trade, 1600–1815*. Cambridge: Cambridge
University Press.

Pratt, A. E.

1906 *Two Years among New Guinea Cannibals: A Naturalist's Sojourn among the*

Aborigines of Unexplored New Guinea. Philadelphia: J. P. Lippincott.

Pratt, M. L.

1992 *Imperial Eyes: Travel Writing and Transculturation.* London: Routledge.

Presilla, M. E.

2001 *The New Taste of Chocolate.* Berkeley: Ten Speed Press.

Price, J.

1995 Tobacco Use and Tobacco Taxation: A Battle of Interests in Early Modern Europe. In *Consuming Habits: Drugs in History and Anthropology.* Edited by J. Goodman, P. Lovejoy, and A. Sherratt. 165–85. London: Routledge.

Raloff, J.

1996 New Signs of Nicotine's Addictiveness. *Science News* 150:38.

Ratner, M., ed.

1993 *Crack Pipe as Pimp: An Ethnographic Investigation of Sex for Crack Exchanges.* New York: Lexington Books.

Raymond, L. C.

1989 *Influence of African Culture upon South America.* Chicago: M. D. Enterprises.

Read, P., and J. Read

1991 *Long Time, Olden Time: Aboriginal Accounts of Northern Territory History.* Alice Springs: Institute of Aboriginal Development Press.

Read, P., and J. Japaljarri

1978 The Price of Tobacco: The Journey of the Warlmala to Wave Hill, 1928. *Aboriginal History* 2:140–49.

Redlich, E.

1874 Notes on the Western Islands of the Pacific Ocean and New Guinea. *Journal of the Royal Geographical Society of London* 44:30–37.

Reece, R. H. W.

1974 *Aborigines and Colonists: Aboriginal and Colonial Society in New South Wales in the 1830s and 1840s.* Sydney: Sydney University Press.

Reed, R. K.

1995 *Prophets of Agroforestry.* Austin: University of Texas Press.

1996 *Forest Dwellers, Forest Protectors.* New York: Allyn and Bacon.

Renard, M. C.

1993 *La comercialización internacional del café.* Mexico City: Universidad Autónoma Chapingo.

Reynolds, H.

1981 *The Other Side of the Frontier.* Townsville: History Department of James Cook University.

Richards, A. I.

1939 *Land, Labor and Diet in Northern Rhodesia: An Economic Study of the Bemba Tribe.* Oxford: Oxford University Press.

Richards, T.

1990 *The Commodity Culture of Victorian England.* Stanford, Calif.: Stanford University Press.

Richter, D.

1992 *The Ordeal of the Longhouse: The Peoples of the Iroquois League in the Era of European Colonization.* Chapel Hill: University of North Carolina Press.

Riesenfeld, A.

1951 Tobacco in New Guinea and the Other Areas of Melanesia. *Journal of the Royal Anthropological Institute* 81:69–102.

Roberts, F.

1989 The Finnish Coffee Ceremony and Notions of Self. *Arctic Anthropology* 26:20–33.

Roberts, J.

1981 Drink and Industrial Work Discipline in 19th Century Germany. *Journal of Social History* 15.1:25–38.

Rodney, W.

1970 *A History of the Upper Guinea Coast, 1545–1800.* Oxford: Clarendon Press.

Rogozinski, J.

1992 *A Brief History of the Caribbean.* New York: Facts-on-File.

Rolls, E.

1993 *Sojourners: The Epic Story of China's Centuries-Old Relationship with Australia.* St. Lucia: University of Queensland Press.

Rorabaugh, W. J.

1979 *The Alcoholic Republic: An American Tradition.* London: Oxford University Press.

Roseberry, W.

1996 The Rise of Yuppie Coffees and the Reimagination of Class in the United States. *American Anthropologist* 98:762–75.

Roseberry, W., L. Gudmundson, and M. S. Kutschbach

1995 *Coffee, Society and Power in Latin America.* Baltimore, Md.: Johns Hopkins University Press.

Roth, W. E.

1904 Notes of Savage Life in the Early Days of West Australian Settlement. *Proceedings of the Royal Society of Queensland* 17:45–69.

1984 *Ethnological Studies among the North-West-Central Queensland Aborigines.* Vol. 1 of *The Queensland Aborigines.* 1897. Reprint, Victoria Park: Hesperian Press.

Roux, C. C. F. M. le

1948 *De bergpapoea's van Nieuw-Guinea en hun woongebied.* Vol. 1. Leiden: E. J. Brill.

Rowley, C. D.

1978 *A Matter of Justice.* Canberra: Australian National University Press.

Rowse, T.

1998 *White Flour, White Power: From Rations to Citizenship in Central Australia.* Cambridge: Cambridge University Press.

Rubel, P. G., and A. Rosman

1991 From Ceremonial Exchange to Capitalist Exchange: How the New Irelanders Coped with the Establishment of Trading Stations. In *Man and a Half: Essays in Pacific Anthropology and Ethnobiology in Honour of Ralph Bulmer.* Edited by A. Pawley. 336–43. Memoir no. 48. Auckland: Polynesian Society.

Rubin, V., and L. Comitas

1976 *Ganja in Jamaica: The Effects of Marijuana Use.* Garden City, N.Y.: Anchor Books.

Rudgley, R.

1993 *The Alchemy of Culture: Intoxicants in Society.* London: British Museum Press.

Rumbarger, J.

1989 *Profits, Power and Prohibition: Alcohol Reform and the Industrializing of America 1800–1930.* Albany: State University of New York Press.

Rush, J.

1990 *Opium to Java.* Ithaca, N.Y.: Cornell University Press.

Ryan, P.

1959 *Fear Drive My Feet.* Sydney: Angus and Robertson.

Sahagún, B. de

1963 *Florentine Codex.* Book 11, *Earthly Things.* Translated by C. Dibble and A. Anderson. Santa Fe, N.M.: School of American Research and University of Utah.

Sahlins, M.

1988 Cosmologies of Capitalism: The Trans-Pacific Sector of "The World System." *Proceedings of the British Academy* 74:1–51.

Salisbury, N.

1982 *Manitou and Providence: Indians, Europeans, and the Making of New England, 1500–1643.* New York: Oxford University Press.

Salomon, F., and G. Urioste

1991 *The Huarochirí Manuscript: A Testament of Ancient and Colonial Andean Religion.* Austin: University of Texas Press.

Samaroo, B.

1982 Missionary Methods and Local Responses: The Canadian Presbyterians and the East Indians in the Caribbean. In *East Indians in the Caribbean.* Edited by B. Brereton and W. Dookeran. 93–115. Millwood, N.Y.: Kraus International Publications.

Sanabria, H.

1993 *The Coca Boom and Rural Social Change in Bolivia.* Ann Arbor: University of Michigan Press.

Sauer, J.

1993 *Historical Geography of Crop Plants: A Select Roster.* Boca Raton, Fla.: Lewis Publishers.

Saunders, W. L., ed.

1885–90 *Colonial Records of North Carolina.* 10 vols. Raleigh.

Schafer, E.

1967 *The Vermilion Bird.* Berkeley: University of California Press.

Schapera, I.

1960 *A Handbook of Tswana Law and Custom.* London: Oxford University Press.

1966 *Married Life in an African Tribe.* Evanston, Ill.: Northwestern University Press.

1980 *A History of the BaKgatla-bagaKgafela.* Mochudi, Botswana: Phuthadikobo Museum.

Schapira, J., D. Schapira, and K. Schapira

1975 *The Book of Coffee and Tea.* New York: St. Martin's Press.

Schivelbusch, W.

1992 *Tastes of Paradise.* New York: Vintage Books.

Schultes, R. E.

1987 Coca and Other Psychoactive Plants: Magico-Religious Roles in Primitive Societies of the New World. In *Cocaine: Clinical and Biobehavioral Aspects.* Edited by S. Fisher, A. Raskin, and E. H. Uhlenhuth. 212–50. New York: Oxford University Press.

Scott, J.

1985 *Weapons of the Weak.* New Haven, Conn.: Yale University Press.

Scully, P.

1992 Liquor and Labor in the Western Cape, 1870–1900. In *Liquor and Labor in Southern Africa.* Edited by J. Crush and C. Ambler. 56–77. Athens: Ohio University Press.

Searcy, A.

1909 *In Australian Tropics.* London: Robertson.

Segal, B., and L. Duffy

1992 Ethanol Elimination among Different Racial Groups. *Alcohol* 9:213–17.

Select Committee of the Legislative Council on the Aborigines

1899 Minutes of Evidence and Appendices, South Australia no. 77.

Sen, S., XV

1979 *Tea Life, Tea Mind.* New York: Weatherhill.

Sewell, W. G.

1861 *The Ordeal of Free Labour in the British West Indies.* London: Cass.

Shalleck, J.

1972 *Tea.* New York: Viking.

Shao, Q.

2000 Tempest over Teapots: The Vilification of Teahouse Culture in Early Republican China. *Journal of Asian Studies* 57:1009–41.

Sherry, T. W.

2000 Shade Coffee: A Good Brew Even in Small Doses. *Auk* 117:563–68.

Shineberg, D.

1967 *They Came for Sandalwood: A Study of the Sandalwood Trade in the South-West Pacific 1830–1865.* Carlton: Melbourne University Press.

Shively, C. A., and Tarka, S. M., Jr.

1984 Methylxanthine Composition and Consumption Patterns of Cocoa and Chocolate Products. In *The Methylxanthine Beverages and Foods.* Edited by G. A. Spiller. 149–78. New York: Alan R. Liss.

Shivute, O.

1999 Joy Grips North. *Namibian,* 2 August:7.

Shostak, M.

1983 *Nisa: The Life and Words of a !Kung Woman.* New York: Vintage.

Shurtleff, N., ed.

1853–54 *Records of the Governor and Company of the Massachusetts Bay in New England.* 5 vols. Boston. Reprint, New York: AMS Press, 1968.

1857 *Records of the Colony of New Plymouth in New England: Judicial Acts, 1636–1692.* Boston. Reprint, New York: AMS Press, 1968.

Siiskonen, H.

1994 Namibia and the Heritage of Colonial Alcohol Policy. *Nordic Journal of African Studies* 3:78.

Silver, T.

1990 *A New Face on the Countryside: Indians, Colonists, and Slaves in South Atlantic Forests, 1500–1800.* New York: Cambridge University Press.

Singh, K.

1974 East Indians and the Larger Society. In *Calcutta to Caroni: The East Indians of Trinidad.* Edited by J. La Guerre. 39–68. London: Longmans.

Sitahal, H.

1967 The Mission of the Presbyterian Church in Trinidad among the Descendants of the East Indians. S.T.M. thesis, Department of Divinity, McGill University.

Smith, P. J.

1991 *Taxing Heaven's Storehouse.* Cambridge, Mass.: Harvard University Press.

Smith, S. D.

1996 Accounting for Taste: British Coffee Consumption in Historical Perspective. *Journal of Interdisciplinary History* 27:183–214.

Smith, W.

1995 From Coffeehouse to Parlor: The Consumption of Coffee, Tea and Sugar in North-Western Europe in the Seventeenth and Eighteenth Centuries. In *Consuming Habits: Drugs in History and Anthropology*. Edited by J. Goodman, P. Lovejoy, and A. Sherratt. 148–64. London: Routledge.

South Africa

1949 *Official Yearbook of the Union of South Africa*. Pretoria: Government Printer.

Southwest Africa

1923 *Report of the Administrator for South-West Africa for 1922*. Pretoria: Government Printer.

1927 *Report of the Administrator for South-West Africa for 1926*. Pretoria: Government Printer.

Spedding, A.

1997 The Coca Field as a Total Social Fact. In *Coca, Cocaine and the Bolivian Reality*. Edited by M. B. Leóns and H. Sanabria. 47–70. Albany: State University of New York Press.

Spence, J.

1975 Opium Smoking in Ch'ing China. In *Conflict and Control in Late Imperial China*. Edited by F. Wakeman and C. Grant. 143–73. Berkeley: University of California Press.

1990 *The Search for Modern China*. New York: Norton.

Spencer, W. B.

1901 Diaries, Charlotte Waters, 22 March–3 April. Mss., Australian Institute of Aboriginal and Torres Strait Islander Studies.

1928 *Wanderings in Wild Australia*. London: Macmillan.

Spencer, W. B., and F. J. Gillen

1904 *Northern Tribes of Central Australia*. London: Macmillan.

1912 *Across Australia*. London: Macmillan.

Spiller, G. A., ed.

1984 *The Methylxanthine Beverages and Foods*. New York: Alan R. Liss.

Spiller, M. A.

1984 The Coffee Plant and Its Processing. In *The Methylxanthine Beverages and Foods*. Edited by G. A. Spiller. 75–90. New York: Alan R. Liss.

Stanner, W. E. H.

1979 Durmugam: A Nangiomeri. In *White Man Got No Dreaming: Essays 1938–1973*. Canberra: Australian National University Press.

Starn, O., C. I. Degregori, and R. Kirk, eds.

1995 *The Peru Reader: History, Culture, Politics*. Durham, N.C.: Duke University Press.

Stevens, F.

1974 *Aborigines in the Northern Territory Cattle Industry*. Canberra: Australian National University Press.

Stinchcombe, A. L.

1995 *Sugar Island Slavery in the Age of Enlightenment: The Political Economy of the Caribbean World.* Princeton, N.J.: Princeton University Press.

Stöcker, H., ed.

1986 *German Imperialism in Africa.* London: Hurst.

Stone, A. C.

1911 The Aborigines of Lake Boga, Victoria. *Proceedings of the Royal Society of Victoria,* n.s. 23, pt. 2:433–68.

Stone, O. C.

1880 *A Few Months in New Guinea.* London: Sampson, Low, Marston, Searle and Rivington.

Suggs, D.

1996 Mosadi Tshwene: The Construction of Gender and the Consumption of Alcohol in Botswana. *American Ethnologist* 23.3:597–610.

1998 "These Young Chaps Think They Are Just Men, Too": Redistributing Masculinity in BaKgatla Bars. Paper presented at the International Congress of Anthropological and Ethnological Sciences, Williamsburg, Va., July 1998.

Sullivan, J.

1983 *Banggaiyerri: The Story of Jack Sullivan (as Told to Bruce Shaw).* Canberra: Australian Institute of Aboriginal Studies Press.

Swan, M.

1991 Indentured Indians: Accommodation and Resistance 1890–1913. In *Essays on Indentured Indians in Natal.* Edited by S. Bhana. 117–36. Leeds, England: Peepal Tree Press.

Synge, F. M.

1908 *Albert Maclaren, Pioneer Missionary in New Guinea: A Memoir.* Westminster, Scotland: Society for the Propagation of the Gospel in Foreign Parts.

Tapscott, C.

1990 The Cuca Shops of Owambo. *Namibian,* 19 June.

Taylor, J. L.

1933 Patrol Report. Purari River Headwaters Area. Ts. [Torres Straits]. Australian Archives, Canberra, Australia.

Taylor, W. B.

1972 *Landlord and Peasants in Colonial Oaxaca.* Stanford, Calif.: Stanford University Press.

1979 *Drinking, Homicide and Rebellion in Colonial Mexican Villages.* Stanford, Calif.: Stanford University Press.

Tench, W.

1996 *1788 Comprising a Narrative of the Expedition to Botany Bay and a Complete Account of the Settlement of Port Jackson. Watkin Tench.* Edited by T. Flannery Melbourne. 1789. Reprint, Melbourne: Text Publishing Company.

Thomas, H.

1997 *The Slave Trade.* New York: Simon and Schuster.

Thompson, E. P.

1967 Time, Work Discipline, and Industrial Capitalism. *Past and Present* 60:56–97.

Thompson, R. W.

1900 *My Trip in the "John Williams."* London: London Missionary Society.

Thomson, B. H.

1889 New Guinea: Narrative of an Exploring Expedition to the Louisiade and D'Entrecasteaux Islands. *Royal Geographical Society, Proceedings*, n.s. 11:525–42.

Thomson, D. F.

1939 Notes on the Smoking Pipes of North Queensland and the Northern Territory of Australia. *Man* 39:81–91.

1949 *Economic Structure and the Ceremonial Exchange Cycle in Arnhem Land.* Melbourne: Macmillan.

Thornton, R.

1987 *American Indian Holocaust and Survival: A Population History since 1492.* Norman: University of Oklahoma Press.

Thwaites, R. G., ed.

1896–1901 *The Jesuit Relations and Allied Documents: Travels and Explorations of the Jesuit Missionaries in New France 1610–1791.* 73 vols. Cleveland: Burrow Brothers.

Tinker, H.

1989 The Origins of Indian Migration to the West Indies. In *Indenture and Exile: The Indo-Caribbean Experience.* Edited by F. Birbalsingh. 63–72. Toronto: TSAR.

Trocki, C.

1999 *Opium, Empire and the Global Political Economy.* London: Routledge.

Trotman, D. V.

1986 *Crime in Trinidad: Conflict and Control in a Plantation Society 1838–1900.* Knoxville: University of Tennessee Press.

Trumbull, J. H., and C. J. Hoadly, eds.

1850–90 *Public Records of the Colony of Connecticut.* 15 vols. Hartford.

1894–96 *Colonial Laws of the State of New York from the Year 1664 to the Revolution.* 5 vols.

Turner, T.

1968 The Work of the Presbyterian Church of Canada and Its Successor, the United Church of Canada, in the Field of Secular Education in Trinidad, West Indies 1868–1953. M.A. thesis, Department of History, University of New Brunswick.

Turner, W. Y.

1878 The Ethnology of the Motu. *Journal of the Royal Anthropological Institute* 7:470–99.

Ukers, W.

1935 *All about Coffee.* New York: Tea and Coffee Trade Journal Company.

1936 *The Romance of Tea.* New York: Alfred A. Knopf.

UNCTAD

1993 *Commodity Yearbook.* New York: United Nations.

1995 *Commodity Yearbook.* New York: United Nations.

Uphof, J. C. Th.

1968 *Dictionary of Economic Plants.* Würzburg: J. Cramer.

Uribe, C. A.

1954 *Brown Gold.* New York: Random House.

van Onselen, C.

1976 Randlords and Rotgut 1886–1903. *History Workshop* (fall):33–89.

Verano, J. W., and D. H. Ubelaker, eds.

1992 *Disease and Demography in the Americas.* Washington, D.C.: Smithsonian Institution Press.

von Gernet, A.

1995 Nicotine Dreams: The Prehistory and Early History of Tobacco in Eastern North America. In *Consuming Habits: Drugs in History and Anthropology.* Edited by J. Goodman, P. Lovejoy, and A. Sherratt. 67–86. London: Routledge.

Wagner, G.

N.d. A Survey of the Windhoek District. Ms.

Waley, A.

1958 *The Opium War through Chinese Eyes.* Stanford, Calif.: Stanford University Press.

Walker, H. F. B.

1917 *A Doctor's Diary in Damaraland.* London: Edward Arnold.

Walker, R. B.

1980 Tobacco Smoking in Australia 1788–1914. *Historical Studies* (October):267–85.

1984 *Under Fire: A History of Tobacco Smoking in Australia.* Melbourne: Melbourne University Press.

Walther, D.

1998 Creating Germans Abroad: The Policies of Culture in Namibia, 1894–1939. Ph.D. diss., Department of History, University of Pennsylvania.

Washburne, C.

1961 *Primitive Drinking.* New York: College and University Press.

Bibliography

Watson, P. L.

1983 *This Precious Foliage: A Study of the Aboriginal Psycho-active Drug Pituri.* Oceania Monograph no. 26. Sydney: University of Sydney.

1998 *Frontier Lands and Pioneer Legends: How Pastoralists Gained Karuwali Land.* St. Leonards, New South Wales: George Allen and Unwin.

Watts, D.

1987 *The West Indies: Patterns of Development, Culture, and Environmental Change since 1492.* Cambridge: Cambridge University Press.

Weber, M.

1946 *From Max Weber.* Edited by H. Gerth and C. W. Mills. New York: Oxford University Press.

Webster, H. C.

1898 *Through New Guinea and the Cannibal Countries.* London: T. Fisher Unwin.

Weinberg, B., and B. Bealer

2001 *The World of Caffeine: The Science and Culture of the World's Most Popular Drug.* New York: Routledge.

Weinberg, C.

1975 *Fragments from a Desert Land.* Cape Town: Howard Timmins.

Weiser, C.

1737 Narrative of a Journey, Made in the Year 1737, by Conrad Weiser, Indian Agent and Provincial Interpreter, from Tulpehocken in the Province of Pennsylvania to Onondaga Translated by H. H. Muhlenberg. *Historical Society of Pennsylvania Collections* 1:117.

Weller, J. A.

1968 *The East Indian Indenture in Trinidad.* Rio Piedras: Institute of Caribbean Studies, University of Puerto Rico.

Westermeyer, J.

1982 *Poppies, Pipes and People: Opium and Its Use in Laos.* Berkeley: University of California Press.

Wetherell, D.

1998 First Contact Mission Narratives from Eastern Papua New Guinea. *Journal of Pacific History* 33:111–16.

White, R.

1983 *The Roots of Dependency.* Lincoln: University of Nebraska Press.

1991 *The Middle Ground: Indians, Empires and Republics in the Great Lakes Region 1650–1815.* London: Cambridge University Press.

Wilbert, J.

1987 *Tobacco and Shamanism in South America.* New Haven, Conn.: Yale University Press.

Wilk, R. R.

2002 Food and Nationalism: The Origin of "Belizean Food." In *Food Nations*. Edited by W. Belasco and P. Scranton. 67–89. New York: Routledge.

Wills, J. E.

1993 European Consumption and Asian Production in the Seventeenth and Eighteenth Centuries. In *Consumption and the World of Goods*. Edited by J. Brewer and R. Porter. 133-47. London: Routledge.

Wilson, G. C., and A. Kelly

1987 *Preliminary Analysis of Clay Tobacco Pipes from the First Government House Site*. Canberra: Heritage Research Services, ANUTech.

Wolf, E. R.

1971 Specific Aspects of Plantation Systems in the New World: Community Subcultures and Social Classes. In *Peoples and Cultures of the Caribbean*. Edited by M. M. Horowitz. 163–78. Garden City, N.Y.: Natural History Press.

1982 *Europe and the People without History*. Berkeley: University of California Press.

Wood, D.

1986 *Trinidad in Transition: The Years after Slavery*. New York: Oxford University Press.

Woolmington, J.

1973 *Aborigines in Colonial Society 1788–1850: From "Noble Savage" to "Rural Pest."* Melbourne: Cassell Australia.

World Health Organization, International Agency for Research on Cancer (WHO–IARC)

1991 *IARC Monographs on the Evaluation of Carcinogenic Risks to Humans*. Vol. 51. Lyons: World Health Organization.

Wright, L. B., ed.

1966 *The Elizabethans' America: A Collection of Early Reports by Englishmen on the New World*. Cambridge, Mass.: Harvard University Press.

Wrigley, G.

1988 *Coffee*. London: Longmans.

Yawney, C.

1969 Drinking Patterns and Alcoholism in Trinidad. In *Studies in Caribbean Anthropology*. Edited by F. Henry. 34–48. Montreal: Centre for Developing Area Studies, McGill University.

Yerbury, J.

1986 *The Subarctic Indians and the Fur Trade, 1680–1860*. Vancouver: University of British Columbia Press.

Young, A. M.

1994 *The Chocolate Tree: A Natural History of Cacao*. Washington, D.C.: Smithsonian Institution Press.

Young, J. A.

1974 *Business and Sentiment in a Chinese Market Town*. Taipei: Orient Cultural Service.

Young, M. W.

1977 Bursting with Laughter: Obscenity, Values and Sexual Control in a Massim Society. *Canberra Anthropology* 1.1:75–87.

Yu, L.

1974 *The Classic of Tea*. Translated by F. R. Carpenter. Boston: Little, Brown.

Zeisberger, D., and G. Sensemann

1768 Diary of David Zeisberger and Gottfried Sensemann's Journey to Goschgoschink on the Ohio, 8 May 1768–20 February 1769. Box 135, folder 7. Records of the Moravian Mission among the Indians of North America, Archives of the Moravian Church, Bethlehem, Pa. (Microfilm copy available at the American Philosophical Society Library, Philadelphia, and at Harvard College Library, Cambridge, Mass.)

Contributors

Charles Ambler is professor of history and dean of the Graduate School at the University of Texas at El Paso. He received a Ph.D. in African history from Yale University. He has been a research associate at the University of Nairobi, the University of Zambia, and the School of Oriental and African Studies, London, and has received a Fulbright-Hays Grant, a Mellon Faculty Fellowship at Harvard University, and an NEH Fellowship. His recent scholarship has focused on the social and cultural history of modern Africa and on debates around the relationships between ideas about alcohol and race in British imperial thought. His publications include *Kenyan Communities in the Age of Imperialism* (1988), *Liquor and Labor in Southern Africa* (coedited with J. Crush, 1992), and a number of articles, including, most recently, "Popular Films and Colonial Audiences: The Movies in Northern Rhodesia," *American History Review* (2001). With Emmanuel Akyeampong he is editing a special issue of the *International Journal of African Historical Studies* on leisure in modern African history that will appear in 2003.

E. N. Anderson is a cultural and political ecologist with special interests in ethnobiology and traditional management of plant and animal resources. He also works in the area of nutritional and food anthropology. He has studied fisheries in Hong Kong, Malaysia, British Columbia, and elsewhere and more recently has carried out research on contemporary Maya agriculture and forest management in Quintana Roo, Mexico. He has a B.A. from Harvard College (1962) and a Ph.D. from the University of California, Berkeley (1967). He has taught anthropology at the University of California, Riverside, since 1966.

Michael V. Angrosino, professor of anthropology at the University of South Florida, earned his Ph.D. in anthropology from the University of North Carolina, Chapel Hill, in 1972. He has conducted ethnographic field research in various parts of the Caribbean, most notably, Trinidad, focusing on questions of labor migration and ethnic relations. His research in the United States has been concerned with mental health policy and service delivery and with the role of organized religion in secularized modern societies. His most recent books include *Opportunity House: Ethnographic Stories of Mental Retardation, Talking about Cultural Diversity,* and *Doing Cultural Anthropology.* A textbook on the anthropology of religion will be published in 2003.

Contributors

Eliana Belmonte, M.S., is a researcher at the Museo Arqueológico of the Universidad de Tarapacá in Arica, Chile, specializing in the botany of prehistoric and modern northern Chile.

Daniel Bradburd is professor of anthropology at Clarkson University. His fieldwork with Iranian pastoralists resulted in the publication of *Ambiguous Relations: Kin, Class and Conflict among Komachi Pastoralists* (1990), *Being There: The Necessity of Fieldwork* (1998), and numerous articles on the economy and political economy of Southwest Asian pastoralists. His current research focuses on drugs and labor and on commodities and consumption.

Maggie Brady, Ph.D., is a social anthropologist with research interests in the health and substance use of indigenous peoples in Australia and elsewhere. She has undertaken fieldwork in remote and rural Australia for several major studies on Aboriginal alcohol use and published a study of the social epidemiology of gasoline sniffing entitled *Heavy Metal: The Social Meaning of Petrol Sniffing in Australia* (1992). She has also focused on applied research, publishing a manual of strategies for managing indigenous alcohol misuse (*The Grog Book,* 1998) and a collection of interviews with Aboriginal people who quit drinking without treatment (*Giving Away the Grog,* 1995). She has been a technical advisor to the World Health Organization Program on Substance Abuse and has worked on alcohol strategies in South Africa. She is currently a fellow with the Centre for Aboriginal Economic Policy Research at the Australian National University in Canberra.

Larry Cartmell, M.D., is staff pathologist in the Department of Pathology at Valley View Hospital. He can be reached at cartmell@chickasaw.com.

Vicki Cassman, Ph.D., is assistant professor of anthropology at the University of Nevada, Las Vegas. She specializes in Andean archaeology and the preservation of archaeological and historic materials, especially textiles. She can be contacted at cassmanv@unlv.edu.

Robert Gordon is professor of anthropology and African studies at the University of Vermont. Among his books are *Law and Order in the New Guinea Highlands* (with Mervyn Meggitt), *The Bushman Myth,* and *Picturing Bushmen.* He is currently working on the anthropology of colonialism.

Terence E. Hays received his Ph.D. in anthropology from the University of Washington in 1974 following the completion of fieldwork in Papua New Guinea. Since then the peoples of New Guinea have remained his specialization and the subject of his numerous ethnographic and large-scale comparative projects. He is the author of *Anthropology in the New Guinea Highlands: An Annotated Bibliography* (1976); coeditor with L. L. Langness of *Anthropology in the High Valleys: Essays on the New Guinea Highlands in Honor of Kenneth E. Read* (1987); editor of *Oceania: Encyclopedia of World Cultures,* volume 2 (1991) and *Ethnographic Presents: Pioneering Anthropologists in the Papua New Guinea Highlands* (1992); and author of dozens of scholarly articles, chapters, and reviews. Since 1973 he has taught in the Department of Anthropology at Rhode Island College, where he is currently professor of anthropology.

William Jankowiak is professor of anthropology at the University of Nevada. He has written numerous scholarly articles and chapters. His books include *Sex, Death and Hierarchy in a Chinese City* (1993) and an edited volume, *Romantic Passion* (1995). Presently, he is working on two projects: a study of Huhhot, a northern Chinese city, and an examination of daily life in the oldest and largest polygynous community in North America.

Stacy A. Lewis, A.B., Kenyon College, is currently a master's candidate in the Department of Anthropology at the University of Arizona.

Jeremy Long is an Australian historian and writer with a background in Aboriginal affairs. He was a field officer and then a research officer with the Northern Territory Administration before working as a senior advisor on policy and research with the Department of Aboriginal Affairs. In the 1980s he was commissioner for community relations with the Australian Human Rights Commission. Since leaving the Commonwealth Public Service in 1987 he has worked as a consultant and writer and published several articles and a book, *The Go Betweens: Patrol Officers in Aboriginal Affairs Administration in the Northern Territory 1936–1972* (1992). He has recently been engaged in historical research for native title claims.

Peter C. Mancall, professor of history at the University of Southern California, is the author of *Deadly Medicine: Indians and Alcohol in Early America* (1995). His writings on alcohol use by indigenous peoples have appeared in the *American Indian Culture and Research Journal,* the *Journal of the Early Republic,* and the *Australian & New Zealand Journal of Psychiatry.* In 1998 he was the inaugural recipient of the ALAC Research Fellowship from the Alcohol Advisory Council of New Zealand.

David N. Suggs, Ph.D., University of Florida, is professor of cultural anthropology at Kenyon College. His research has focused on the BaKgatla of Botswana and ranged from discussions of the life course to understanding the construction of gender and age in alcohol consumption. He has published numerous articles and edited or authored three books, most recently, *A Bagful of Locusts and the Baboon Woman: Constructions of Gender, Change and Continuity in Botswana,* Case Studies in Cultural Anthropology, George Spindler, series editor (2002).

Index